Desi Delicacies

AF655919

Also edited by Claire Chambers

Rivers of Ink:
Selected Essays

A Match Made in Heaven:
British Muslim Women Write about Love and Desire

Desi Delicacies

Food Writing from Muslim South Asia

EDITED BY
CLAIRE CHAMBERS

PICADOR INDIA

First published in India 2021 by Picador India
an imprint of Pan Macmillan Publishing India Private Limited
707 Kailash Building
26 K. G. Marg
New Delhi 110001
www.panmacmillan.co.in

Pan Macmillan, The Smithson, 6 Briset Street, London EC1M 5NR,
Basingstoke and Oxford
Associated companies throughout the world
www.panmacmillan.com

Any royalty payments from this book will go to charities working to provide food for people in need in South Asia.

ISBN 978-93-89104-57-8

Copyright © Claire Chambers 2021

All rights reserved. No part of this publication may be reproduced, stored in or introduced into a retrieval system, or transmitted, in any form, or by any means (electronic, mechanical, photocopying, recording or otherwise) without the prior written permission of the publisher. Any person who does any unauthorized act in relation to this publication may be liable to criminal prosecution and civil claims for damages.

4

This book is sold subject to the condition that it shall not, by way of trade or otherwise, be lent, re-sold, hired out, or otherwise circulated without the publisher's prior consent in any form of binding or cover other than that in which it is published and without a similar condition including this condition being imposed on the subsequent purchaser.

Typeset in Perpetua Regular by SÜRYA
Printed and bound in India by Repro India Ltd

FSC
www.fsc.org
MIX
Paper from responsible sources
FSC® C047271

Copyright Acknowledgements

'The Homesick Restaurant' © Nadeem Aslam

'Qissa Qorma aur Qaliyya Ka (All about Qormas and Qaliyas)' © Rana Safvi

'Paye, Pressure and Patience: Life in Pakistani Cooking' © Sauleha Kamal

'Alhamdulillah: With Gratitude and Relish' © Kaiser Haq

'The Rise of Pakistan's "Burger" Generation' © Sanam Maher

'Jootha' © Tabish Khair

'Chewing on Secrets' © Annie Zaidi

'Stone Soup' © Sarvat Hasin

'High on Chai and Samosa' © Sadaf Hussain

'Aftertaste' © Tarana Husain Khan

'A Brief History of the Carrot' © Rosie Dastgir

'The Hairy Curry' © Asiya Zahoor

'The Origin of Sweetness' © Uzma Aslam Khan

'The Night of Forgiveness' © Farah Yameen

'What's Cooking?' © Aamer Hussein with Sabeeha Ahmed Husain

'But There Are Angels' © Farahad Zama

'Jackfruit with Tamarind' © Mahruba T. Mowtushi and Mafruha Mohua

'Hungry Eyes' © Sophia Khan

'The Homesick Restaurant' was first published in the *New York Times.*

The aphorism and the poem in 'Alhamdulillah: With Gratitude and Relish' are both from Kaiser Haq, *Published in the Streets of Dhaka: Collected Poems* (Dhaka: Dhaka University Press, 2015).

'The Rise of Pakistan's "Burger" Generation' was first published in *Al Jazeera* online.

Versions of 'What's Cooking?' have appeared in collections brought out by ILQA Publications in Pakistan and HarperCollins India.

Arts & Humanities Research Council

Desi Delicacies and the broader research project 'Forgotten Food' are supported by the Arts and Humanities Research Council (AHRC) in the United Kingdom of Great Britain and Northern Ireland.

For Derry: chef's kiss

Some men drink the blood of other men,
All I drink is wine.

–The Sabri Brothers' Qawwali 'Saqia aur Pila'
Translated from Urdu by Mohsin Hamid in *Moth Smoke*

Good morning, Bangladesh, good morning.
How are you?
Bangladesh, sometimes you're busy husking rice
in a cheap striped sari . . .
At times you carry a pitcher on your hip
to fetch water, fall to chatting
at the ghat . . .
At siesta time in hot summer
offer paan and areca nut to a guest,
cook a delicious fish curry . . .

– 'Good Morning, Bangladesh' by Shamsur Rahman
Translated from Bengali by Kaiser Haq

O ye who believe! Eat of the good things
wherewith we have provided you, and
render thanks to God.

– Quran, 2:172

Measurements

Volume

Metric (ml)	Imperial (fl oz)	US cups
250	8	1
180	6	¾
150	5	⅔
120	4	½
75	2 ½	⅓
60	2	¼
30	1	⅛
15	½	1 tbsp

Weight

Imperial (oz)	Metric (g)
½	15
1	30
2	60
3	90
4	110
5	140
6	170
7	200
8	225
9	255
10	280
11	310
12	340
13	370
14	400
15	425
1 lb	450

CONTENTS

PART TWO: STORIES

Foreword: Appetizer

Bina Shah

Food and cooking have so often been compared to alchemy that I hesitate to use this overworked metaphor to describe the culinary arts of Muslim South Asia. Yet I cannot help but think of the early Muslim scientists in the classical age of Islam, who looked at the efforts of Chinese, Egyptian, Greek and Christian alchemists to prolong life and turn metal into gold. The alchemists believed that the four elements – earth, air, water, fire – needed a fifth element, quintessence or aether (variously interpreted as the air the gods breathed, a vacuum, nothingness), to make this transmutation possible, to turn base materials into noble ones.

These medieval Muslim scientists began their explorations into the same endeavours, but somewhere along the way they turned away from the more occult and superstitious aspects of alchemy. Notable among them were Al-Kindi, who distinguished alchemy from chemistry, and Ibn Khaldun who, a century later, wrote against disguising silver with a thin layer of gold. These thinkers distilled their experimentation into what became the basis of modern chemistry, which has a magic all its own for its proponents and for humanity, which benefits so greatly from scientific discovery.

The preparation, cooking and serving of food in Muslim South Asia, with its attendant science, rituals, folklore, superstition and occult arts, parallels the dance between alchemy and chemistry of the Islamic Golden Age. But in a Muslim South Asian kitchen, there is no need to separate the two. Cooks and chefs, bawarchis and khansamas of all ages and genders perform their work of taking a myriad of elements and turning them into gold, or concoctions that prolong life. Along the way, they imbue the food they prepare with a fifth element. And in Muslim South Asia, this is not quintessence, but the Divine. Practising Muslims firmly believe that it is this element which raises their food from the stuff of mere subsistence to a treasure that has come their way because of God's mercy and beneficence, and which bestows blessings upon anyone who consumes it.

Many cooks will invoke Allah, start their preparations with a 'bismillah', pray and blow duas – prayers or invocations – into the food as they prepare it. How many chefs in the Mughal region must have bowed in supplication to God that their culinary creations would please their kings and emperors? How many women in Muslim households create food for the Ramadan meals of sehri and iftar in the hope that their toil will bring them sawab or reward for enabling their households to keep their fasts? How many people make food and distribute it among the poor in times of need, believing that in preparing a dish of sujji on Shab-e-Barat or a deg of biryani at a funeral, they are building a house for themselves in the afterlife (presumably without a kitchen in which to toil)? This is strong magic.

Or, if Allah is not foremost in the mind when preparing food, then it is love which is the quintessence, the fifth element which transforms food into feast, drudgery into service, toil into pleasure. Muslim South Asian cookbooks abound with tale after tale of a young child growing up watching a beloved grandmother preparing elaborate meals, sitting at the family dastarkhwan amid dozens of relatives and friends, participating in an Eid feast or perhaps wooing a possible lover with the dishes that one grew up eating in one's ancestral home. The recreation of these meals, the offering of household menus or secret recipes is the desire to feel again that love, remember it, spread it, bask in it, no matter how badly the onions and garlic and spices make the clothes smell or the curtains reek.

Muslim South Asian cooking performs many magical deeds which we might assign to the Sufi saints. It facilitates time travel: one bite of the siri paye takes you back to a wintry morning in a village in Punjab when you were a child. It brings back the dead: opening a cookbook that your long-deceased nani compiled returns the sound of her voice instructing you how to cut the vegetables just so, and the sight of her hair braided or tied up in a bun. One glass of lassi, and you may find yourself as deeply asleep as one of the Companions of the Cave in Surah Kahf.

The Hadith showcase miracles through food, as in the story of the wedding of the Prophet Muhammad (peace be upon him) to Zaynab bint Jahsh, when a small number of dates suddenly multiplied into a feast for three hundred. Or the seventy men whose bellies were filled by a single loaf of rye or a small amount of bread, along with a goat that fed a thousand people. Each of these stories may be taken not just literally but also metaphorically, to show that abundance can come from faith rather than greed and waste.

This is a lesson that is constantly repeated in Muslim South Asian kitchens even today, where the discrepancy between the rich and the poor is most readily apparent in the amount of food each family has to eat, where people are admonished not to prepare giant wedding feasts and let the food go to waste, and where low-income families must feed many mouths with very little. The majority of people in South Asia go hungry every day. The highest proportion of charity in Pakistan where I live goes to the distribution of food and rations among the needy. It is that fifth element, in this case generosity (another attribute of the Divine), which turns the preparation of food in Muslim South Asia into a life-saving act that sends ripples beyond the walls of one's immediate household.

In many households, the kitchen is seen as the heart of the home. Muslim South Asian kitchens are the engines of an entire culture. The alchemy that takes place within them affects nations and economies, politics and history.

This is strong magic indeed.

Introduction: Food in the Time of Corona

Claire Chambers

The last book I edited, *A Match Made in Heaven*, was about love and desire. For the present volume I have turned my attention to another kind of love – the love of food, and of its preparation. It is love in a more complex sense than mere carnality, a relationship that is as layered as a paratha. Through this love we nourish our bodies and feed others. Indeed, food is intimately connected with hospitality, a trait rightly associated with South Asia. Communal eating is a superb way of breaking down barriers and bringing different people together, especially in contexts where caste and religious scruples usually prevent such exchange. Akbar Ahmed evocatively writes, 'Islam is sharing your food.' Moreover, as Bina Shah suggests in the Foreword, memories of love and fellowship season our food, infusing particular meals with much more than the sum of their ingredients.

I was musing on these ideas as I began commissioning and editing this anthology of Muslim South Asian food writing. But before I could finish my work, the coronavirus pandemic really took hold and went global. This initially paralysed me with fear so that I was unable for some time to do any further reading or writing. I know that I wasn't alone in experiencing writer's block at the beginning of the lockdown. In an illuminating and curiously uplifting article, Aisha S. Ahmad, a political scientist who is no stranger to dangerous situations, puts the current health crisis in the context of other emergencies. Since reading her work, my paralysis no longer worries me. As Ahmad writes, 'the legacy of this pandemic will live with us for years, perhaps decades to come. It will change the way we move, build, learn, and connect ... Your first few days and weeks in a crisis are [when] I would focus on food, family, friends, and maybe fitness.' This is sound advice. And there is no reason to feel guilty if it's impossible to concentrate on reading, writing and other creative or intellectual tasks at this time.

In that confusing early period of the crisis, people in the UK seemed fixated on buying things to see them through the lockdown. As a result, shops were selling out of all sorts of products such as medical supplies, hand sanitizer and toilet roll, and also of foodstuffs with a long shelf life, including pasta, tinned tomatoes, flour and rice. I refused to panic-buy, but after our younger son got ill with suspected Covid-19 and we had to self-isolate, I almost came to regret not getting involved in the consumerism frenzy. One colleague felt so concerned about my family's chances of catching scurvy that he was eager to drive a fifty-mile round trip just to deliver some brassicas for us from his allotment. This generous offer came despite the fact that he was in his early seventies and therefore belonged to a high-risk group!

Happily, our son recovered and I soon managed to find a vegetable-box company willing to deliver to a new customer, thus sparing my septuagenarian friend the trouble. But his kindness alerted me to the good deeds and community spirit that the crisis has engendered, alongside unedifying examples of selfishness and stockpiling. As David Miliband put it recently on the World Economic Forum podcast *World Versus Virus*, 'Survival now is a team sport, and life is a team sport.'

A group who have particularly distinguished themselves all over the UK in these testing times are British Muslims, a majority of them with familial links to South Asia. *Al Jazeera* reports that the Green Lane Mosque in Birmingham immediately started a food-delivery service for vulnerable individuals. Meanwhile the British-based charity Muslim Hands launched a campaign to get meals to those in need. This comes as no surprise, for food is a spine running through one of Islam's five pillars, that of zakat or charity. Feeding the sick or poor is a crucial aspect of such good works. During Ramadan, when the devout deprive themselves of sustenance from dawn to dusk for a month (no mean feat during the long summers of northern countries like England), zakat becomes even more central to faith, and many Muslims donate even more of their money and time to the needy. Lockdown meant that many believers worldwide were deprived of breaking their fasts communally. The mosque is usually a popular space to take iftar, the evening meal to break the fast. This year, Muslims had to think creatively and use technology to convey the accustomed sense of togetherness.

In Britain, as I write this, the state of play regarding Covid-19 is changing weekly. Until the end of May 2020, each Thursday evening at 8 p.m. we celebrated those on the metaphorical battlefield of the National Health Service by joining in with a round of robust applause. My husband is a family doctor who put in shifts at the red zone for coronavirus patients, so I had mixed feelings about this sweet but empty gesture. We quickly became aware that we should also be applauding those who were fulfilling other essential services – including that of providing food. Greater plaudits ought to have gone to the unsung heroes of the supply chain, from truck drivers to shelf-fillers and cashiers, and also the refuse workers who were taking away our food and other waste, all of them taking great personal risks.

Having been summarily shut by government decree, many cafés and restaurants are going out of business, although some have survived by serving takeaway orders. My family and I live close to Harehills, an area known affectionately as 'little Pakistan' in the city of Leeds. The desi cuisine here is already well established. Furthermore, the district has been experiencing a foodie efflorescence in recent years, with a number of excellent and affordable eateries serving dishes from Afghanistan and South Korea to Ethiopia and Syria. Over the same period, the array of South Asian outlets became more diverse, with a high-end gelato joint, two chai bars and a halwa puri outlet rubbing shoulders with the usual fried chicken shops and mainstream tikka masala places. The last time I went to one such establishment, Chai Walay, just before the lockdown, the British-Pakistani owner was visibly jittery about his young business's future and how he would pay his employees. I really hope when all this is over, his fine café is still standing.

Restaurants with greater capital to draw on reinvented themselves to feed the poor, the vulnerable and key workers. Finding themselves suddenly stripped of their orders, wholesale suppliers like Bradford's Delifresh opened themselves up for emergency online shopping by the general public.

The panic-buying and stockpiling has calmed down now. It's still difficult to get quite a few culinary items, though, and I miss being able to pop into the shops for random ingredients. Yet I'm well aware that to have this niggling concern is a luxury when many people around the world do not have enough to eat, a problem exacerbated by this crisis. That is why any royalty payments from this book will go to charities working to combat food insecurity in South Asia.

Women's rights groups around the world are reporting that lockdown has led to a spike in domestic violence. More positively, the editor of *HuffPost Japan* was quoted as saying that the stay-at-home order in East Asia contributed to a more equal gender distribution of household chores and cooking along the lines of gender. It will be interesting to see whether this trend continues once workplaces reopen fully and everyone is busy again. Certainly, even the most ardent cooks have found themselves ground down by the relentless pressure to put food on the table thrice daily for children who would usually spend a lot more time away from home.

Food is not only for nutrition but also comfort. With more leisure time yawning in front of us, many people turned to baking to occupy their days, quieten their nerves and fill their bellies. Writing for *Good Food*, Emily Laurence covered the transnational craze for banana bread during this pandemic. She accounts for this loaf's popularity because of its wholesomeness, its long tradition stretching back to the Great Depression, and its purse-friendly cost, in addition to some nostalgic and mood-boosting properties.

People simultaneously turned to books, e-books and audiobooks to get them through quarantine. In fact, according to *WIRED*, sales have risen in most genres except, unsurprisingly, the travel book market. The eighteen essays and short stories collected here allow for travel of another kind – of the mind – as the contributors, established and emerging authors from India, Pakistan, Bangladesh, Kashmir, the UK, Denmark and the US, explore the issue of food in Muslim South Asia and the diaspora.

There is a thirst – or perhaps in this context 'hunger' – for writing from Muslim South Asia; and the topic of food has a universal appeal. What could be more important than food? And what is food about if not the ever-present topics of power relations, sensuality and love? In their honeyed words, the authors reflect on ideas of good living, culinary traditions, family, domesticity and sexuality, as well as food scarcity. There is much focus among the writers on the sensation of taste – whether taste as a sumptuous pleasure or its corollary of disgust.

The subject of food and the pleasures of eating was, in part, chosen because it differs from the issue-based or problem-centred topics Muslims are often expected to write about. The pieces collected here are at once specific and ordinary. In their specificity, they reflect the range of circumstances experienced by Muslims in particular South Asian (diasporic) communities, and the ways in which these circumstances are negotiated. In their ordinariness, the narratives contradict some received ideas about the otherness of Muslims: stereotypes about halal meat, abstemiousness and carnivorous tastes, at a time of deep socio-cultural divisions, food shortages and beef lynchings. Stylish but far from shallow, these pieces reflect on sociability, prejudice, sensuality, hunger, bereavement and many other subjects. Characters try to move in the direction of happiness, and the authors depict the truth about their own and others' lives, meals and human connections.

'Forgotten Food', the broader project out of which this book comes from, offers a platform from which the voices of South Asian Muslim writers and foodies can be heard. I myself am from a non-Muslim, white Irish background. My interest in the literature of the Indian subcontinent and the Muslim world was originally ignited by the year I spent prior to university teaching in Peshawar, Pakistan. My interest continues to be informed by return visits to the region, and by working with diasporic communities. As a middle-class white academic occupying a position of power, my editorial interventions may inadvertently change the conversation, and I have had to be careful not to privilege some voices over others. Remaining mindful of Gayatri Spivak's warning not to speak for the other, I want to keep this introduction short to give as much space as possible for the chapters to exude all their rich aromas. I admit, though, that my vegetarianism has contributed to there being more meat-free recipes in this volume than might be expected. The authors too were conscious of financial hardship and environmental degradation as they offered up delicious vegetarian or pescatarian meal ideas.

As the pandemic eases, we are slowly moving into what Aisha S. Khan has called the 'new normal phase'. Literary critic Muneeza Shamsie wrote in an email to me about this crisis: 'So strange, one's known world and all the certainties of what one should or should not do, all gone for a six.' She's right; the things we take for granted have shifted tectonically almost overnight.

Yet, if music (and writing and other kinds of art) be the food of love, play on – especially in the time of corona. Hold your loved ones close, eat hearty meals, listen to your favourite album on repeat, and, as soon as you can concentrate, read on!

part one

Essays

The Homesick Restaurant

Nadeem Aslam

In March this year, I telephoned a friend in Pakistan and asked him to pick a bowl's worth of flower buds from the kachnar tree in his garden. They appear only at that time of year. He was to put them in the freezer until I visited from England some time at the end of April or the beginning of May. Each beautiful leaf of the kachnar tree resembles a child's drawing of an apple, and the large blossoms are a deep pink striped with white, though they can be completely white also. The buds are seldom given the chance to open, however, as they are harvested to be cooked soon after they form. The kachnar flower buds are a great delicacy in Pakistan, a delicacy unavailable in England, and it is one of the things I miss most about my homeland.

My brother and sister were visiting me at the time, and an hour or so after my phone call to Pakistan, we went out for a meal. The restaurant we chose, more or less at random, was staffed by Pakistanis – one of the countless such places in the London area that are referred to by the white clientele as Indian. I hadn't been living in this particular neighbourhood for long, but I felt sure that most of the waiters had only just arrived in England from small towns and villages in Pakistan. They often come after having arranged marriages to British-born Pakistani girls. They have little or no English and little choice except working in restaurants or driving taxis. A lot of such men do manual labour at a nearby factory that the British-born Pakistani teenagers call 'the factory of the newlyweds'.

We ordered. As always, my brother, my sister and I searched the food that evening for our mother, for our aunts, and for our grandmothers. Each Pakistani woman spices her curries in her own way; each pan has a different aroma, the way each human body smells slightly different. The thickness, texture and the width of each woman's chapati is also unique to her, depending on the size of her hands, the shape of her fingers, and the strength with which she kneads the dough. And that evening all three of us were overcome with emotion very soon after we began the meal: the food – the flavour of the mutton, of the samosas – was the best we had tasted since our visits to our eldest aunt's home in Lahore. That was twenty years ago, and the aunt had been dead for ten years.

We reminisced as we ate, each new mouthful sending us deeper into our memories. We talked about how our aunt used to dye her hair a bright orange with henna, something that made us smile when we came to live in England as teenagers, where only punks dyed their hair that colour. She was the best cook in the family, but she could be bad-tempered at times. Her husband, our uncle, was gentle and kind but impractical and a dreamer, like all his brothers, including our own father. The uncle had, for example, taken his children out of what was arguably the best school in the city and enrolled them in one that had very poor standards – but it was owned by a friend of his and was threatened with closure because there were not enough pupils on the register.

'This is too incredible,' I said, pushing the small steel wok of spinach and fenugreek across the table towards my sister. 'How did the cook learn to do all this?'

My brother raised his hand for the waiter, and when he arrived, my brother asked: 'Who is your cook, please? Would it be possible for us to talk to him?'

'It's not a man,' he replied. 'It's a woman.'

We three looked at one another. The kitchen workers in these restaurants are almost invariably male.

My sister put down her fork and rose from her chair without a word. She went into the kitchen with the waiter, and then my brother and I heard her give a small shout. We rushed to the kitchen and found her in the arms of our cousin – the eldest daughter of our dead aunt.

We learned that she and two of her brothers were living illegally in England – having arrived in the country hidden in a shipment of Christmas trees via France back in December. They hadn't contacted us or our parents because they were too ashamed of their circumstances, preferring to wait until they had managed to get a foothold in England. They were also concerned that we might get into trouble for harbouring illegal immigrants.

We left after a while but went back for her at 2:30 a.m., when the restaurant closed. She took us to her place, and we stayed up talking until her two brothers, our cousins, who were out driving taxis, came back at around 4 a.m., and then there was more talk.

It was almost dawn when we took our leave. At one point our beautiful cousin smiled sadly and said: 'Come back this evening. Someone brought me a bagful of kachnar flower buds from Pakistan yesterday. I'll cook them for us.'

SPINACH AND FENUGREEK (PALAK AUR METHI)

1 tbsp butter
200g fresh fenugreek (methi) leaves
200g spinach leaves

2 medium onions, chopped
2 tsp ground coriander
1 tbsp double cream
12 cloves of garlic (crushed)
4 tsp ginger–garlic paste
1½ tsp turmeric
2 tsp cumin seeds
2 tsp ground coriander
3–4 green chillies (to taste)
½ tsp ground ginger
Salt to taste
½ tsp sugar
½ tbsp mustard oil
50g paneer (optional)
Generous handful of coriander leaves

Method

1. Wash the fenugreek leaves and spinach leaves (both without the stems) thoroughly. Boil them together and blend them to a fine paste.
2. In a deep-bottomed saucepan or pot, heat the butter and oil together.
3. Add the cumin seeds and let them splutter.
4. Add the onion and fry until brown. Then add the turmeric, garlic, green chillies and ginger–garlic paste, and sauté everything.
5. Add the blended paste of the greens, sugar and salt, and mix well.
6. Add the coriander powder and ground ginger, and fry until the oil seeps out by the sides. Cook on a slow flame.
7. If the mixture is very thick, water can be added to make the desired consistency.
8. Add the cream and paneer slices (if using) and cook for another 3–4 minutes.
9. Garnish with coriander leaves.

Qissa Qorma aur Qaliya Ka (All about Qormas and Qaliyas)

Rana Safvi

Food has always been a serious business for people from the city of Lucknow in northern India, irrespective of their religion. In times gone by, in the metropolis and the wider princely state of Awadh (in modern-day Uttar Pradesh), food was also about refined tastes, as well as *tehzeeb-o-adaab*, or etiquette, hospitality and a highly syncretic culture. This was made evident from the setting of the dastarkhwan (the eating area covered by a sheet), which would have had invocations for blessing the food and house printed on it, to the laying of *rakabis*, as plates were called in our childhood, with tin bowls for drinking water cooled in earthen pots. Those present would wait for the eldest in the house to take his or her place at the head of the dastarkhwan, after which the meal would start with a prayer. We youngsters would say 'adaab' if some elder passed a dish to us, and in turn were blessed with a 'khush raho' (stay happy). Meals like this were a way of life which has all but vanished.

Like everything else in life, cultural practices were derived from religion.

As we often say, '*Nosh farmaaiye, bismillah kijiye*.' It is difficult to translate these terms as they don't have exact equivalents in English. The closest for 'nosh farmaiye' would be 'Please come and sup.' Meanwhile, 'bismillah kijiye' would be 'Start in the name of God.' Food is a blessing and so can never be eaten without thanking God for it, whichever religion one belongs to.

In many houses which are influenced by Persian culture, *nosh-e-jaan* is another polite way of inviting people to share a meal, or even to politely decline with a gesture.

Despite being Muslim, my husband studied in a boarding school run by the Church of North India, and to this day he doesn't start a meal without saying grace.

Islam is regularly described as a way of life and so it is not surprising that there are many dos and don'ts for cooking and eating which were and are followed. Chief among them are, of course, a list of foods which are forbidden (haram), those that are better avoided (makruh), those that are permitted (halal), and those which are positively encouraged for their wholesome qualities (tayyab). These are found in the Quran as well as in the body of Hadith or sayings of Prophet Muhammad.

Food has to be given the utmost respect. I remember being taught, and I follow this teaching to the present day, that while we can wait for the food, food must not be made to wait for us as it is Allah's blessing. Similarly, nothing should be wasted. Waste is frowned upon. One must take care not to hurt the sentiments of the person preparing or offering the food, and guests are also a blessing from God.

There is a beautiful story which, though it is not an authentic Hadith, exemplifies this about Prophet Muhammad. One day a poor man gifted the Prophet a bunch of grapes. The Prophet was sitting in the mosque of Medina with his companions. He ate one grape and then finished them all with a smile on his face but without offering any to his companions. Once the man who had gifted it departed, the Prophet was asked why he didn't share the fruit. He answered that the grapes were in fact sour and he didn't want his companions' expressions giving that information away to the poor man.

To understand recipes and methods, it is important to understand the ethos behind them too.

Since wastage was frowned upon, as long as time and ease of life allowed, food was cooked fresh every day and only in as much quantity as could be consumed during the meal.

One of my most enduring memories is of my mother sitting in front of the storeroom where food supplies were kept, discussing her menu with the bawarchi (cook), and then having the ingredients weighed on a small set of old iron scales. As only modest quantities were cooked, it would be a pinch of this and a handful of that. Most recipes were passed down through the generations within the family and never written down with precise measurements. All wet ingredients would be bought fresh. No powders were used, for all masalas had to be ground from scratch. I still remember the grinding stone and the smell of turmeric being pounded. We had a family retainer whose job it was to do the daily shopping and tally the amount with Amma every day. Considering we were not a very big family or lavish eaters, our shopping in the 1970s and 1980s would have come to a small amount. Amma would diligently record it in her diary and the money given for the shopping was all accounted for.

Once Amma went to stay with my grandmother and I found myself running the house. I am totally deficient in mathematical skills, so although I could plan the menu, get the daily portions for cooking taken out of the storeroom, and give orders for the shopping, I could never balance the total. Eventually, Fazal Bhai, our family retainer, said in despair, 'Baby madam, I thought you were educated! We come to a different sum every time you add it up. Let it be. We will reconcile accounts once Begum Sahiba is back.' Back in those days, we were raised to treat our family retainers with esteem, adding a term of respect to their names, and they could rebuke us if they felt we were in the wrong.

Among all the things I miss, it is the sense of family and belonging that food and our age-old dining etiquette brought with it that I miss the most. Having grown up in Lucknow, I imbibed this culture and still try my best to keep it intact.

However, it has become increasingly difficult. Higher prices and pressures in our time have taken their toll. After I got married, I could never emulate my mother's practices. Instead, I started cooking in bulk, using readymade powdered masala, and freezing leftovers. There was no time to plan daily meals, enjoy cooking them, or even savour the meal. Chewing a morsel the prescribed thirty-two times is of course out of the question these days, though I'm told it helps in burning calories during digestion and leads to better digestive health.

Since everyone is now rushing around, we have begun taking a lot of shortcuts. We have reduced the fine art of cooking and eating into just mechanical belly-filling. As a result, our age-old heritage of cuisine and table manners have taken a hit and often it is, 'I just threw some things together,' or 'Let me see what I can rustle up.'

We no longer have the resources, financial or temporal, to maintain well-equipped kitchens and cook elaborate meals. These have become confined to fine-dining restaurants or big celebrations in the family.

Lack of time also means that my recipe books are now more for reading pleasure than cooking from. I have always been interested not only in cooking but in reading recipes, and have a collection of more than a hundred books on cuisines from all over the world. One of the first books that I was given by my father was a collection of recipes from the families of Awadh and the Deccan Plateau, entitled *Ismati Dastarkhwan*. This was a compilation by Begum Amina Nazli of Delhi, which showcased recipes collected from the women of Awadh who belonged to royal households or whose husbands were highly placed government officials, doctors or army officers. The year is not given but it appears to be from the mid-twentieth century.

To me, the discovery of similarities and differences between recipes that were cooked so many decades ago and those that we make today has been exciting and productive.

A few years ago, my cousins collected some family recipes so that they might stay forever in our collective memory, especially to make sure that they live on through our younger relatives. This book is called *Dastarkhwan-e-Shamsabad* and it is from this volume that I have taken the recipe for Tehsildari qorma given at the end of this chapter.

I was recently presented with a copy of an old cookbook called *Khwaan Neamat-e-Kalan*. The cover page bears the inscription that not only dishes from royalty and noblemen's families are inventorized, but also with great difficulty English and French recipes have been collected. It makes the claim that any ordinary cook can become a great chef with the help of this book. The volume was in a tattered state, with termite damage and many pages missing. I was helped by the Rekhta Foundation, who digitized those pages which remained intact so that I could read this treasure-trove of recipes.

The year of its publication is again missing but I have estimated it as being from some point in the early twentieth century because of the style. Tying in with the culture I had seen as a child or heard from my parents, that we have to thank God at every step, the book proper begins not just with a bismillah but also an invocation to Him:

> *Bismillah hir Rahman ir Raheem*
>
> Uncountable Praise be to Allah for He made man the chosen one and gave us countless blessings and made us capable of cooking these foods which we desire. He blessed us with intelligence to recognize His uniqueness and unity.
>
> One can never praise Allah enough.
>
> When Allah created man He also created delicious fruits and dry fruits and other foods for him. And the ability to cook delicious food.

The book has many recipes that have been divided into eight chapters dealing with flatbread, non-vegetarian, vegetarian, rice, dessert, various sherbets and tea, relish, achar (pickle), chutney, and of course those English and French recipes I mentioned earlier. Each section is about the same length and accorded the same care, with detailed instructions being imparted.

Yet somehow, when we talk of the Muslim cuisine of North India, we use the term Mughlai very loosely for any non-vegetarian dishes. The food eaten by the Mughals was delicately flavoured and cooked under the supervision of a hakeem (physician) so that it was absolutely balanced. The tomato- and cream-based dishes that are served today were definitely not served on the Mughal dastarkhwan, as tomato was introduced by the Portuguese in India and it took some time for Indians to adopt the ingredient. Even today, we use yoghurt rather than tomato to add tanginess to our dishes in traditional cooking

Yet most Mughlai food the world over is tomato-based. The Mughals also ate a lot of vegetables, as is apparent from *Nuskha-e-Shahjahani*, written in the seventeenth century, but we don't have any Mughlai bhartas, a vegetarian dish in which vegetables are mashed and cooked.

The Central Asians were nomadic warriors and, for them, cooking was done on the go. Many a time they would ride their horses while carrying marinated meat in their saddlebags. These pre-spiced provisions would take less time to cook when they set up camp at night.

What we eat today is an amalgamation of the food eaten in medieval times, influenced by indigenous and Persian cuisines. In India, most dishes use generous quantities of oil and spices, especially chilli, which are not native to the Central Asian food of the Mughals.

In the eighteenth century, the Mughal Empire began its decline following two sackings of Delhi, one in 1739 by Nader Shah and another in 1757 by Ahmed Shah Abdali. Provincial governors like the Nawab of Awadh began gaining prestige and power. Awadh is the land of sangam (confluence), where the rivers Ganga and Jamuna meet. It's also here that many cultural streams met and derived their unique 'Ganga–Jamuni' identity. The cuisine reflects a mélange of Persian influences that came with the nawabs of Awadh, that influx of people who migrated to Lucknow after the attacks on Delhi by Nader Shah and Ahmed Shah Abdali. Their customs and eating habits were absorbed into the existing culture of this rich Indo-Gangetic plain. For instance, the kebab was eaten with a paratha – inspired by fried puris, the deep-fried, puffed bread which is such an intrinsic part of the Hindu cuisine. Even today, if you visit the narrow alleys of old Lucknow, you will find puri–kebab and puri–alu ki sabzi being sold, along with samosa and jalebi.

Whenever Mughlai food is spoken of, we immediately think of that most famous offering of them all, the qorma. While in the Perso-Arabic script we write it with a 'Q,' it is normally spelt korma and not qorma.

Like the rose, it tastes just as spectacular by any name.

History tells us of a Central Asian dish called 'ashqorma, qorma or kuverma', and it is this repast that was adapted in India.

Another interesting aside is that while *Nuskha-e-Shahjahani* does not contain any recipes for qormas, the dastarkhwan of Emperor Bahadur Shah Zafar served some variety of it. This is attested to by Munshi Faizuddin, in his *Bazm-e-Aakhir*, which was published in 1885 and which I recently translated under the title *City of My Heart*. So qorma made its appearance on Indian tables in the late eighteenth and early nineteenth centuries. Later in the nineteenth century, it had become a staple item, and no festive meal whether for special guests or celebrations was complete without a qorma.

As the renowned Urdu poet, Dilawar Figar – known for his humour and satire – writes:

Yaa Rab mere nasiib mein akl-e-halaal ho
Khaane ko qorma ho khilaane ko dal ho.

O Lord, may my destiny be replete with lawful food
May I eat qorma and be able to feed [others] dal.

The joke here is that poets are celebrated and given qorma to eat, but can only afford to feed dal (lentil curry) to others!

When we were growing up, qorma was made only for parties, as its preparation involves tedious labour in the roasting of the meat and masalas. But considering its delicious taste I'm sure that, like Figar, many people would have preferred it to the lowly dal which he was content to feed to others.

To summarize, the food we eat today was perfected in the kitchens of the Awadh nawabs with a generous dash of Persian influence adapted to Indian tastes. In Iran itself, food is more unadorned and uses far fewer spices than we do in India.

Qorma literally means 'braising the meat'. For qorma, the meat is braised in oil (traditionally, desi ghee was used), yoghurt and spices. It is then simmered in water till tender.

For festive occasions, blanched and finely ground cashews are also used as thickening agents. For everyday use, peanuts can be used as a substitute.

My grandmother was known for this culinary precept:

'*Masala aise bhuno jaise dushman ka kaleja!*' Roast the spices as passionately as if they were the enemy's heart!

This instruction – not meant to be taken literally – is the story of qorma, a dish that is infused with labour, love and passion, but one that delivers magic when done right.

Time devoted to cooking and to understanding food has changed over the years, so before I give the recipe I want to present a few dos and don'ts, for these can make or break a dish. Here are the three don'ts of traditional north Indian qorma:

1. Do not add turmeric.
2. Do not use tomatoes.
3. Do not garnish the qorma with coriander leaves. This herb garnish is normally reserved for those dishes which use turmeric as an ingredient.

And the rules for getting it right are:

1. The onions should be finely sliced and fried to just the right golden-brown colour. If underdone, the colour and

taste of the qorma will be pale and dull. If you burn or over-brown the onions, you'll be back to a dullish brown colour, this time with an unpleasantly bitter taste.

2. During the roasting process, keep adding dashes of yoghurt so that the masala doesn't stick to the pot. The reason hotel or restaurant qorma tends to be so oily is that their cooks add lots of oil while roasting, in order to cut down on the time and effort. If you love your arteries as much as you love good food, use yoghurt!
3. The meat should be well cut. Trim all the fat from it, since fat gives it a very oily appearance and taste, as well as an uninviting smell. The best meat is from the shoulder or rump (raan).
4. Open the pot or pressure cooker only when the steam has completely escaped, otherwise the dish will lose colour and the meat will becomes tough.

India has seen the rule of many dynasties. The last dynasty was the Mughal Empire, which was ended by the British East India Company in 1857. India later became a colony of Great Britain. This brought about many changes. The Mughal Emperor was exiled to Rangoon, now Yangon, in Myanmar.

Immediately after the Uprising of 1857, the Mughal princes were either killed or escaped from Shahjahanabad (Old Delhi). It took many years for the remaining Mughals to be rehabilitated in Delhi and given pensions.

One prince had escaped to Farrukhabad district in Uttar Pradesh and, when some restructuring was taking place, the British appointed him as the tehsildar of Farrukhabad. He became very close to the ancestors of my in-laws who had settled in Shamsabad in the same district. They had come to India from Iran during the reign of Shah Jahan after the fall of the Safavid dynasty, from which they are descended.

The most popular dish of this branch of the family is called Tehsildari qorma, which is said to have come from the Mughal prince's kitchen.

The dish is a rich and creamy delight with very few spices. The use of rabdi (condensed milk) and khoya (closer to ricotta cheese) in this mutton recipe makes it burst with robust flavours. It is not a dish for the faint-hearted and definitely not for anyone watching their calories. The desserts in my husband's house are extremely sweet. All these are supposed to be signs of a noble palate.

As a young bride, I remember a conversation between two uncles-in-law in chaste Persianized Urdu as to why their digestive systems were not being repaired despite following all the instructions given by the doctor. What were these instructions? That they eat vegetarian khichdi so that the stomach would get a rest. It turned out that although Nawab Sahib was eating khichdi, his cooks were adding plenty of dried fruits and meat to it as per his instructions.

Abdul Halim Sharar (1860–1926), Awadh's chronicler, mentions a khichdi made of pistachios and almonds cooked in the same slow, simmering way as rice and lentils. Sure enough, I found a qorma khichdi recipe in *Khwan Neamat-e-Kalan*.

However, daily meals at home were primarily qaliyas, a meat preparation with turmeric and vegetables. We were taught that the base of qorma is fried onion paste and yoghurt; turmeric is never added to it. Qaliya, on the other hand, uses turmeric and raw onion paste.

The trick to cooking any meat dish is in the 'bhuna' or sautéeing of the masala. Too little and it looks pale and tastes insipid; too much and it will taste bitter.

Some of the vegetables that are cooked with the meat are unusual, to say the least.

I often cook a mutton dish, a winter favourite, with baby turnips and leaves, according to my late aunt Mrs Motahira Hasan's recipe. In the old days, my aunt used to tell me, they would just put all the ingredients in lots of desi ghee and cook them overnight on a slow fire till the embers died out, but she also had an easier recipe for today's times.

I am quite convinced this was a ploy by the women of the house to make the family eat vegetables, as most meals in the olden days consisted of meat. The arrays of qaliyas that we cook are mind-boggling and range from beetroot, bitter gourd, turnips, cabbage, beans and bottle gourd to all kinds of greens, peas and carrots. Indeed, my grandfather, a tennis player and a health-conscious man, ate a meat curry with bottle gourd throughout the summer because it was considered to have a cooling effect, and a carrot and mutton curry during the winter. He would only eat the shorba (soup) and vegetables from it. One qaliya recipe from *Khwan Neamat-e-Kalan* has potatoes in it. Alu ka salan, as this dish is known, is a comfort food, especially for north Indian families like ours, and is often cooked at home. When I was studying in Aligarh Muslim University and living in the hostel, that was the staple meal.

What is fascinating for me is to see how a single dish like the qorma evolved over the years. In *Guzishta Lucknow*, translated as *Lucknow: The Last Phase of an Oriental Culture*, Sharar writes that 'in those days [the late eighteenth or early nineteenth century] the best food was considered to be that which appeared light and delicate but was in fact heavy and not easily digestible.'

The two recipes of Qorma Khasgi Zafrani that I studied in *Khwan Neamat-e-Kalan* and *Ismati Dastarkhwan* are very similar as they come from the same era, give or take a few years. They both involve copious amounts of cream and ghee, and a long cooking time. However, the family recipe that was passed on to me from my mother has many differences. One can see that it is much lighter in calories. It is not only light but quick, with a pressure cooker being used.

The reason for calorie-heavy foods a few centuries ago was that people only ate two meals a day. Their first meal was enjoyed at 11 a.m. or so, and another was served after six in the evening.

In between, smoking a hookah and chewing paan (betel leaf) were all that was taken. It was the British who introduced breakfast and afternoon tea, as well as snacks along the way. Our physical exercise has reduced as we use our fingers and brains far more than our legs these days. This has led to worries about weight gain and associated health problems.

I miss the days of my childhood. In winter afternoons we would sit in the sun and eat our meals; at night we sat around a log fire, competing for hot bread from the fire. In summer, afternoons were languid and with light meals. In the evenings we would be seated outside in the courtyard around the dastarkhwan, listening to narratives ranging from fairy tales to stories with a moral or from the scriptures. These were told to us by our parents and grandparents, as we soaked up their values and earnestly tried to learn to become better people. Perhaps that is why Muslim belief insists that life increases the longer we sit around the dastarkhwan.

Abdul Halim Sharar writes in *Guzishtha Lucknow*, 'The most important activity in human life is eating. As any community or nation progresses, its diet is the most salient guide to it.'

Food is such an important part of our heritage and culture and, for me, a wonderful raconteur when it comes to the history of human evolution. It describes the progress of technology which has made cooking so much easier, and the decline of a culture due to the fast pace of life and our newfound lack of time.

Tehsildari Qorma

(late nineteenth-century recipe)

500g mutton
2 onions (fried, then ground or blended to a paste)
2 tbsp ginger–garlic paste
¼ cup yoghurt
¼ cup cream
2 tbsp khoya, grated (you can use ricotta if you can't get khoya)
¼ cup rabdi or condensed milk (½ litre of milk reduced to ¼ cup by boiling)
Pinch of nutmeg powder
Pinch of mace powder
2 tsp of red chilli powder (or to taste)
1½ tsp salt (or to taste)
4 tbsp oil

Method

1. Heat oil in a pan and add the onion paste. Fry for 5–6 minutes till it turns golden brown.
2. Add the ginger–garlic paste and fry for another 3–4 minutes.
3. Now add the mutton pieces and sauté for 8–10 minutes on medium flame.
4. Beat the yoghurt with a spoon and add to the pan. Stir immediately.
5. Then one by one add the red chilli powder, salt, cream, khoya, and rabdi. Mix well and cook for 5–6 minutes.
6. Add half a cup of water. Cover and cook on low flame for 20–30 minutes till the mutton is completely cooked.
7. Once the mutton gets cooked, sprinkle the nutmeg powder and mace powder over it.
8. Switch off the flame and serve.

Paye, Pressure and Patience: Life in Pakistani Cooking

Sauleha Kamal

It is nearly mid-summer, just before the break of dawn in Cambridge, and the Jesus College May Ball is in full swing. Canopies and Ferris wheels have taken over the massive expanse of grounds at Jesus, a college known for sports. A fortune-teller answers questions in one corner and students run in giant inflatable water zorbs at the other end. Food flows freely; there are curries and rice, and chocolate-dipped strawberries, hot cocoa and an impressive list of mini-desserts. The name May Ball is a misnomer in many ways because these events are more carnivals than balls and because they happen in June, not May.

We arrive a few hours early, just before sunset, and queue up in our floor-length gowns and tuxedos, heels sinking into the soft grassy grounds, eyes just recovering from exam-season bleariness. Some of us break our fasts here because it is also Ramadan. The May Ball is oddly convenient in that way. There is enough food for an iftar feast and, because the festivities continue into the next day, for sehri too. We are back at the tents, piling up food on our plates about half an hour before the Fajr call to prayer would have rung out, if that sort of thing happened here.

'What do they have over there?' Sohaib asks Sara and me.

When we both reply 'Pie,' his brain registers, 'Siri paye,' and, for a second, he is full of excitement.

As I said, it is early in the morning, and Sohaib is Lahore-born and bred. Of course, there is no paye here at the Jesus May Ball, and he realizes it soon enough. We laugh at the absurdity of the moment.

Siri paye is a Pakistani delicacy that tastes better than it sounds. It is a gluey, gelatinous, meaty stew, sticky to the touch, congealing over fingers, welcome on a cold winter's day, scooped up into a spongy tandoor-fresh naan. If I try to describe it in English, though, it sounds weird because siri paye literally translates to 'heads and hooves'. *Who would eat that?*

I have never attempted to cook siri paye but I have seen my mother make it sometimes. It is a painstaking task, and one that, like many desi delicacies, starts the night before. The beginning is almost gruesome: roasting the bones over a flame to burn off any leftover hairs and smells. After that, you scrape the bones clean and rinse off the burned bits. Simmer them down in water with garlic, ginger and onions. Then come the roasted spices: bay leaves, cardamom, cinnamon sticks and all the usual suspects: cumin, coriander and ground chilli powder, or a box of Shan masala, which blends the spices just as well. My mother – Ami, as I call her – and I have complete faith in the boxed blends. She sometimes makes her own, sometimes relies on the boxes – with a tweak here and there to make them her own.

Ami only learned how to make paye after she married my father. They are both Punjabi, but Abu is a big fan of Lahori foods from his time living with his nana in the old Mughal city as a student at the University of Engineering and Technology. Abu is not much of a cook himself. The only recipe of Abu's I know is his tuna salan, an invention from grad school days abroad. It is surprisingly good, lemony, tangy and fragrant with Pakistani spices that drown out the pungent smell of canned tuna.

There are perhaps few cuisines that demand as much time and patience as Pakistani food. We do have our quick karahis, balti goshts and tikkas, but the bulk of Pakistani cooking is a masterclass in patience. The secret behind paye is the same as that behind nihari, haleem or a host of other delicacies: overnight cooking. Before this dish can make it to the table with its sliced ginger and coriander garnish and stacks of steaming naan fresh from the fiery furnace of the neighbourhood tandoor, the paye cooks for hours and hours. Shank of lamb, known as raan – the pièce de résistance of any Eid-ul-Adha feast – is marinated for hours before slow-roasting. Every minute of the hours spent over it is worth it when the meat falls off the bone, each fibre steeped in flavour.

Similarly, spinach blanched and buttered might be good but it is never as flavourful as palak simmered in spices over a low flame. Roasted or fried aubergine can be delicious cooked many different ways, but aubergine as baingan ka bharta has undergone a sea change, transformed into something rich and strange. However, to get to bharta, you must roast the aubergine, peel it, smash it, and only then can you cook it, with all the standard base vegetables of Pakistani food and a blend of roasted spices picked specifically to accompany the star of the show.

The passage of time has brought certain innovations to desi cooking. There's the newer wave of appliances, including the Rotimatic which dispenses fresh, round rotis from just the raw materials. There are also older innovations that have become mainstays of home cooking: the pressure cooker comes to mind. Ubiquitous, fast, convenient and dangerous, the pressure cooker is responsible for the faded yellow circular stain on the kitchen ceilings of most households, which you can just about make out if you know where to look. Every Sunday, a man can be heard bellowing in the streets, 'Pressure cooker wallah, pressure cooker wallah,' going from neighbourhood to neighbourhood, advertising repairs for pressure cookers and other kitchen appliances.

My mother is a pragmatic woman who encapsulates universes within her and works with an efficiency and energy that would put anyone to shame. One thing she cannot tolerate is a waste of time; this makes sense for a woman who is always doing something. She gave me her handwriting and her face (although my eyes are a few shades darker, and hair lighter and straight where hers falls in waves that she keeps caged in a sensible bun). But I have nowhere near her levels of energy. When we watch a movie together, she must pause it many times to go and complete one of the many tasks she always has in motion. Not one to squander even a second of her time, she has, over the years, streamlined her cooking process: preparing masala blends in advance; on weekends pre-cooking salan bases for the week ahead; and grinding up shami kebab mix from fresh beef and dal, shaping it into fat discs to be stored in the freezer, ready to fry at a moment's notice. All her chopping is done at a dizzyingly fast pace, with the knife skills she first picked up from *Yan Can Cook*, a Chinese cooking show from public broadcast television.

From her, I have also inherited a love of making food, of improvising (cooking is an art, baking is a science), and received a list of time-efficient shortcuts long before the internet popularized five-minute hack videos. In our household growing up, we would prepare jars of Kashmiri chai concentrate ready for the winter. Our atta was kneaded with a Kenwood K-beater attachment, and our gulab jamuns made with Nido milk powder. Everything from scratch but with maximized efficiency. Many urban women of her generation who could afford servants would outsource the task of cooking. Ami has always insisted on making food herself and sharing it with the household help who assisted with other tasks.

If I love to cook, it's because I learned from my mother how to make recipes my own. Cooking has been a way for us to spend time together, to experiment with ingredients and, yes, to have control over what we eat. Knowledge is power, and cooking is too. As a largely female occupation, though, it has not been associated with power.

In April 2019, *Queer Eye*'s British-Pakistani designer Tanvir 'Tan' France uploads a roti-making tutorial onto his YouTube channel. As he rolls the atta into a perfect round and fires up the tawa, it is quickly apparent that France knows what he's doing.

Sure enough, within seconds over the flame, his roti begins to bubble and balloons into a flawless sphere of hot steam. Deflated once it's off the heat, his roti is light, even and circular. France's Urdu may be endearingly accented but his roti is authentic and, as many joke, very rishta-worthy.

What is remarkable about this video is not that a man has filmed a cooking tutorial but that a man has filmed a tutorial on a highly gendered household staple, the humble roti, at once inconsequential and vital to the desi household. (Of course, France and his public image archly refuse to conform to heteronormative conventions.) But television has long lifted male chefs – for men are almost always chefs where women are home cooks – to celebrity heights. In the hands of a man, cooking becomes a skill and an art form instead of a duty, which it often is for women. When they choose to cook, then, men favour recipes that are impressive and artsy, worthy of celebration. Meanwhile France wants to elevate comfort foods and teach roti and dal. He is, of course, aware of this tension and begins his video by noting that, 'It's not typical, in a Pakistani household, for a boy to learn really young (or ever), which I know is archaic but that is just how the culture is. But my mum taught me when I was really young.'

Food is political and, in a culture so enamoured with food, it can consume the lives of the women who are tasked with making it. On Twitter, a historian posts a picture of a page from a Punjab home economics textbook. Rendered in saccharine pink is a timetable entitled *Khatoon-e-khana ke liay waqt ke goshawaray ka misali khata*, or 'An example of a timetable for housewives'. Added up across the day, it allocates a whopping seven hours to kitchen-related tasks.

On International Women's Day, 8 March, in 2018, women marched through the streets of Pakistan in what was dubbed the Aurat March. As expected, the protest was divisive and sparked national debate. The placard at the centre of the debate? A plain orange poster that read *Khud khana garam kar lo*, or 'Heat up the food yourself'. Not an unreasonable suggestion by any means, yet the most patriarchal facets of society interpreted these words as an assault on Pakistani culture. A common complaint took issue with the construction of the informal 'kar lo' over the respectful 'kar lein' which represented not just a rejection of gender roles but an end to the respect that is the birthright of sons and husbands in South Asia.

Lost in much of the outrage was what lay behind the words and the plea for shared domestic responsibility: the fact that for many women, domestic labour is linked to violence. A month after the Aurat March, in a fit of rage, a middle-aged man murdered his wife for not preparing his dinner on time. In 2016, a man received a death sentence after being found guilty of murdering his daughter for failing to make a 'gol [round] roti'.

Most of us remember fondly our grandmothers' and mothers' kitchens but it can hardly be true that all of them enjoyed cooking. For most of history, and even today, cooking has not been a choice for women and, in the most extreme of cases, it has been the reason for their deaths. The luxury to be able to choose to cook is a class privilege. What to make of it, then?

My nani, my mother's mother, passed away when I was three. I was still too young to know her as a person, being barely a person myself back then. Yet I do remember 'cooking' with her. Slathering slices of Dawn bread with Happy Cow cream cheese – foil-wrapped triangles with a plastic string running through; pull at the red tab and the string would slice the foil away revealing sharp, creamy cheese – topping them with discs of juicy red tomatoes and sprinkling on top just a touch of rock salt and freshly ground black pepper. I was too young to be allowed near an actual stove at the time, and she was probably too sick to cook. Yet I cherish those memories.

Ami, who has never met a dish she couldn't master, whose food has many fans amongst family, friends and acquaintances, who teaches her ninth graders about yeast with a cherished tradition of holding a special pizza-making class every year, and who can whip up flaky croissants and airy choux pastry at a moment's notice (from scratch, of course), nonetheless considers herself a lazy cook compared to her mother who never took any shortcuts at all. She fondly remembers their home on Embassy Road in the 1980s, always overspilling with the neighbours and friends who flocked to her mother's food, the house brimming with chicken roasts with crunchy fried peas and French fries, Nargisi kofta – the original inspiration for scotch eggs – and shahi tukray, best described as a Mughlai bread pudding, although that does not do justice to the cardamom-scented dessert – and my grandmother's signature chocolate walnut cake covered in warm ganache made from fresh cream and cocoa powder.

My biology teacher mother becomes fascinated with organs every Eid-ul-Adha, even taking cow hearts to class for demonstrations. So devoted is she to life that she has taken in and raised generations of cats, peacocks, chickens and rabbits. She and I try to eat meat sparingly and, always, with a measure of guilt. As a young university student, she had attempted to set free a fluffy white rabbit she had been assigned in her lab.

During my second semester of college in New York City, a Pakistani restaurant called Shahi Biryani & Grill opens up on 109th between Columbus Avenue and Manhattan Avenue. The restaurant is just a short walk from campus, although it feels longer in the biting January air. It's a small operation, the brainchild of a sweet middle-aged couple – an uncle and an aunty – who run and own the place. The food, neatly laid out in containers behind glass panels like ice cream in a gelato shop, is the standard Pakistani fare you might find at a relative's dinner party: deep-fried shami kebabs, sabzi ki bhujia, bone-in chicken biryani, rich chicken makhani and the occasional beef nihari, plus creamy, bright orange chicken tikka masala, a cultural concession to the British invention that is synonymous with Indian food in the Western part of the world but unrecognizable back home. Every now and then, I want to order it but it is always a risky endeavour in the company of compatriots who would no doubt tease me for this choice. It does not help that I grew up in Islamabad, the city of burgers – an artificial, modern construction grafted onto the country's storied history.

Inside the Shahi & Biryani Grill, Urdu flows uninterrupted and *Geo News* plays without pause. Dessert we never order but always receive, and they insist we take it – thick, creamy bowls of kheer or pieces of sugar-soaked mithai such as gulab jamuns or barfi. The Shahi, as we call it, becomes our go-to caterer for cultural events on campus, and is also our little sanctuary from homesickness. We're quick to petition to put the restaurant on the university's list of approved vendors. When I google Shahi to order delivery one day, I find a negative Yelp review. The reviewer's outrage is palpable as he complains that the food is not made to order but pre-cooked and reheated. We laugh to ourselves. Only someone unfamiliar with Pakistani cooking would expect it to be prepped in an instant because, for most dishes, the flavour comes from the slow-cooking.

When I attempt biryani in our small dorm kitchen on 116th and Broadway, I am not afraid to improvise. I make the biryani salan, with the help of a box of Shan Sindhi biryani masala, and parboil the rice then layer it all in an aluminium tray because I do not have a pot large enough to contain it all. As I'm layering, I think of my sister who, when we were learning how to make it, had observed that biryani is like desi lasagne. I seal the aluminium tray and place it in the oven. The small oven can barely be closed and when I force the door shut, it pushes up the foil lid in a corner so that the dum – that crucial rice seal – is broken. I attempt to fix it but am not entirely successful. In the end, I decide to let it go and allow the stones to fall where they may, a laissez faire attitude I have nowhere else in life except my kitchen.

As the biryani cooks, I marshal the ingredients for a chocolate-orange mousse while watching what is then a new show on the CW Network, *Jane the Virgin*, a comedic remake of a Venezuelan telenovela. At its heart, the programme is a story of love shared across three generations of women who are as different as they are close. *Jane the Virgin* is a celebration of Latin culture, and my cooking is rooted in a desire to celebrate mine. A few hours later, the kitchen smells of kewra and the biryani is done. There must be magic in the air because despite the technical difficulties, the rice turns out as it should: grains all separate and half-dyed yellow and orange.

Perhaps I should have eschewed cooking. Perhaps that would have been the more obviously feminist thing to do, I think sometimes, but then I remember that feminism is about choice and it is my right to make this one. Still, I feel guilty at the privilege that has bolstered my right to choose, even as I am angry that most women do not get to choose. A generation ago, a more urban modern woman who had the option would have rejected the kitchen, but a strange change has occurred in the world of food. The kitchen, with all its secrets, has entered the popular consciousness. In a world where Instagram foodies thrive, cooking has become an on-trend hobby. Perhaps this change can help loosen up the rigidity of gender roles. The cracks are already showing. Tan France films roti and dal tutorials. Shan Foods airs a Biryani Masala ad in which a man wins over his very macho intended in-laws with his biryani. At social gatherings in homes, we still do that dance where men and women split off into the drawing room and the kitchen, the women discussing food and lawn collections, the men talking politics. Female hosts still bring in trolleys laden with food and serve their guests. Hospitality is one of the bedrocks of culture but I have seen men of my generation participate in it too and perhaps that is the way forward, not to reject food culture and hospitality but to indulge in it outside of gender roles.

I initially learned to cook because it was a fun thing to do and because it allowed me to make my favourite foods – poached eggs, first with vinegar and trepidation and then with plain water at just the right simmer; chicken karahi, fragrant with bright red in-season tomatoes and hot with seed-still-in green chillies; and pastas, spaghetti puttanesca because that's what author Lemony Snicket's Baudelaire children made for Count Olaf, and lasagne because it's the crown jewel of Italian cuisine.

I knew how to brew coffee before I could make chai because I am an ardent coffee drinker. I joke that this is anti-colonial resistance because coffee has its origins in the Muslim world while tea is all wrapped up in British colonialism. Really, I just like the taste. I learned how to prepare coffee because I wanted to drink it and, later, chai, because my parents drink it. Neither skill was developed to present ceremoniously to a set of rishtay-wallay – prospective in-laws – who would view this practice as a test, another opportunity to scrutinize and criticize. If those had been my associations with the kitchen, if I had been taught how to cook so that I would make a good wife, perhaps I would have hated it too.

When I am about to leave my first full-time job for graduate school, I make goodbye cupcakes for the office. It is a small gesture of gratitude towards colleagues who have made hours spent writing policy briefs, budget reports, and negotiating donor meetings not only bearable but fun. The night before, I cream butter and sugar, separate eggs, and fold the wet ingredients into the dry. Then I bake my cupcakes and leave them to cool overnight. The next morning, I wake up a little earlier than usual to inject lemon curd into each cupcake and finish them with bright blue frosting, piled high like mounds of cartoon snow. It occurs to me that baking for work is such an odd novelty in a place where being able to work away from home and outside of domestic household tasks is an opportunity few women get to experience.

The cracks in the Pakistani glass ceiling have been slow to form and they only materialize with a combination of education, class privilege and familial support. So, when women like me who have been afforded such immense privilege choose to step into the kitchen, we do it on the shoulders of entire communities. What a strange and fraught thing it is to be able to study and work and yet come back to the kitchen to preserve our heritage, to feed loved ones, to keep traditions alive, or simply to satisfy a craving.

Baingan ka Bharta

For the Aubergine (Eggplant or Brinjal) Mix

75 ml or 5 tbsp vegetable oil
2 medium onions, chopped
1 tbsp finely sliced ginger
1 tsp finely sliced garlic
2 medium tomatoes, chopped
2 large aubergines (eggplants)
Fresh coriander (cilantro) and chopped green chillies for garnish
Juice of 1 lemon (optional)

Spices

½ tsp chilli powder
½ tsp turmeric
½ tsp coriander powder
1 tsp salt (or to taste)
½ tsp cumin
½ tsp mustard seeds
1 tsp fennel seeds

Method

1. Roast the aubergines in the oven at 200°C (400°F, Gas Mark 6) for at least half an hour, drizzled with about half of the oil until the skin becomes taut and easily falls away. Then peel and roughly chop the aubergines.
2. Dry roast the spices in a pan until nicely browned and then grind them together.

3. Sauté the onions in oil until light golden, and then lower the heat.
4. Add the garlic and ginger and sauté until just fragrant.
5. Add the tomatoes and stir fry until the water evaporates.
6. Add the ground spices.
7. Add the aubergines (already roasted, peeled and chopped). Sauté until they are incorporated into the dish.
8. Lower the heat and cover to steam for about 10 minutes or until the oil starts to separate out.
9. Garnish with coriander and green chillies.
10. Squeeze lemon juice on top if the dish isn't tart enough from the tomatoes.
11. Enjoy with roti or rice!

Alhamdulillah: With Gratitude and Relish

Kaiser Haq

Most early memories sink into oblivion like the pebbles children delight in chucking into ponds. However, the memories that do not sink but stick in the mind provide enjoyable topics for reminiscence.

Just like that most memorable of feasts at Grandmother's chehlum. This is the Muslim rite of passage marking the end of forty days' mourning following a person's death. The observances are similar to those on the Qul Khani, four days from the death. The complete Quran is recited by a team of Hafiz-e-Qurans, religious professionals who have memorized the holy book by heart. There is a collective prayer for the departed soul, and the congregation are treated to refreshments, as are any beggars who have gathered outside. Usually, snacks are distributed at the Qul. A typical middle-class family would hand out packets containing savouries and sweets; a poor man's Qul could end with the distribution of simple jalebis or batashas. More often than not, mourners at a chehlum are served dinner, nowadays increasingly in boxes ordered from caterers. This meal generally consists of a combination meat and pilau dish, biryani (goat) or tehari (beef) or murgh pilau (chicken); or it could be khichuri with meat.

For Hindus the fortieth-day rites, called sraddha, end with a satvik feast, which is supposed to be conducive to spiritual development. In concrete terms, such cuisine is vegetarian but without onions or garlic, vegetables which are said to make for spiritually deleterious excitation. Partaking of such a refined repast in our ancestral village is one of my memorable culinary experiences in childhood.

The sraddha was that of one of the elders in a family with which we had close social ties. Virtually the entire village had been invited. Brahmin priests droned Vedic mantras in one corner, but the centre of attention was the local trencherman, a lightly built, nondescript Muslim chap. The menu included labra, a delicately flavoured dish of mixed vegetables cooked in ghee, and luchis, thin, deep-fried, white-flour flatbread. As an appreciative crowd watched, the man, eating quietly, unhurriedly, polished off a mountain of labra and hundreds of luchis.

Feasts honouring the dead no doubt fulfil multiple purposes. It is hoped that prayers from well-fed mourners will carry more weight. Sharing a meal is also a life-affirming act and cements social bonds.

Father and his elder brother were both deeply attached to their mother, but Father's attachment – he was Grandfather's posthumous child – had more of an emotional edge to it. Father wanted the very best katchi biryani for Grandmother's chehlum. A reputed baburchi (bawarchi or chef) and his assistants came from Old Dhaka, a part of the city whose Mughal connection is reflected in its culinary traditions. The team spent the greater part of the day preparing the meal that would be served after Maghrib prayers. Accompanying the biryani would be borhani, a sour, peppered yoghurt drink, and alu bokhara chutney, a thick gravy. Dessert would be zarda, a sweetened rice dish with yellow food-colouring, ghee, cardamoms, raisins and various nuts.

Though the word is of Persian origin, biryani, as we know it, developed in Mughal India. According to one legend, Empress Mumtaz Mahal when inspecting the troops found them undernourished and instructed the cooks to prepare a composite meal of rice and meat to build up their strength. The dish spread to every part of the empire, acquiring a local flavour wherever it went. The baburchis who accompanied Nawab Wajed Ali of Awadh (Oudh) into exile in Calcutta after the 1857 Uprising added the potato to the biryani, and baburchis in Dhaka picked up the innovation.

The classic Dhakai katchi biryani should have goat, rice and potato in the ratio 4:2:1, together with ghee (the richer the better) and a host of ingredients in small portions that make for a refined flavour, such as alu bokhara (local prunes), saffron, onions, lime juice, ginger paste, garlic paste, dry ginger, red chilli powder, cumin seeds, cloves, cardamom, cinnamon, caraway seeds, cubeb pepper, black pepper, grated nutmeg, mace, salt, yoghurt, soya oil, sugar, edible oil, rosewater and milk. The rice may be basmati or the sweet-smelling chinigura (literally 'grains of sugar'). But in my view what sets the Dhakai biryani apart is the meat. It has to be the meat of the 'Black Bengal', a resilient, fast-breeding variety of goat that thrives in Bangladesh and eastern India. Muslims introduced the practice of neutering the male kid to turn it into what is called a khasi, whose finely textured and tender meat, now with a little extra fat and without the pong that would otherwise linger in the he-goat, gives the Dhakai biryani an edge over other varieties.

Katchi (also spelt kachchi), as opposed to the pukki variety, indicates that the meat, duly marinated, is raw (katcha) when it is placed in alternating layers with rice and the other ingredients. The lid of the degchi (pot) is sealed with dough, and charcoal embers placed underneath between several bricks, and spread on the lid as well. This is a form of slow-cooking called 'dum', or 'breath', in Persian, Urdu and Hindi: the rich concoction trapped in the degchi 'breathes' in the low heat. The moment of truth is when the massive lid comes off the giant degchi, and the dum rises several feet high and proportionately portly, like something out of *One Thousand and One Nights*. I still remember the cloud of aromatic vapour that cast an ineffable enchantment over my seven-year-old olfactory nerves.

Many are the humorous accounts of jousts of wit between denizens of Dhaka, the old Mughal capital of Bengal, and the babus of Calcutta, the upstart colonial capital. One such has to do with food. A Calcutta babu reminisced about a feast in his native city: 'I can still smell the bouquet of the puris when I think about it.' The Dhakaiya retorted: 'Last year we had such a delicious biryani at a family wedding, I can still feel the ghee on my fingers. Look, I can't even snap my fingers; they slip noiselessly over each other.' The dish at Grandmother's chehlum was that kind of biryani. Neighbours were talking about it months after the event.

As with everyone else, barring a few sad exceptions no doubt, my experience with food began not with culinary creations but with suckling, a word whose mild connotations hardly do justice to the vigorous action of strong albeit toothless jaws devouring the maternal – or wet nurse's – breast.

What has that got to do with food culture, one might interject. Well, every culture lays down certain ground rules for breast-feeding, weaning and introducing infants to solid nourishment. Al-Baqarah, the longest surah in the Quran, specifies two years as the limit for breast-feeding unless for some reason the parents want an earlier weaning.

At two and a half years – Mother pregnant again – I refused to surrender my right to the primal nourishment. A distant aunt who lived next door and was known for her wicked sense of humour held whispered colloquy with the women in our family. I smelt conspiracy but couldn't put my finger on it. I felt the urge to go for Mother's breasts and moved towards her. Strangely, there were no interdictory words. Nor did Mother try to fob me off. But as my lips touched her warm nipples, I recoiled and burst into loud wails before rolling on the dirty courtyard in frustration and rage. The nipples had been anointed with quinine.

After such bitterness, what forgiveness? Not only did the quinine poison my relations with Mother, but my food habits also had to change overnight. And by and by I became an avid reader; years later, I would read somewhere that for bookworms, books serve as a substitute for the maternal nipple.

Ours was a joint family comprising my childless uncle and aunt, my parents and, in due course, several siblings. Aunt and Mother were sisters and first cousins to their husbands. Grandmother, whose chehlum was so memorable, was their father's sister. Only Muslim families can become intertwined in such a semi-incestuous fashion. For us children it was like growing up with two sets of parents, one more indulgent than the other.

In those days we had our meals in the small kitchen that had been built, like the three other huts that originally made up our rural-style home, of bamboo matting, with a tin roof. Often I would eat with Uncle, sitting cross-legged on madoor mats made of reed grass while Aunty served us rice, veggies, fish curry and dal by the amber light of a hurricane lantern, since electricity would take a few more years to reach our home. We ate with our right-hand fingers off enamelware plates. Uncle emphasized the importance of tartib, Arabic for discipline and order, even in the act of eating. Unnecessary chatter was discouraged. In raising a morsel to the lips, one silently mouthed bismillah ('I begin in the name of Allah'); subhanallah ('Glory be to Allah') while chewing slowly, mindfully; and alhamdulillah ('All praise and thanks to Allah') while swallowing. I don't remember how long I kept this up, but it was long enough to create a permanent niche in my memory. I haven't heard of anyone else going to such lengths, though it isn't uncommon to hear people start a meal with a bismillah in an undertone, and end with an alhamdulillah.

Meal ended, we'd drink water from enamel mugs and then pour some to wash the right hand over the plate, rubbing the fingers together. Uncle taught me to dip the right index finger in the water that collected in the plate and let a drop fall into each eye, making it burn a little. He said it was good for the eyesight. A similar claim was made for squirting the juice of orange peel into the eyes. Neither did Uncle much good, for he developed cataracts in middle age and in his last years was purblind.

Occasionally when Mother served dinner, for some odd reason lost to memory, I would go into a sulk and refuse to eat. This would elicit a resounding slap. I would then bolt out of the house but never go very far, and loiter, waiting for Uncle or Father to come and coax me into going back to a cold dinner. During the brief spell of rebellion, I'd weave fantasies of lonely independence, like that of a waif or a beggar for whom Islam has a special place. Giving alms is one of the five pillars of Islam, so if there were no paupers – 'miskins' and 'miskinas' in Arabic – the faithful would not be able to fulfil their religious obligations. They might have to fall back on relativism, like the wealthy Arab sheikhs who dish out food and other necessities to pilgrims from poorer countries, often to the latters' chagrin. 'Do I look like a miskin?' plaintively asked an affluent Bangladeshi pilgrim into whose unwary arms a sheikh's servant thrust a pile of goodies.

In much of the Muslim world and the globalized planet as a whole, there are of course plenty of miskins and miskinas, many of whom can be considered to create an informal fraternity that affirms its right to exist with a certain pride.

'I have seen Spanish beggars,' notes Emil Cioran, a Romanian essayist, 'and I should like to have been their hagiographer.'

These 'saints of indigence' defy the ethos of Homo economicus. Many among them, particularly the disabled ones, have evolved distinctive repertoires of chants and songs that qualify them as performance artists. I once essayed a rather cold-hearted aphorism on the subject: 'The beggars on the streets are actors; the traffic lights their footlights. With their woeful expressions, their spectacular deformities, their carefully maintained sores, their laments, chants, ululations, they depict a broad range of human misery, and thus fulfil the same function as serious drama. But unlike their counterparts on stage, they do not crave applause, only a few coins. Such modesty is exemplary.'

I know of beggars who are quite well off, owning a house and farmland in their villages. One shouldn't grudge them such riches; their property has been bought with hard-won money. Arguably, beggars will be around not only as long as alms-giving is believed to earn one spiritual points but also, as Marxists would claim, as long as capitalism keeps breeding unemployment. Those who find this state of affairs morally reprehensible might think of supporting the idea of a universal basic income.

Meanwhile, the thought of hundreds, thousands, of poor people being fed – as they are at iftar, marking the end of the Ramadan fast, at the Eids, and on Fridays after Jumma prayers – offers some emotional relief, since hunger in a world that has enough to feed everyone is an unmitigated evil. Some years back, out of thoughts such as these, I produced a modest poem:

Poor Man Eating

Were I a painter
I am sure
My signature theme would be
The title of this poem.

The sun races to the zenith,
Imperious as an oriental autocrat.
The poor man crouches
In imitation Tommy Hilfiger rags
In the dwindling shade
Of a denuded tree.

His hands cradle
A bowl of fired earth –
It could be a Ouija board
To conjure up goodies,
Courtesy of the weak of conscience.

And when they come
How he falls to it!
Eyes focused in mystic concentration,

Left arm protectively around
The pile of comestibles,
As right hand shovels them
Into an eager mouth.

I would paint the scene
Over and over
In luscious oil:
The painted proliferation
Might work magic,
Converting seeming impossibility
Into palpable reality:
All the world's poor
Men, women, children
Gathered as if on the mythic day

Of final reckoning,
On this lowly earth,
Devouring earthly fare:
O the gods would come down
To bless and share!

The big difference between Hindu and Muslim eating habits has to do with animals. Many Hindus regard cattle as sacred and the eating of beef as sacrilegious. On the other hand, there is the Judeo-Islamic taboo on pork, which is considered 'unclean'. This apart, in any particular region, there is more similarity than difference in the cuisine of the two communities. The differences are rather subtle.

Take, for instance, rice pudding, which is a popular dessert in Bengal. Hindus cook payesh (from Sanskrit payasa, milk), using wholegrain rice boiled in milk, with ghee, raisins, cardamom and nuts added. The Muslim phirni (from Persian fereni, rice custard) is the same, only the rice is ground before being cooked in milk.

The fare for feasts and festivals gives a good idea of what is distinctive in a community's cuisine. Shab-e-Meraj, the night of the Prophet's journey via hell to heaven and an interview with the Almighty – described in Surah Al-Isra, which might well have inspired Dante's *Divine Comedy* – is commemorated by feeding the poor, but there is no specification as to the menu.

Shab-e-Barat or Laylatul Barat, the night when Allah decides everyone's fate (barat) for the following year, used to be like the Hindu Diwali, with unending fireworks, which must have helped those who wanted to stay awake for night-long prayers. The special halwas and flatbreads of ground rice were a delight for children. Besides feeding them to beggars, they were exchanged between families as a goodwill gesture. But the practice is on the wane.

Milad-un-Nabi, the Prophet's birthday, is ritually celebrated in gatherings called milads where sweets are distributed. Frowned upon by Wahhabis, the celebrations had gone into a decline but are now regaining their popularity. No doubt the most important festivals from religious as well as culinary points of view are the two Eids: Eid-ul-Fitr, which follows Ramadan, the month of fasting; and Eid-ul-Adha, the festival of the Abrahamic sacrifice that comes at the time of the Hajj pilgrimage.

Whether Ramadan is a month of fasting or intermittent feasting is a question on the minds of many. It was different when I was growing up. For children, it was a rite of passage. They didn't have to fast every day of Ramadan; a single day was enough to earn one's laurels, so to speak; and the younger the age one could do it, the greater the credit. I was not quite seven when I made my first attempt. It was only partially successful. By 3 p.m., with another three hours to go, I could feel my knees shaking. The elders decided that was achievement enough, and urged me to break the fast. At thirteen, when I was in a boarding school, we were allowed to fast for five days, if we wished. I decided to fast, more as a test of endurance than anything else. I had been reading about adventurers in the Wild West going without food for days. The fast didn't excuse us from the usual exercise, though: physical training or PT at six and games in the afternoon. Iftar was relished all the more; the sherbet to break the fast most of all.

Those in the food business have always tried to capitalize on Ramadan by turning iftar into an epicurean indulgence. Chowk Bazaar in Old Dhaka has long been famous for iftar specialities. In a feature titled 'Chawkbazar: The Original Iftar Market of Bangladesh,' the *Daily Star* (19 May 2018) listed the grandiosely named 'shahi jilapil' and 'shahi paratha' (shahi means 'royal'); the slangily and piquantly named 'Boro Baper Polay Khay' (What a Rich Dad's Son Eats). The latter is 'a mixture of chickpeas, minced meat, potatoes, brains, chira, egg, chicken, spices and ghee'. Other delicacies include 'beef, chicken, mutton, pigeon and quail roasts; keema roll; keema paratha; borhani; doi bora; different types of kebabs, including shami, sutli, jaali, Irani and tikka.' Upmarket restaurants and hotels have lately got in on the act, offering not only lavish iftar buffets, but at sehri as well, this being the pre-dawn meal before starting the fast. No wonder the affluent put on weight in the month of abstinence.

On the Eids, the day starts with sweet dishes – traditionally semai or vermicelli, either ghee-based lachcha semai or the dudh semai, cooked in milk – and meals are usually pilau with chicken qorma, goat and beef curry.

But it's Eid-ul-Adha that witnesses a splurge on meat. In 2019, an estimated ten million goats and cattle were sacrificed. The extravagance is the sign of a rapidly growing economy. During my childhood the count would have been a tiny fraction. In our corner of the town, seven households would collectively sacrifice a modest-sized cow or ox. The number is significant. A goat or sheep counted for one merit point, cattle or even larger animals, like camels, seven points. The children of the seven households would actively take part in the skinning of the animal. One of the neighbourhood elders, whom we addressed as uncles, said it was good training for us; it was early familiarity with gore that made Muslims good fighters. I remember wondering why in that case the Muslim armies in the wars of the past several centuries had tended to be at the receiving end. But the pleasure of gorging on beef put politics in the shade. Normally in those days we would buy a pound of beef once every week or fortnight. Eid-ul-Adha was then, as it still is for most people, the season of beef-eating. Till we acquired our first fridge when I was sixteen, the meat was partially cooked and left in pots; the fat collected as a thick layer on top and acted as a preservative.

Until I entered my teens, my school holidays were spent in the villages – mainly Mother's ancestral village – where I acquired a fair acquaintance with rural eating habits. Supreme importance is attached to the quantities consumed, and trenchermen are figures of legend. After Grandfather was married to Grandmother, my great-grandfather paid a visit to his son's in-laws. He was massively built, renowned for his strength and notorious for his temper. He asked his hosts what was cooking for lunch. Koi machh, he was told: the climbing perch, *Anabas testudineus*. How many? Seventy. When the meal was served, the guest counted the fish and found them a dozen short. He pushed his plate away. Placatory sounds were made and the remaining fish quickly fetched. He fell to with relish. Seventy cooked koi machh of average size would have weighed three and a half kilogrammes. Such are the believe-it-or-not tales that lend charm to the days of yore.

I have seen guests at village weddings put away enormous quantities of food, so we, perhaps, ought to be more generous with belief. The wedding guests are first received with a broad assortment of pithas, traditional rice cakes of varied design, texture and flavour. If the groom's party is peckish after an arduous journey, they will eat more pithas than they ought to, and shortly afterwards find the floor being laid with dastarkhwans for the main meal. These are strips of cloth embroidered with traditional motifs, which are laid all around the room. Guests sit in rows, wash their right hands with water poured over spittoons, and are served out of huge bowls. Rice and beef are the main items. The plates are invariably soup plates, for much gravy and dal are consumed. Interestingly, the local name for a chinaware plate is *chinir bashon*, obviously a corruption of 'china', but in Bengali the phrase means 'plate of sugar'. The glasses are thick half-pint tumblers with straight sides. The men serving must be sharp-eyed, for it is bad manners to let a guest's plate become empty. A curious choreography marks the delivery of a fresh serving. As the serving spoon, filled with rice or meat, is thrust forward, the guest's left hand makes a show of refusal but draws back as the spoon advances and graciously submits to the task of devouring the fresh pile. This pas de deux is repeated until both parties silently agree to a cessation. The spittoon bearer comes to help the guest wash. As for the ladies, their meal is eaten in the inner quarters, and is far from a gargantuan affair.

The denizens of Chattogram (Chittagong) have kept alive the practice of hosting feasts called mezbani, mezban being Persian for 'host'. Throwing a mezbani adds to one's prestige, and it may or may not be for marking a particular occasion; for example, a chehlum, a son's circumcision, or the birth of a child. It is an open-to-all party lasting from morning till afternoon, in which an endless stream of guests are treated to a meal comprising steamed rice, beef, nawla kanji (cattle bone soup) and kaloi (chickpea) dal.

What makes the feast distinctive is mezbani beef, a dark curry prepared by specialist baburchis who are loath to part with their secret recipes. Social clubs in Dhaka and other cities arrange annual winter mezbanis for which they fly in chefs from Chittagong. In a mezbani thrown by a Hindu, fish replaces beef. For their everyday diet Chittagonians have a yen for dried fish, which may be added to vegetable, fresh fish or meat dishes, and hot dishes in general. There is a joke about a Chittagonian buying a kilogramme of green chillies and a hundred grammes of dried chillies; the green chillies were the vegetables to be cooked with the dried chillies. Strange to think that chillies were brought to the region from Mexico by the Portuguese as late as the seventeenth century!

Another noteworthy style of cooking beef comes from the northeastern Bangladeshi district of Sylhet, ancestral home of ninety per cent of the 'Indian' restaurateurs in Britain. The special ingredient in this case is shatkora, *Citrus macroptera*, a semi-wild citrus fruit native to the region as well as to Malesia and Melanesia. Shatkora makes a zingy chutney and adds a tart edge to beef curry or a fish dish. The boal, a kind of catfish, is a great favourite with Sylhetis. The sequence of dishes at a typical Sylheti feast may come as a surprise. I was once invited to a feast thrown by a Sylheti family in London, where pilau was accompanied by beef, lamb and boal fish – in that order.

Arguably, eating out is the essence of a modern food culture. Bangladeshi cities, especially Dhaka and Chittagong, have undergone a dizzying spike in the number of restaurants and cafés that might be dubbed international. Their Chinese, Thai, Japanese, Italian or Indian cuisine, or fast-food joints – KFC, Pizza Hut and Burger King among them – are no different from what any other city could offer. But Old Dhaka can boast that eating out is the norm there. No Old Dhaka family cooks breakfast; the meal is consumed as a takeaway from one of the traditional eateries in the mohalla, or locality. So are the teatime snacks, like the deep-fried puris or samosas and singaras or the crispy layered flatbread called bakarkhani, delicious with the local cheese or a light sweetmeat, and the tea itself, the strong, milky variety that recalls the earlier English phrase 'a dish of tea'. Often other meals are also ordered from the local eateries.

For those of us living in the newer part of Dhaka, a culinary trip to the Old Town is a welcome outing. Recently, I accompanied a couple of young colleagues to a well known restaurant there for breakfast. We started with khasir paya, soup of khasi leg bones, thickened with a little flour and garnished with coriander, and moved on to khasi curry and liver, a mixed vegetable dish, with oil-free parathas, baked rather than fried on a tawa pan, finishing with rice phirni and 'a dish of tea'. We agreed it was a most satisfying meal. The restaurant, and others like it, has a simple sign: 'We Serve No Beef.' There is a praiseworthy philosophy of inclusivity behind this; the restaurateur welcomes both Muslim and Hindu patrons. Kebab joints, where beef items are prominent on the menu, are patronized mainly by Muslims. My colleagues are eager to go on more culinary forays into Old Dhaka, and anyone coming this way is welcome to join us.

Bon appétit!

Katchi Biryani

This recipe comes, with the language slightly edited, from *Recipes from the Rasoi* by Shawkat Osman, published in 2010 by Dhaka Club Ltd, by kind permission of the author and the copyright holder, his daughter Ms Rukhsara Osman.

Shawkat Osman, in his notes to the recipe, writes:

> 'It is a basic Katchi recipe, obtained from the migrant Awadhi Baburchis; the potato was adopted during their transitional stay in Calcutta (Kolkata). The Ustad [master chef] with all his assistants takes fifteen to eighteen hours to cook this biryani at a leisurely pace. The recipe requires a fair amount of time management,

so follow the steps in the order outlined above, and you will not need more than 1 hour of preparation and 2 hours of cooking time. Correctly and carefully made, it is an epicure's delight.'

1½ kg chevon (use castrated Black Bengal he-goat for best results; if you can't get goat meat, use mutton or lamb), cut into 10 pieces
½ kg basmati rice
½ kg potato, peeled
1 cup onions, finely chopped
2 tsp lime/lemon juice
2 tsp ginger paste
4 tsp garlic paste
2 tsp sonth (ground ginger)
3 tsp red chilli powder
2 tsp cumin seeds
5 + 5 cloves
5 cardamoms, de-podded
5 cardamom pods, gently cracked
2 + 2 (2.5-cm-long) cinnamon sticks
1 tsp caraway seeds
1 tsp cubeb pepper
¼ tsp grated nutmeg
1 tsp mace, pounded
1 tsp freshly ground black pepper
2 tsp + 2 tsp + ½ tsp + ½ tsp salt
1 cup ghee
½ cup yoghurt
1 cup soya oil (if you can't get soya oil, use any vegetable oil)
2 tsp sugar
5 drops edible yellow food colouring
2 drops edible red food colouring
½ cup rosewater
2 cups sliced onions
Pinch of saffron
½ cup milk

Method

1. In a metal mortar (hamam–dista), pound the following ingredients: cumin, 5 cloves, 5 de-podded cardamoms, 2 cinnamon sticks, caraway, cubeb pepper, nutmeg, mace and black pepper.
2. After you obtain a fine powder, transfer the spices to a mixing bowl. Add the following: red chilli powder, 2 tsp salt, garlic paste, ginger paste, ground ginger, yoghurt, lime/lemon juice. Mix and blend to get a smooth paste.
3. Drop the meat into the mixing bowl and meticulously apply the paste to coat the meat pieces. Marinate for 4 hours.
4. Spread the rice on a kula (a winnowing tray of woven bamboo) or a clean surface, pick out and discard any grit, as well as dark or discoloured grains.
5. Wash the rice in a fine sieve or colander held under warm running water until the draining water runs clear.
6. Place the rice in a large bowl, add 2 tsp salt, cover it with 2.5 cm (1 inch) of cold water, and soak for 2 hours.
7. In a small glass bowl, soak the saffron in lukewarm milk and let this stand (covered) until required.
8. In a separate glass bowl, mix the following: yellow food colouring, red food colouring and rosewater. Let this stand (covered) until required.
9. Heat oil in a korai (wok), throw in the sugar, and cook until the sugar caramelizes.
10. Chuck in the potatoes and sauté them until their coat acquires a caramel colour, strain the potatoes and keep them aside. Discard the oil.
11. Heat ghee in a large, heavy degchi (pot), lob in the sliced onions and sauté until they are golden. Using a slotted spoon, strain out the fried onions (baresta), and set them aside. Reserve the ghee as well.
12. In a separate stainless-steel pan, bring 6 cups of fresh water to a boil over a high flame.
13. Drain the rice. In a slow, thin stream, so that the water does not stop boiling, pour in the rice and sprinkle with ½ tsp salt.

14. Stir once or twice, then brisk boil, uncovered, for 5 minutes.
15. Occasionally pick out a few of the rice grains with a spoon and chew on them to see if they have softened.
16. When the rice is half-crunchy, half-soft, take the pot off the flame and drain the excess water through a fine kitchen strainer.
17. Lightly fluff the rice with a large fork to remove all moisture, and to keep the grains separated.
18. Divide the rice into three portions.
19. Colour the first portion with the yellow–red colour concoction (Step 8) and set aside.
20. Mix the reserved ghee (Step 11) with the second portion of rice, and set aside.
21. Keep the remaining rice untouched and white.
22. Lay the potatoes at the bottom of a large degchi or a heavy saucepan with a 30 cm (12 inch) base. Sprinkle these potatoes with ½ tsp salt. Pile up the yellow-red-coloured rice (Step 19) loosely on top of the potatoes.
23. Take half the quantity of meat and arrange the pieces on top of the rice. Scatter half the 'baresta' on top of the meat.
24. Cover the meat with the ghee-mixed rice (Step 20) and lay out the remaining pieces of meat.
25. Scatter the cracked cardamoms, 5 cloves and 2 cinnamon sticks over the meat and cover the entire surface with the remaining baresta.
26. Loosely cover the second layer of meat with the remaining white rice (Step 21).
27. Sprinkle the saffron-infused milk over the rice so as to create irregular patches of saffron colouring.
28. Make a soft dough with the 2 cups of plain flour and enough water. Roll out the dough into a long, thin strip.
29. Place the strip on the rim of the pot, covering the entire circumference. Rest the lid on the strip of dough, and press firmly to attach the lid tightly to the dough.
30. Place the pot on a high flame for about 5 minutes. Then take the pot off the stovetop and place it in a preheated oven.

31. Cook on low to moderate heat (170°C or 330°F) for 50 minutes. (As cooking time varies from oven to oven, please experiment with the timing to find out how to obtain the best result, of 'neither overcooking the rice nor undercooking the meat'.)
32. Switch off the oven and wait for about 5 minutes before taking out the pot.
33. Insert the handle end of a metal khunti (cooking spud or spatula) right through the centre of the food until it reaches the bottom of the pot. Gently pull it out and check to see if the end is well coated with fat.
34. If there is no fat coating the spatula's handle, return the pot, covered with its lid, and cook for 10 minutes more over a very low flame. At this stage you should be able to hear a slight spattering sound from the fat which has collected at the bottom.
35. To serve, open the lid, take a ceramic dinner plate and use it to cut vertically into the biryani. Push the plate down until the edge touches the bottom, and with one deft scoop, take out a plateful. It will contain all the six layers: potato, rice, meat, rice, meat, and again rice.
36. Slide the biryani onto a serving dish in such a way that all the layers are discernible.

The Rise of Pakistan's 'Burger' Generation

Sanam Maher

On the evening of 24 April 2015, Sabeen Mahmud, the director of The Second Floor, a beloved café and communal space in Karachi, was shot and killed. Mahmud's murder, and the resounding question of who was responsible, made news within and outside Pakistan. Less than a month later, the authorities announced that they had a culprit: a twenty-seven-year-old man named Saad Aziz.

For many, Aziz seemed to be the unlikeliest of suspects. Media reports painted him as a mild-mannered man who had graduated from a reputable Karachi business school with good grades. He was the father of a baby girl, and a restaurant owner who loved football.

Aziz was 'a burger kid', explained one unnamed friend interviewed by the Pakistani newspaper the *Express Tribune* at the time of his arrest. 'He was funny, acted in plays and danced.'

In Pakistan, the label 'burger kid' is a loaded one.

'The implications of being a "burger" are that you are spoilt, and detached from what is going on in the country,' says Monis Rahman, forty-five, the founder of Rozee.pk, Pakistan's biggest online jobs portal.

'A burger lives in a cocoon and is enamoured by things outside of Pakistan – by the West,' Rahman explains. The word is often used to describe well-to-do Pakistanis who may have

American or British-tinged accents after years spent studying or working outside Pakistan, he says.

'Fully dressed with matching accessories even for 8 a.m. classes at university, they always own the latest in fashion, cars and gadgets,' is another definition suggested by the *Express Tribune*. 'Their "parties" mimic nightclubs in foreign countries since the poor souls don't have any clubs here and have to recreate the experience on their own.'

Despite the connotations, being a 'burger' in Pakistan has value, says Rahman. 'People who have stronger English-speaking skills and more international exposure are valued higher in the jobs market.'

Since 2013, there has been a slow but steady evolution of the term 'burger' beyond its pejorative context.

That year, Pakistanis voted in the first general elections in which power was transferred from one democratically elected government to another.

Former cricketer Imran Khan, the leader of the Pakistan Tehreek-e-Insaf (PTI) party, was dismissed as a 'baby boy' or a 'burger boy' by older political leaders, while his supporters were called 'burgers'.

'It's the first time that the burger group will also come out to vote,' quipped politician Sheikh Rasheed Ahmed before the elections in May 2013.

'They're going to join the chapati-and-salan [curry] folk. They might need to carry their laptops on their heads to protect them from the sun.'

While Rasheed hinted that PTI supporters were more suited to campaigning on social media from the comfort of their homes, he made one crucial point: 'If they do come out to vote, they'll do amazingly well.'

An estimated 46.2 million people voted in these elections, compared with the 36.6 million voters from the previous 2008 elections. The 2013 election saw the highest voter turnout in Pakistan's history. Thirteen million were first-time voters and more than half the registered voters were aged between eighteen and twenty-nine.

Rasheed was proved right. Khan's base of young, educated urban 'burgers' helped the PTI emerge from the elections as the second-most powerful political party in the country. With 7.7 million votes, the PTI knocked President Asif Ali Zardari's party, the Pakistan People's Party (PPP), which had garnered 6.9 million votes, from its perch and into third place.

PTI's burgers began to wear the label with pride; literally, in some cases, as the party's supporters turned up at rallies and on election day wearing T-shirts emblazoned with the words 'Kaptaan's Burger Army' (Kaptaan is a moniker that pays tribute to Khan's time as captain of the Pakistani cricket team).

That an American fast food has become a catch-all phrase for a generation of Pakistanis who flocked to a political party which promised change, including an end to the decades-old hold of the two ruling parties, and the rooting out of corruption, has its origins in the story of how the food itself first came to Pakistan. This story begins in 1953, a handful of years after the Partition of India and Pakistan, when a man named Syed Musa Raza arrived in Karachi.

Originally from Lucknow in pre-Partition India, Raza spent several years after Partition in 1947 working in the Middle East. Although he knew no one in Karachi when he arrived, his son, Ashfaq Raza, fifty-three, says: 'My father dreamed of starting up a business that would ensure people would know of us and know our family's name.'

As his nine sons moved to the United States and England for their studies, Musa Raza, who is no longer alive, urged them to return to Karachi as soon as they could to start a business.

Ashfaq's older brother, Iqbal, a flight engineer, travelled frequently to Europe and had witnessed the arrival of McDonald's there in the 1970s. 'He saw the long lines outside McDonald's restaurants and hit upon the idea of bringing the franchise to Pakistan,' says Raza.

In 1978, the brothers approached the McDonald's corporation. They were promptly turned down. 'They told us that Pakistan was not ready for burgers,' Raza recalls.

They made an offer to Burger King who gave them the same answer.

'So we took that as a challenge,' Raza explains. 'We wanted to prove these multimillion-dollar chains wrong.'

To learn the ropes, the brothers spent a few months working at a McDonald's near their family home in Hartford, Connecticut. At one point, Raza and five of his brothers worked at the same outlet.

Their colleagues did not know that they were there to soak up all the information they could about running a fast-food enterprise.

'We even offered to work for no pay,' says Raza, who spent three months at McDonald's while in high school.

The brothers were paid $1.80 an hour and worked their way up from cleaning the restrooms to learning to make the food, handle equipment and manage staff. In late 1978, the Raza brothers returned to Karachi and began testing burger recipes.

'Our friends warned us that this was a bad idea,' says Raza. 'At that time, there were no burgers in Pakistan – just bun kebabs.' The bun kebab, a local variant of the burger, consists of a slender minced-meat patty and a potato or lentil patty. Slapped inside a bun and garnished with a fried egg, onions, chillies and chutney, the bun kebab is a staple at roadside cafés or street vendors' carts and is gulped down in three or four bites. But the brothers didn't want to make what Raza refers to as this 'poor man's burger'.

'I'm sure many people told McDonald's in the 1950s that American households weren't interested in what they had to offer,' Raza says. 'But McDonald's changed the game. That's what we wanted to do – change the model of how and what people ate in Pakistan.'

They spent three months perfecting a tender beef patty with a peppery spice and the slightly sweet 'secret sauce' that cut out the need for what Raza calls 'frills', like tomatoes or onions.

In the following months, the brothers laid down the foundation for Pakistan's first burger joint, and created a blueprint that would be replicated in hundreds of fast-food outlets in the country for years to come, its simplicity belying the mammoth task of creating an entirely novel approach to eating out.

The brothers were determined to source all the food products locally – this was to be a proudly Pakistani enterprise – and so, while equipment had to be brought in from the US, everything from ketchup to straws and paper ramekins for sauce had to be made in the country.

'You won't believe it, but at that time, there was only one supplier in the country who made disposable cups, and it was selling them to the national airline only,' Raza recalls. 'They refused to sell the cups to us because they didn't think it was worthwhile and they didn't understand what we were trying to do.' It took the family five years to convince the company to produce the sixteen-ounce cups they needed.

Following the McDonald's model, the Raza brothers wanted to hire students to work at the outlet. But they did not anticipate the stigma associated with working in a kitchen.

'Kids from Karachi were embarrassed about getting a job at a restaurant and, moreover, they didn't want to do basic chores like cleaning the floor,' Raza says.

Some employees would appeal to Raza: 'I'm a Sayed [families believed to be direct descendants of the Prophet Muhammad], how can I mop the floor?' Raza laughs at the memory now. 'They didn't realize I am a Sayed as well. I cleaned the floors and tables for two years until the employees came around to it.'

One year later all that remained to be decided was the name. 'There used to be a restaurant in Hartford named Mr Steak,' Raza recalls. 'When we were trying to come up with a name for our business, that name clicked.'

And so Mr Burger was born. 'It was simple, easy to remember and whether someone was educated or not, it was easy to pronounce,' Raza says.

His brother Iqbal, the flight engineer, often flew to Paris, and after the name was settled on, he strolled down the Champs-Élysées and found an artist who sketched a logo for the business.

In 1980, the Raza brothers opened the doors of the first Mr Burger in Karachi's Nazimabad neighbourhood. They served five kinds of burgers – Mr Burger, Beef Burger, Chicken Burger, Egg Burger and Veggie Burger – for five rupees each (five cents today), French fries (Rs 2) and flavoured slush (Rs 2 a cup). The prices ensured that even students on shoestring budgets could buy a meal of fries and slush.

'Within minutes we had nearly a hundred and fifty people crammed into this tiny space,' Raza recalls. 'People in the neighbourhood had been watching as the restaurant was being constructed and they were so curious about what we were selling that we didn't even need to advertise our opening – the news just spread through word of mouth.'

The brothers did not just introduce a new food to Pakistani consumers – they served up the fast-food culture that they had seen in the US, one that a majority of Pakistanis had never been exposed to as international travel was a privilege reserved for the rich.

While some customers were annoyed that the restaurant only served burgers – 'You won't believe how many people asked us why we didn't have nihari or biryani on the menu,' Raza says – others wanted a taste of this 'American food'.

'They wanted to try it, but they were confused about how to eat a burger,' Raza says. 'Some would pick it apart and then use the bun as roti to scoop up bites of the patty.' Raza and his brothers would then demonstrate how to unwrap the burger's paper covering, and pull it down halfway to form a pocket while eating.

Customers would sit at a table and holler at servers to bring their food over or get angry that they weren't being waited on. 'They had no clue about self-service, takeaway food or disposable items – people returned wrappers and cups to us until they learned they could throw leftovers in the trash.'

Mr Burger's no smoking policy was an alien concept too. At the time, there was a marked shift in behaviour towards more gun-toting as AK-47s, brought by Afghan refugees fleeing the Soviet invasion in their country, flooded the black market. 'Some people – especially the big shots – would pull a gun on my employees if they asked them not to smoke inside the restaurant,' Raza remembers. 'They felt insulted.'

Back then, the brothers couldn't find a Pakistani company making sliced cheese. 'One of my customers walked in with a packet of Kraft cheese slices he bought in America,' Raza says. 'He was used to eating a burger with cheese abroad and that's what he wanted.'

Raza tracked down a small company that manufactured butter and desi cheese or paneer in Sahiwal, Punjab. 'They tasted the Kraft cheese and then spent months trying to make it,' he explains. Once the taste mimicked the yellow plastic-wrapped Kraft slices, the suppliers proudly brought a large block of cheese to the restaurant.

'I looked at it and I said, "What is this?" You see, they didn't have a slicer for the cheese,' Raza says, laughing. They imported a cheese slicer from the US and taught the supplier how to use it.

So who came to Mr Burger? 'Everyone,' Raza says.

In the first fifteen years of business, Nawaz Sharif, the prime minister of Pakistan until July 2017, used to come for the chicken burgers, as did former President Asif Ali Zardari, who at the time was Prime Minister Benazir Bhutto's fiancé.

During the day, queues would spill out of the restaurant and on to the street.

'Everyone, no matter how important or rich they were, had to get in line,' he says. Initially, the space was a great equalizer.

High-ranking police officials and businessmen briefly rubbed shoulders with students and labourers at Mr Burger. But soon there was a return to the well-worn grooves between these classes.

'We had space for only four hanging tables – no chairs – inside the restaurant, so we'd clean and wash down a space outside where people could sit,' Raza says. 'Some movie stars, rich people and celebrities who wanted to avoid the aam aadmi [common man] began to come in after 10 p.m. and would sit on this cleaned floor to eat their burgers.'

While the fast-food concept was new for a majority of people, it thrilled others to finally have access to a beloved staple of life outside Pakistan.

'Members of foreign consulates and diplomatic missions in Karachi were so happy they could finally have a burger here,' Raza recalls. His first sweet taste of success came from these customers. 'You are the McDonald's of Pakistan,' they would tell him.

By the mid-1980s, there were five Mr Burger outlets in Karachi. The tantalizing brush with American culture that Mr Burger offered trickled past the palate and into other parts of customers' lives in a way that Raza had not anticipated.

'Customers began objecting that the teenagers who came to Mr Burger were behaving in a very "Westernized" way – they would come there for dates,' Raza says. '"The kids are sitting too close together, they are holding hands,"' he recalls customers complaining.

For Raza, this was a source of pride. 'I felt very happy that this was a safe space for these teenagers,' he says. 'To this day I have customers coming in with their wives and they tell me, "Our first date was at Mr Burger." Their children call me Uncle Burger.'

These 'Westernized' customers were given a name: burgers.

According to Raza, the phrase was coined by Pakistani comedian Umer Shareef back in the 1980s. 'He saw that people of a certain class and from certain well-off neighbourhoods such as Clifton and Defence would come to Mr Burger a lot and he started calling them "burgers",' claims Raza.

In an interview last year, Shareef confirmed that the term was used to describe people from this 'certain class', and he used the analogy of food to describe 'burgers' as distinct from the aam aadmi.

'[In the 1980s] I started noticing women in restaurants who were the kind of people to pick up a roti using a tissue paper,' he said. 'We had never done anything like that, so I asked myself, "What class do these women belong to?"' It was a class that preferred to align itself with the West, and behaved as though it did not even know how to eat a common roti, he implied.

By 1995, the Raza brothers were flipping more than 100,000 burgers a month. A year later, they received word that they were being 'watched'.

'Some of our customers told us that they had been employed to thoroughly research Mr Burger, to see how it had done so well in Karachi,' Raza claims. McDonald's was coming to town, and Mr Burger was no longer the only option for Pakistanis in search of fast food.

In 1993, Pizza Hut was the first foreign franchise to land in Pakistan, followed by KFC in 1997, and McDonald's a year later.

Today, KFC reportedly has the largest share – thirty-seven per cent – of the fast food market in the country, followed by McDonald's at twenty-six per cent, while other foreign franchises have made inroads here too such as Hardee's, with six per cent of the market share.

For consumers under the age of nineteen, who account for forty-five per cent of Pakistan's population of more than 185 million, burgers have always been a part of life, whether by way of the small roadside kiosks or international brands.

In 2013, BIL Foods, the franchiser for Fatburger, predicted that the demand for fast food would continue to grow and estimated a thirty per cent increase in Pakistan by 2017. By 2017, Foodpanda, the food delivery marketplace popular in Asia, predicted that the meal delivery industry would increase in Pakistan by more than a hundred per cent to $2 billion by 2021.

Industry sources say that it is difficult to put a number on the market share for homegrown fast food businesses, but they agree that it is swiftly growing to cater to the demand.

Shahvez Fazail, thirty-three, founder of the online delivery service Food Genie, has for instance signed on more than sixty burger chains in the last year, including Mr Burger, and of these, new local businesses outnumber the foreign entities.

One of Fazail's clients is Ali Raza, thirty-eight, owner of Burger Inc. Raza studied and worked in the US before returning to Karachi in 2004. He, like many fast-food restaurant owners in Karachi I spoke to, spent his formative years abroad where he got his first job. He believes that the local burger-chain boom has arisen partly because of the lucrative growing demand, but also from a need to cater to consumers like himself – a generation that has been exposed to international fast food trends and franchises.

'Part of our personalities [is] very rooted in another culture,' he explains. 'It's not just those of us who have returned to Pakistan, though – everything is so accessible via the internet and we travel so much now that we all want to be part of an international culture that we see so much of.'

While those who have returned to Pakistan relish traditional food, they also crave American burgers, he says. That's where the local chains step in.

'The international brands are great, but they're all about convenience and volume,' he explains. 'They can nuke you a burger in three minutes, but I'll make it from scratch, with the freshest of ingredients and the best quality beef in the market.'

Despite the friendship between Pakistan and the US being lukewarm, at best, over the past decade – a 2014 Pew Research Centre poll found that fifty-nine per cent of Pakistanis view

Americans unfavourably – our palate still takes its cues from the US.

Local burger chains try to offer the best of both worlds, bringing fresh, homegrown produce to a menu with a decidedly American flavour.

Naveed Savul, forty-seven, the owner of Burger Lab, which he started nearly four years ago, also feels the local market is spurred on by food trends outside of Pakistan.

'We were very used to overly processed, synthetic-tasting fast food, but then we saw a change in the US and Europe – a return to organic, fresh cuts and locally sourced ingredients,' he says.

In the years Burger Lab has been operating, Savul has noticed greater demand for 'gourmet burgers' – burgers with blue or gouda cheese, for instance – which, costing more than Rs 700 ($6.68), have become staples on restaurant and café menus, catering to customers with deep pockets. According to the consumer research firm Euromonitor International, the annual disposable income of Pakistanis increased by 23.1 per cent between 2008 and 2013 and expenditure jumped by 24.5 per cent.

'Unlike my generation, kids today have a lot of money and there's an entrenched culture of eating out or ordering in,' says Raza of Burger Inc.

Since the day Mr Burger came to Pakistan, burgers – the food, the concept – have become harbingers of change.

'I feel so happy when I hear people using this term "burgers",' Ashfaq Raza says, laughing. 'It makes me think of Mr Burger. It reminds me of how people doubted us when we were starting out, but then called us pioneers and began to follow us.'

'The Pakistani market is very trend-oriented, but it's a small percentile of consumers who start these trends,' says Savul, owner of Burger Lab. These consumers manage to spark something. 'One definite reason for this demand for burgers is the idea that, "The cool people are eating them",' feels Savul.

The PTI and its supporters arguably hope to capitalize on the possibilities that such trendsetters offer, and perhaps redefine what it means to be a 'burger'.

'I think that when they [critics] refer to us as "burgers", they are talking about people who are from the educated class,' says Arsalan Taj Ghumman, thirty, the former president of the Karachi chapter of PTI's student wing, Insaf Students Federation.

'We have never been involved in corrupt politics, we aren't afraid to question what we are told, and we don't believe that politics must be a game of fear and threats.'

For Ghumman, it is a source of pride that the party was able to bring a generation of 'burgers' into the fold.

'The most ignorant people are those who belong to the upper class in Pakistan,' he says. 'They have been given every opportunity in life by God and they have everything that one could desire. It is very difficult to attract these kinds of people to political activism, and if PTI has done so, it is a big victory for the party.'

When the PTI's critics comment on the branded clothes that these party supporters wear, their income or accents, and use the word 'burger' as a slur, Ghumman has a simple retort: 'Would you call Mohammad Ali Jinnah a "burger"? He lived abroad, he was educated in London and he worked there, and he liked to dress a certain way. Can you call the founder of our country a "burger"?'

Vegetarian Bun Kebab

½ kg potatoes, peeled and boiled
1 medium white onion
1 small red onion
1 green chilli, chopped
Salt to taste
2 tsp garam masala
2 tbsp lemon juice
½ tsp ground coriander
2 eggs
3 tbsp mayonnaise
Lettuce leaves and tomatoes for garnish
100g or ½ cup yoghurt
1 tsp fresh or dried mint leaves
¼ tsp garlic paste

Method

1. In a bowl, mash the peeled and boiled potatoes together with the chopped red onions, white onion, green chilli, salt, lemon juice, ground coriander and half the garam masala.
2. Now make burger patty-sized cakes (kebabs) out of the mixture.
3. Beat the eggs and dip these potato cakes in it. Heat oil in a pan and shallow fry these cakes. Flip in the middle so you heat on each side until golden brown. Take them out and place on a plate.
4. For the yoghurt dip, in a bowl add the yoghurt, salt, mint, the other half of the garam masala, and the garlic paste. Mix well.
5. Spread some mayonnaise on one side of the potato 'kebab', and on top layer sliced tomato and sliced lettuce. Cover it with the burger buns. Serve with 1 tbsp of yoghurt mixture at the side of the plate, for dipping.

Jootha

Tabish Khair

Food, as the anthropologist and cultural theorist Mary Douglas has highlighted, is a primary marker of identity: not just what *cannot* be eaten, but also what *can* be eaten. Born in a Muslim family in small-town India, I have never had to be reminded of this. If pork was forbidden to us, the permitted consumption of beef – as recent lynchings of Dalits and Muslims on the mere suspicion of killing a cow highlight – came with grave risks.

My family lived outside the Muslim mohallas, and we had grown up in what scholars call a syncretic tradition, though, as my contribution to this anthology will argue, traditions are as difficult to name across cultures as words can be difficult to translate across languages. For instance, the 'syncretism' or pluralist nature of weddings in my immediate family was fraught with sometimes indelible lines of difference. They all required two sets of cooks and two separate dining areas. The larger set made traditional wedding dishes, which had to include murgh mussalam, mutton qorma, mutton and chicken kebab (which, in pre-Independence days had been beef kebab, it was said), pullao, bakarkhaani roti, roomaali roti, meetha paratha, chapati and what I, perforce, will call vegetable 'curries', one of them containing hard-boiled eggs. All this was made by a Muslim cook and his helpers.

A smaller tent was set up for a Brahmin cook and his high-caste helpers, who made purely vegetarian dishes, with puris, kachoris, roti and rice. The demarcation, I was told, went back to times when many Hindu friends of the family would not eat with Muslims, let alone consume food cooked by a Muslim. When I was growing up, the custom was still maintained because many of our Hindu friends continued to be strict vegetarians. Even the last wedding in my family – my sister's, who is a decade younger than me – involved these two tents. Interestingly though, the desserts – makuti in small earthen plates (essential in our view), not on china ones, shahi tukra, gulab jamun and so on – were common to both the tents, as was the tea (sheer chai) and coffee, at least within my memory.

Coming from a family that took its food seriously, it is inevitable that dishes have crept into my fiction. I am not exceptional in this. Food has become a marker of South Asian fiction. To an extent, it is a marker of postcolonial fiction in general. In the case of recent South Asian literature, or even recent literature about South Asia, elaborate dishes, the naming of spices, the listing of recipes and similar gastro-literary devices have completely obscured whatever poverty of description might have existed in the past. I, for one, distinctly recall V. S. Naipaul describing roti or chapati as 'an uninspired kind of pancake' in one of his texts, probably a travel book.

Of course, this visibility of food in current fiction has also coincided with its recovery in scholarly fields, for instance in Sidney Mintz's *Sweetness and Power: The Place of Sugar in Modern History*, his seminal study of the role of the eighteenth-century sugar trade in creating Western modernity. To this I can add the various enlightening studies of food in slave narratives. However, I am not convinced that food in South Asian fiction, especially fiction in English, operates only along these necessary and often radical lines of subaltern recovery. This is so because such narratives of food in South Asian fiction in English are sometimes served as a middle-class 'Indian' spread for a middle-class 'global' palate, with subalterns, such as servants and cooks, appearing only on the periphery.

As confessed, I have contributed my pinch to this ingestion of South Asian food and its makers in fiction, most obviously in my second novel and first internationally published book, *The Bus Stopped* (2004). The domestic spaces of *The Bus Stopped* teem with dishes and spices, both Indian and 'continental'. One of its significant characters, the semi-feudal khansama-not-cook, Wazir Mian, lists some of the latter with aplomb: ishtake (steak), esstoo (stew), chicken allah kaatey (chicken à la carte), tamater boss cat (tomato basket), karma puteen (caramel pudding) . . . Along with these colonial reminders, my novel – like so many other Indian novels – also chants the names of South Asian dishes.

The Bus Stopped is not an autobiographical novel, but it is firmly set in the kind of family and place I had known well into my twenties, when I finally managed to leave my hometown. My father always claimed that we were 'proud, independent and impoverished farmers' before *his* grandfather studied his way to a medical degree in the late nineteenth century, after which – until I broke the tradition in the late twentieth century – almost every male member had studied medicine. My grandfather and father were doctors too. They were also gourmets. This trajectory from 'impoverished farmers' to a family with a very well stocked pantry – or dastarkhwan, to be exact – never made full sense to me. The family wedding dinners were good arguments against my father's origin myth of impoverishment. As were the more mundane dinners.

Until the last years of his old age, when he lost interest in things in general, my father expected at least three or four dishes at every meal, apart from breakfast. Mind you, weekend and vacation breakfasts had to be elaborate. All this, we were told, was far less than what had been served in *his* father's time. We grew up not just with various kinds of Muslim and Hindu cuisines, including a family devotion, unusual among Muslims, to vegetarian 'Marwari' cooking, but even got a fairly good introduction to 'continental' (British- and French-origin) cuisine, which demanded dexterity with fork and knife, and

Indo-Chinese dishes, though without chopsticks. Incidentally, eating with chopsticks was the first skill I cultivated when I made friends with Tibetans.

Pork was, of course, never on the table; neither was alcohol. But, apart from that, the family interpretation of halal cooking was distinctly Sufi rather than Wahhabi. Even 'rustic' dishes, such as the working-class litti chokha of Bihar (the litti are stuffed wholewheat balls with the chokha chutney served alongside), were made and eaten with relish: there was an almost puritanical insistence on cooking and serving dishes the 'right way'. For instance, litti chokha is cooked by the (mostly Hindu) poor on an open goitha (dried cowdung cake) fire in Bihar. Genteel Muslims frown on goitha as fuel, considering it disgusting. And goitha was not used in my family either – except when litti was being made. Litti had to be made on a goitha fire. My father insisted on this. It was the way litti was made, just as a fish cutlet had to be eaten with fork and knife, not with one's fingers; and a paratha had to be broken and swirled in curry with one's fingers, not sliced insipidly with a knife. In this, we ran against both religious and class prejudices, as we discovered when we served litti chokha made on such a goitha fire to one of my father's upper-caste Hindu friends, recently back from England after obtaining an FRCS or MRCP. My father's friend, who did not eat beef in India but had eaten it in England where, as he noted, the cow is not holy, refused to eat the litti chokha, sticking carefully to the other fare on the table. My brother and I ate his share of littis with alacrity.

In short, there was nothing impoverished or insular about the meals we used to have, and no sign of past impoverishment either!

It was only when I grew up and visited our ancestral village on my own that I discovered that my father had embroidered, unconsciously, on the family history. It is true that when his grandfather abandoned the family fields and set out to study medicine, reportedly walking to town and back in order to save money, the family had been in straitened circumstances.

But it was still a family of landlords, one of the three in the village.

'What do you mean, landlords?' I asked the villagers, shocked to the core of my socialist being. 'You mean elephants, you mean carriages?'

'No landlord in these [impoverished] parts of Bihar had elephants or carriages,' they told me. 'But you were landlords because you had inherited land from your ancestors, and you employed people to work them.' Suddenly I understood the dinners in my parents' home and my grandparents' house when I was growing up. Such replete dastarkhwans, such elaborate recipes, such insistence on many courses and their proper presentation: all these things take time and privilege to accumulate.

I understood something else from my childhood. The old servants in my grandfather's house – all of whom retired to their villages while I was still a teenager – had a strange relationship to our food: they would eat food from our plates, when they took them back to the kitchen to be stacked and washed. The new 'professional' servants employed by my parents never did so, but these old village retainers still did. As a child, I used to be fascinated and faintly repelled by this, because like all middle-class Indians I had a strong sense of food that is 'jootha'. This is a caste Hindu inheritance, and some religious Muslims try to guard against it by eating from a large common plate at times, a gesture that stresses the egalitarianism of Islam and satisfies the religious Indian Muslim's misplaced nostalgia for his or her – in most cases entirely fictitious – Arab roots. But we were not religious like that. The idea of eating food that had already been partly eaten by someone else was disgusting to us.

Jootha is a reminder of all that cannot be translated, and hence narrated, about food in South Asia. It is not *jhoota*, which would mean 'liar'; it is also not *joota*, which would mean 'shoe'.

It is jootha.

Jootha is food that has been already tasted by others. It has a long history in South Asia. Caste squats heavily on it; penury lurks in tatters all around it. And while stories about our food get 'translated' into literature, stories about jootha have a more precarious existence. Perhaps the only major book in any Indian tongue that uses the word in its title is Omprakash Valmiki's Hindi-language *Joothan*, published in 1997. The English translation (2003) is subtitled *A Dalit's Life*, and the *Joothan* of its title is a dialect version of what we, in genteel Urdu, called 'jootha'. There is obviously a strong connection between Valmiki's joothan and my family jootha, but there are also differences.

Valmiki's joothan has to be understood in the context of upper-caste Hindu prejudices, a socio-political economy in which, as Valmiki himself notes, it was permissible for the Hindu upper castes to touch a dog or a cat, but not to let even the shadow of a Dalit fall on them. This is how he describes the 'tradition' of joothan in his book:

> During a wedding, when the guests and the baratis, the bridegroom's party, were eating their meals, the Chuhras [the Dalit caste to which Valmiki belongs] would sit outside with huge baskets. After the baratis had eaten, the dirty pattals or leaf-plates were put in the Chuhras' baskets, which they took home, to save the joothan sticking to them. The little pieces of pooris, bits of sweetmeats, and a little bit of vegetable were enough to make them happy. The joothan was eaten with a lot of relish. The bridegroom's guests who didn't leave enough scraps on their pattals were denounced as gluttons. Poor things, they had never enjoyed a wedding feast. So they had licked it all up. During the marriage season, our elders narrated, in thrilled voices, stories of the baratis that had left several months of joothan.

As the above extract indicates, Valmiki's book provides a fascinating insight into a Dalit's life in the recent past – structured by poverty, impacted on by the violence of the 'upper' castes, forced to survive on leftovers, including food that had been eaten and discarded by others. The pieces of pooris, he goes on to narrate, would be dried in the sun and preserved, to be soaked and eaten much later during the 'hard days of the rainy season'.

This was not the case with jootha in my grandmother's house. There were various differences: the servants were Muslims, the plates were china or (in later years) metal. And the jootha was not given to the servants to eat; they chose to do so on their own. But it was revealing. Even though food was cooked for the servants, such was the chasm of affluence between the delicacies we savoured and the ordinary fare they consumed that they freely chose to eat our jootha. Caste is closely linked to poverty, and was even more so in the past.

The servants who later replaced these old village retainers would *not touch* our jootha. We knew that they would be offended if we ever gave them a delicacy from off our plates. How did we know that, for it was never openly said? Probably from the way they handled our dirtied plates and bowls, the way they dumped the remaining food in the garbage bin, claiming only items that had not been put on our plates. Surely, some of this difference – the parents who ate our jootha and their children who recoiled from it – had to do with a certain tradition of poverty and of power, which, happily, has been broken in recent decades. Today, jootha has only one living connotation in families like mine: as when a parent eats his or her child's jootha, or a sibling eats his or her sibling's jootha, or a lover eats his or her lover's jootha. This still happens. It is considered the ultimate sign of closeness. *We are one*, the gesture proclaims, *your body is my body, your saliva is my saliva*. And I recall that in the past, when I once questioned a village retainer in my grandmother's house as to how she could eat my jootha – I must have been nine or ten then – she had put it in that light.

'How can you eat food I have been eating, Bua?' I had asked. 'How could you take a chicken wing I had bitten into and put aside?'

'It is because you are like my son,' she had replied.

However, this was not true for her daughter. When the latter visited us for festivals and sometimes helped out in the kitchen, she would never touch food from the jootha plates. As stated above, none of the new servants would have dreamed of doing so.

How would one attempt to translate 'jootha' in English? I don't believe this is possible. 'Contaminated' or 'polluted' will be as one-sided as 'shared' or 'partaken'. 'Half-eaten' would be a technocratic joke. 'Tasted' would be worse, while 'leftovers' is about as accurate as Naipaul's 'uninspired pancake' for roti. Perhaps dishes themselves can be translated, though I am not sure about this, but some of the cultural contours of its consumption appear impossible to translate. Just like 'jootha'.

I recall my mother explaining some of her inherited recipes to me. She seldom bothered with measurement. 'A bit of salt,' she would say to me. 'A little garam masala. *Andaaz se.*'

'How much, Ammi?'

Andaaz se. You did it by experience, by touch, by guess, by instinct. It is as difficult for me to translate her 'felt' verbal recipes (which I can only approximate) as it is to explain 'andaaz' or 'jootha'.

'Those who sit at meal together are united for all social effects; those who do not eat together are aliens to one another, without fellowship in religion and without reciprocal social duties,' wrote Robertson Smith, one of the founding fathers of anthropology. But what of jootha, where one had fellowship in religion but did not sit at meal together, yet partook in an eating that was intimate *and* at the same time removed?

And what of joothan, where one could never sit down to eat with the upper castes, for even one's shadow was 'polluting', but must subsist on what had been partly eaten then discarded, without fellowship in religion (if you pressed Ambedkar to answer), or *with* fellowship in religion (as Gandhi insisted)? In either case, people were pegged down for centuries by 'reciprocal social duties': traditions, customs, rules.

Like most Indian children, my mother and aunts would feed me and the other youngsters with their hands, and then eat from the same bunched-up fingers with which they fed us. Jootha, in that sense, was the ultimate sign of oneness, of belonging.

To say that our old family servants ate our jootha is not to claim that they loved us as much as our parents did. They didn't do it from choice but from hunger. Because no matter how well we paid them, their poverty was a hard fact. It was a fact of history and tradition: no family ever paid servants much more than what other families in the region did. If you were rich and magnanimous, you paid the servants a bit more, but never enough to upset your neighbours and relatives. You did not, as I continue to be told in small towns even today, 'spoil their habits' (*aadat kharaab karna*) or 'spoil the market' (*market kharaab karna*). What you mostly did, apart from paying them maybe ten or twenty per cent more than your neighbours, was to give them clothes, new during festivals and old for the rest of the year, as well as better food, specially cooked for everyone during festivals and on ordinary days the option of sumptuous jootha.

The Chuhras of Valmiki's account were not so far away from such servants, despite the difference of place, religion and caste. I grew up hearing old retainers explain why they worked for my family by alluding favourably to the good food that we served and shared. *Yahan khaane ko bahut achcha milta hai*, I heard one say. One gets to eat well in this household. But of course, Valmiki's Chuhras endured not only the greater poverty of Dalits, compared to our family servants, but also a greater deprivation. To say that this deprivation was due to poverty is not to say enough. You will have to say more. You will have to read more.

You will, at least, have to read texts like Dr B. R. Ambedkar's *The Annihilation of Caste* (1936). You will have to understand why M. K. Gandhi, as he recounts in *My Experiments with Truth* (1929), had so much trouble forcing himself to eat outside caste prohibitions, a taboo that, to his credit, he managed to a large extent to break. Joothan explains why Ambedkar, being a Dalit, had to reject Hinduism as identical with caste, and Gandhi had to reform caste from within Hinduism because, like Ambedkar, he knew that Hinduism and caste were two sides of the same coin and, unlike Ambedkar, not being a Dalit, he believed that Hinduism, like a plate, could be cleansed of caste.

The word jootha in my family, and the related and different word, joothan, in caste India, have a complex but largely unearthed history that a 'multicultural' celebration of food in South Asian fiction cannot even begin to excavate. And yet, only in fiction will these complexities be explored and explained, for fiction permits all contradictions, one in which 'jootha(n)' is both the closest one person can get to another and, simultaneously, the greatest hostility that one person can show towards another, as well as various grades in between. It is both a mother feeding her child, and Dalits forced to subsist on the joothan of upper-caste guests who would not even let a Dalit's shadow fall on them.

Fiction has the suppleness that fact does not allow. It neither abandons meanings, nor pins them down. But for that, fiction has to use food, and its consumption, as something more than an easy marker of identity. It has to reveal how identity is connected to what we eat – and how we eat it. Fiction has to go deeper – and call upon the reader to do so too.

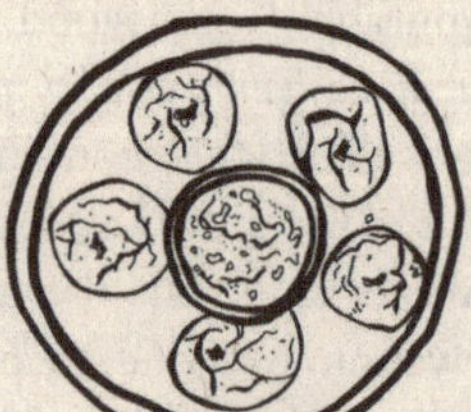

Quick Seafood Broth

This came to me as a simple home recipe, but I am sure it is based on something more standard and traditional. You can vary the quantities according to preference and availability, provided the seafood is *at least* a third of the vegetables.

100g shrimps or prawns, cooked and peeled
100g salmon (cut into small pieces)
100g squid or octopus pieces
100g mussels (without shells)
2 medium peeled potatoes
2 carrots, chopped
1 leek, diced
½ a red and ½ a yellow bell pepper (more for colour than quantity)
1 tsp curry powder (mild, medium or hot according to taste)
1 tsp garam masala
1 tsp garlic paste
1 tsp salt (or to taste)
2 tbsp single or double cream (depending on your arteries and waistline!)
1 tbsp cooking oil (mustard, sunflower or vegetable: any will be fine)
Handful of coriander leaves

Method

1. Lightly fry the seafood with thinly sliced leeks and diced pepper very quickly in as little oil as possible, with salt, garlic paste and garam masala. Put aside. (If using frozen stuff, it is a good idea to defrost the seafood first and drain off the defrosted water.)
2. Cut the potatoes and carrots into inch-long slices, then half-boil them in salted water (enough to cover the vegetables).
3. Add the curry powder. Stir in the seafood, leeks and pepper. Add cream according to taste. The sauce (water + cream) should be about an inch higher than the solid ingredients in

the utensil. Cook on low or medium flame until the potatoes and carrots are fully cooked.

4. Taste to see if you want to add more curry powder or if it is already hot enough. You can also increase or decrease the consistency of the broth according to preference by adding water or cream.
5. Cook for another 3–5 minutes on a low flame.
6. Garnish with fresh coriander leaves. Serve.

Chewing on Secrets

Annie Zaidi

I don't care much for recipes. Anyone can look up, buy, steal, tweak or inveigle themselves into recipes. What I do like are secrets. The sort of secret recipes I like best are revelations in waiting, like a child in a game of hide-and-seek, waiting to be discovered even though she is also afraid of being sought out.

My secrets are like the halwa my middle mumaani took to one of her kitty party lunches in Lucknow last year, sending a frisson of excitement through her friend circle. Unfamiliar with the hosts and with kitty parties in general, I was silent and watchful of the eyes skimming over each edible item on the table, the scales rising and falling with each mouthful. Someone offered easy praise for a dish that was rare in her own kitchen. Someone offered a reluctant 'Hmm' upon tasting a dish that was only too familiar, and yet no fault could be found with it. Someone else simply counted the number of dishes and made comparative notes.

Sultana maami's halwa was good, but the excitement was more about its texture than its flavour. None of the other ladies could guess what it came from. It looked like chane ka halwa, but wasn't as smooth. It was more like milk cake, but it wasn't that either. It was a distant cousin to the habshi halwa, but not a sibling. The ladies kept guessing and my aunt enjoyed teasing them. Smiling, shaking her head all the while, she pressed into their hands the folded paans she had brought along as a post-lunch treat. Her friends were starting to clamour for answers and one of them even pulled me aside to ask what was in the halwa, and looked disbelieving when I said I didn't know. My aunt left the party without telling anyone.

The excitement was infectious and once we left the party, I too demanded an answer. Sultana maami kept me guessing for another few hours, and I kept cajoling her, even though we both knew that my skills do not lie in the kitchen. She told me anyway, releasing the information as if she were handing over an item from her wedding trousseau to a favoured niece, along with the admonishment that I was not to pass it on to anyone else. I haven't tried making that halwa myself and, to be honest, I have forgotten what it tasted like. I know, however, that whenever I do make it, it will taste of my aunt's smile and her momentary enjoyment of her little secret. The scent of paan will always linger over it even if there isn't a paan around for a hundred miles.

My middle mumaani's table is never under-laden. She would scream if you tried to throw a one-dish party. If she says it's just biryani, chances are there will be a couple of starters and perhaps another smallish course, plus dessert. If she says it's a pizza party, there's also garlic bread and dips, and maybe the dry chhole known in our family as my grandmother's chhole.

Grandma's chhole, Grandma's kheer, Grandma's chane ka halwa, Grandma's pindi.

It is said that a dish changes with the hand that cooks it. My grandmother fed her children and grandchildren these dishes for so many years that we all know the difference between 'her' chhole and other people's chhole. Hers was not necessarily the tastiest version of chhole we've ever had, but it was her own thing: neither spicy nor bland; neither wet nor dry; neither garnished nor plain; neither a whole meal nor a snack to be taken lightly.

Grandma wasn't a foodie. Towards the end of her life, she had taken to fasting for three months instead of the single month of Ramzan. Even when she didn't fast, she ate sparingly. What she did enjoy was cooking to show her love. Once she realized that a particular child liked a particular dish, she spent hours slaving in the kitchen and prepared mounds of it. Little mountains of halwa, small lakes of kheer and jarfuls of laddoo. She had to cook enough to feed the more than a dozen people who visited each summer and stayed for weeks. She also cooked enough for us to take away at the end of our vacation.

When she saw how much her grandkids liked it, she even taught herself to make ice cream. For weeks, she'd skim the cream off the daily pot of milk, hoarding it in the freezer and eventually cooking it up with mango pulp. Even now, there are summers when I am filled with an insane craving for Grandma's ice cream – grainy and heavy and shot through with tiny icicles that lend a crunch to the sweet melt.

After she died, for a few years there was no chane ka halwa, no homemade ice cream, no pindi. Or if there was, we didn't know it because it wasn't being shared with the whole family. Then, one year, a cousin was getting married, and Sultana maami showed up with a dark brown gob in transparent plastic. Grandma's halwa, she said. I remember that moment: the ziplock bag on a table already laden with boxes of sweets, the halwa waiting to be warmed up and shared around. It had tasted of our struggle to stay bound together as a family now that the elders were gone.

The family has managed to stay bound even though its members have scattered to different parts of the world. We try to meet at weddings, and eating meals together over several days helps to keep us connected. At another cousin's wedding, my middle mumaani took responsibility for wedding pindis, the type Grandma made. When we cannot meet, we stay in touch through our family WhatsApp group, where everyone shares pictures of what they've cooked. On Eid this year, one of my cousins sent a message saying that, instead of the traditional siwain, she had made Grandma's kheer. Meanwhile I was annoyed that my siwain turned out neither like my mother's version nor like Grandma's siwain.

I was secretly proud, though, that I had learnt to make a vegetable kebab that Grandma used to make for her vegetarian guests. I am quite certain that I will part with this recipe with great reluctance, should anyone ask. I am aware that it is possible to google something very similar, but even so. It is one of those things made more delicious through unnecessary secrecy.

What I hold in the deeper recesses of my heart are the meals and snacks Grandma made strictly for consumption by the family. They could never be offered to guests, and most of us have now stopped eating them. Dishes reminiscent of genteel poverty. Simple three- or four-ingredient dishes, high on carbs and sugar or salt. Dishes bad for the heart. Dishes doubly dear to my heart for, at least some of the time, her effort and her love was mine alone. One of these is a sweet called maleeda.

Maleeda comes from an era before refrigeration, when leftover chapatis were turned into new dishes to avoid waste. I have a vivid memory of sitting on an old carpet beside Grandma as she tore up and crushed bits of chapati between her forefinger and thumb, content in the knowledge that she was doing this for me. After she died, I didn't eat this dish for nearly fourteen years. The one exception came forty days after her death, when the grieving family had gathered for her chalisvaan. Trying to hold on to some tangible piece of her, I expressed a desire to eat maleeda. One of my aunts made some, but it wasn't quite Grandma's maleeda.

Recently, looking for a simple dessert I could whip up without any special ingredients, I remembered maleeda and looked for it online. I was initially amused, then mildly alarmed to see that it had transmogrified from a three-step, three-ingredient leftover dish into a complex recipe that involves cooking up a fresh batch of chapatis or parathas or mothia, only so that you may cut them up and crush them back down again! As for the addition of saffron and dry fruits, all I can say is: there's no end to human folly.

Maleeda

2 leftover chapatis
2 tbsp ghee
1 tsp cardamom powder (optional)
2 cloves
4 tbsp sugar

Method

1. Take the chapatis and tear them up into bits. Crush each piece between your thumb and fingers into the smallest bits possible, but don't grind it down to powder.
2. Heat the ghee in a pan, and add cardamom powder if you happen to have some handy. The cloves will also add flavour.
3. Toss the crushed chapati bits into the ghee and add the sugar.
4. Fry on a medium flame until the sugar appears to have melted.
5. Eat while still warm (if you wait until it is cold, the whole thing hardens).

Stone Soup

Sarvat Hasin

As a child, I played Villager Number Six in a school play entitled *Stone Soup*. The play was based on the Eastern European folk story in which every member of a community is encouraged to add their food to a pot of 'stone soup'. It is a story about sharing but also about duping people into parting with their supplies to make something delicious. I wore a white flouncy skirt and a shawl, and doled out bowls of nothing to my fellow actors. I hated doing it. I would come to hate cooking too. For years, stirring an imaginary pot in a school play was the closest I got to the kitchen.

There is a romance around cooking, especially if you're South Asian. A gift handed down through generations like wedding jewellery, recipes sacrosanct to familial tradition. People who hear I love to cook assume I learned this way – from my mother, who learned from her mother, and so on. In fact, most people in my family don't enjoy cooking and don't do it unless they have to. My mother's attempt to teach me the summer before I went to university was almost entirely useless. I watched her stir a pot of dal in a hot kitchen, everything having already been prepared before I'd woken up and come down to the stove, and knew I would never replicate it.

When I finally started to cook properly, it was out of unhappiness, and a giant loneliness. It was summertime and I was in Pakistan with my family. Hot, sticky July afternoons coloured with boredom and malaise. It was Ramadan and the hours seemed endless, rolling into each other, nothing upsetting the routine of my days. My sadness seemed to accrue around me. I had thought when I got back for the holiday that this would be a pleasant time. I was twenty-one and halfway through my master's, a bawdy, hectic year that had ended dramatically. It had been the sort of crash teenagers usually have after their first year of independence. I came to everything late, even hedonism. Having been caught up in a whirlwind of intensity – the year bringing me a life that unlocked me, both bodily and emotionally, in ways that hadn't seemed possible before this – the things I wanted were suddenly in reach. Friends to write around the kitchen table with, to party with, to eat with, to watch films with at the cinemas on our doorstep, to flirt and fight with. Having gorged on all of this too quickly, I thought I was ready for some quiet.

The solace of my family, the cats, and their warm open home should have been balms. Instead, I felt trapped in a kind of stasis, unable to move. There was no one for me to see: all my school friends were either no longer friends or lived abroad now, in other cities or countries. I snuck onto the roof of my family home and smoked cigarettes, stared at sunsets like an overgrown cliché. I am an only child and had before then been very used to my own company but the sharpness of it now soured in me. In the evenings, I wrote emails to my friends who were far away – praising the solitude, pretending my aloneness was complete. When Ramadan started, I taught myself how to cook, out of a desire to be useful in some way.

I got the recipes off websites. I made a new thing every day for thirty days and by the end of the thirty days, I sort of knew how to cook. I learned that if you cook onions slowly for a long time, they go brown and sweet. Flour can be used to thicken a sauce. Almost all foods other than those at the dessert–baking end of the spectrum can take a little improvisation, a little bending of the recipe to your tastes. I knew the magic of cooking, the glory of starting with a set of ingredients and transforming their shapes, textures and flavours as if with a spell. More than anything, it calmed me. It was easy to forget about things when you were cooking, when you were chopping vegetables or fretting over the consistency of your icing. Heartache and loneliness dissolved in the process, everything melting to the task at hand, to getting to the end of the recipe. Ramadan seemed to me to involve restraint and reward, and that summer cooking was both of those things for me. The activity kept me from thinking about the world carrying on without me, and it brought me satisfaction too, not just in the making of a dish but in the feeding of it.

Chocolate Tart

The thing my family loved best that summer, and the thing they still seem to enjoy the most when I cook for them, is puddings. A household of sweet teeth. My grandmother judged the quality of a dinner party by the standard of its dessert, a metric everyone else seems to have inherited. They smile politely when I roast a chicken or toss pasta into a sauce but it is the sweets they love: swirled cheesecakes baked to fudginess, brownies, crumbles and tarts.

My favourite chef to steal from is obviously Nigella Lawson. She was the first chef I watched on the telly, the only one for a long time because she is beautiful and because she uses her words like a poet. My family, when they want to praise me, call me their Nigella. Imagine being so well known for being good at something that your name becomes a compliment.

The chocolate tart is probably my favourite of her recipes – luxuriously easy to make, deathly sweet, and its method full of wonderfully Nigella words like 'slake'. You make a biscuit base from crumbled cookies and butter, generously mashed together, patted into a pie dish if you have one, or at the bottom of a cake tin if you don't, making sure it goes up an inch around the dish. Let it set in the fridge till it is firm. Then mix melted chocolate, double cream and cornflour in a deep bowl, going gently – this is not a whisk that should make your arms hurt. It is a serene swirl, the sort you might watch Meryl Streep do in her beautiful kitchen in a Nora Ephron film while Etta James plays in the background. You let this cool down to room temperature and pour it into your biscuit shell. Put it to sleep in the fridge. It is magic watching it settle from custardy gloop to velvet. Cut thin slices out of kindness. Let your family have seconds. Lap up the compliments of a tart so rich it belies its own simplicity.

Taco Party

Every venture into the kitchen before that summer had been either totally disastrous or unimpressive. Earlier that year, I'd hosted a surprise birthday party for a friend and overcooked a whole vat of pasta, letting it all congeal together. I had watched someone throw it out, the off-white fleshiness of it like scraping the beginning of a soft demon into the garbage. Mostly I made scrambled eggs, with careless additions of soy and paprika in an attempt to elevate it. I liked food. I always had. I just didn't have any impulse to be the person creating it. For most of my university life, I managed to live near or with people who would cook for me, and it was a strange wizardry, the way they prepared these meals. One housemate had a regular veg-box delivery while I was still making grilled cheese for my dinner, and the gulf between our levels of expertise was so staggering that I didn't bother trying to overcome it. She made beautiful Victoria sponges, biscuits and stews. I could have watched and learned, but I didn't.

In a way, I even found it a point of pride that I could not cook. Domestic goddessing simply had no space in the persona I was trying to build. From the ages of eighteen to twenty-one, my first time living away from home, I was growing into the kind of woman who just didn't cook. It was part rebellion and part habit: no one in my family particularly enjoyed cooking so there was no organic way for me to have absorbed it when I was younger. But there was a hint of bite in it, too. I didn't want to be domesticated, I didn't want to be marriageable and biddable. I wanted, clumsily, to separate myself from the girls who could make round rotis. It was extremely misguided and bullish and a little lazy.

A friend, who could already roll her own pastry, make her own bread, and prepare feasts fit for kings, one day said to me: 'Cooking is sexy.' It is a wisdom that has since sat in me, sculpting my relationship with food into something different entirely. She made us puff-pastry pizzas and we ate them off our knees, spilling drinks onto the carpet, someone else's fluffy cats curling around our ankles. I still think of those evenings when I host now, which is a thing I love to do. If you had told me at twenty-one that my favourite way to spend an evening would be crowding people into whichever place I lived in and slaving over a stove for hours before their arrival, I wouldn't have believed you. Sometimes, I am too ambitious and it is difficult to enjoy. Last summer, I cooked for fifteen people and lost a whole weekend to it, producing veggie biryani, sabzi, keema and slow-cooked kheer that filled the house with the smell of rosewater and milk. But I couldn't relax into the evening, shivering at the precipice of the group all evening and never quite settling into the fun.

The best way to host a dinner party, really, is to make something you can toss in the oven and forget about. It's to make something with bits that you can set people to work doing – have willing guests chop onions, mash avocados and mix drinks. The best kind of dinner party is a taco party.

The next recipe is an adaptation of an adaptation. It was made for me a few years ago, deliciously and extravagantly with a particularly good slaw. When I wanted to make it myself some years later and asked for the recipe, the creator did not have one – he'd done what I usually do, google some recipes and cobble them together. I then did the same with this.

It is roasted cauliflower tacos and is easy enough that you can host upwards of ten people on a weeknight as I recently (madly) did.

You break two cauliflowers into florets, bite-sized chunks. Blend together a paste with chilli, olive oil, garlic and I like cumin too. Toss the florets generously in the mixture – this can be done a day in advance and left in the fridge. Then simply shake onto a baking tray and roast. You will need more cauliflower than you think you do because it is both delicious and likely to shrink in the oven.

Tortillas to warm. Cheese to grate. Make guacamole or ask someone else. Make roasted aubergines as well if you like (I usually do). Sometimes I add gochujang paste to the marinade because these tacos have never been traditional and I like the way the paste deepens the flavour. Chop red onions and squeeze lime over them, then coat them in brown sugar so they pickle together, sour and tangy. Let people make their own plates. Let them choose between hard and soft shells.

Snow Day Stir-Fry

Because I now believe that cooking is sexy. Because there is something special about a meal made for you by someone you're in love with. Because cooking together is intimate, warm and lovely, just like shopping for food is – arguing in the aisle about which soy sauce to buy and over the chopping board about how finely the onions need to be sliced. Because the measure of a relationship can be condensed down to the way you shift around a kitchen together, the way you learn to adjust your dishes to each other's tastes.

A Snow Day Stir-Fry. I braved the length of the city where no one went to work to be at home with someone else. It is late March and the sun is bright and the city stands still, the pale carpet of the morning already turning to thick grey slush.

I wore a big white jumper and a woollen plaid skirt, brushed my hair which whipped around my face by the time I got there, mad at the snow – wearing boots that I was slipping in the slush in, and a fur coat that I inherited from a friend who recently moved to Australia.

We make it as far as the convenience store across the road. I have been planning to cook, imagining fried chicken (a thing I've recently mastered) or steak. But there is only luncheon meat and an array of fresh vegetables, so we do a stir fry instead, lots of chilli and garlic and vermicelli noodles that crackle in the sauce. Planning to cook for someone can be so loving, so considered but merging together, mushrooms torn directly into a sizzling pan while one of you whisks together a sauce. Moving around each other's bodies in a narrow kitchen is even better. You can put anything you like in the stir fry – just make sure the pan is hot, and your oil is hot too. It's an everything-but-the-kitchen-sink kind of dish. I like shiitake mushrooms, prawns, plenty of chopped chilli and spring onions. Sometimes I throw anchovies in. I start my sauces with soy and garlic, add miso and rice wine vinegar – poured over the hot pan till everything sizzles together – and then stir through noodles.

I don't remember exactly what we ate when we made these but I remember that we agreed on the correct number of chillies, that we ate them sitting up in bed with cold beers, that we watched *The Devil Wears Prada*, that outside, everything was cold and bright, a perfectly seized-up evening.

Kali Dal

It was one of those quite spontaneous plans that is rarely possible to make in London. When I lived in Oxford, my life was full of things that could be thrown together at the last minute – trips to the pub at a moment's notice, dinners cobbled together or expanded to include new people. In London, people live by their diaries, playing Tetris with appointments and dates and trips to the cinema, theatres and so on. I text a friend and ask if she wants to come over for dinner, a warm satisfied joy when the answer is yes. I am already making a vat of black dal – I have enough bread for two. Nothing else is necessary.

If making a good dal, nothing else is ever necessary whether you have one person or six. It is generous and satisfying.

First soak your lentils for at least six hours. They will swell in the water like fat little stones. Then bring the water to a hard boil. Cook the lentils in this for a few minutes and then bring down to a simmer, letting them chuckle away for about forty minutes. In a Dutch oven or any heavy-bottomed dish, if you have one, fry onions till they are soft, and add ginger and garlic. Cook till they are brown and your kitchen smells delicious. Add your spices and toast them in the oil. Add tomato paste and cook till it is brown and sticky and all its redness is gone. When the lentils are cooked, toss them in this mixture, coating fully. Add stock if you want – animal or vegetable, depending on your tastes. In a low oven, you can leave this for hours. I finish with some coconut milk to thicken it, so it spoons so creamily into your plate that you could eat it on its own, no bread or rice necessary.

It tastes only distantly like the kali dal we used to eat when I was growing up, usually accompanied by rice. Lately, I find this matters less. I used to think cooking was only about nostalgia, about preserving the past, but I am growing more and more comfortable with the fact that it is about learning, about changing: brown sugar if you don't have white, capers instead of anchovies, swapping out garam masala for nutmeg. Maybe the best thing about the dinner table I grew up eating around was the way it was possible in Karachi for people to stop by unannounced and needing only a chair to be pulled up.

Pasta

Everyone is their own favourite cook. You don't have to be good at putting food together for this to be true, just basically competent. No one else will really cook dishes the way you like them – no one else will add exactly the right amount of salt, the ratio of turmeric to cumin that is precisely suited to your taste buds. You can love a restaurant for its pasta or biryani, or the specific fluffy bread they serve, or the perfectly rolled dumplings. But if that chef came over to make you breakfast, they would still probably not put enough salt on your eggs or butter your toast exactly how you might like. Their pancakes might be too thin, too crisp, when you prefer yours pudgy.

Late in the evening, in an empty house, you can cook for yourself – snacking on nuts while you wait for the simmer of a sauce because there is no one to judge you or to split the snacks with. A tomato sauce, Marcella Hazan-style perhaps – something simple, rich, luxurious. Or the Alison Roman-recipe shallots. I own one good piece of cookware, a blue Le Creuset that I could only afford because they were discontinuing the size: probably because it is too small to do any real cooking with. But it is perfect for caramelizing four to five shallots, which have been thinly sliced and left to cook in a cast-iron pan over a low flame with a generous pinch of salt till they turn soft and jammy. When you taste one, the flesh will be as tender and sweet in your mouth as a piece of fruit.

Put on the music that you like the most, that no one else shares a love for – Whitney Houston, Dolly Parton – and sing badly along to it. Try out your best Nick Cave. Then add anchovies and chilli flakes and a whole tube of tomato paste which seems like too much but is not. Season as you go, always. Wait for the tomato to also go jammy, dark. It is a generous recipe – you save half in a jar as a gift for your future self, to spread on good bread or eat with eggs. The other half is softened up with pasta water and the spaghetti draped into it, shiny and satin-brown.

Eat in silence, with a drink you've earned just for making yourself a delicious meal, or with the kind of a lazy podcast that makes you feel as if friends are in the room but you don't have to participate in the conversation. Or watch again the movie everyone else is sick of sitting through with you even though you yourself find it so homely, with every viewing the jokes landing deeper in you. Mine is *Moonstruck*, a good film about food; each time they make eggs in that movie, I feel hungry. Or *Goodfellas*, which is the best film about pasta – the thinly sliced garlic cloves melting in a way that I do not believe is gastronomically possible.

Because cooking is an expression of true, earnest love, the desire to feed and delight. When you were cooking for your family, your friends, your lover, you were trying to tell them something true. And you can tell yourself that too, even if the truth is that you like bucatini better than most or that you had to use two tins of anchovies because you began spreading the first on crackers and ate them while you waited for the shallots.

Cook to make time stop, to make pain stop but also just because food is good. You do not need to learn anything from the act of chopping onions. Just let yourself cry and enjoy them when they're crispy. There are no lessons here, only the simple pleasure of greed.

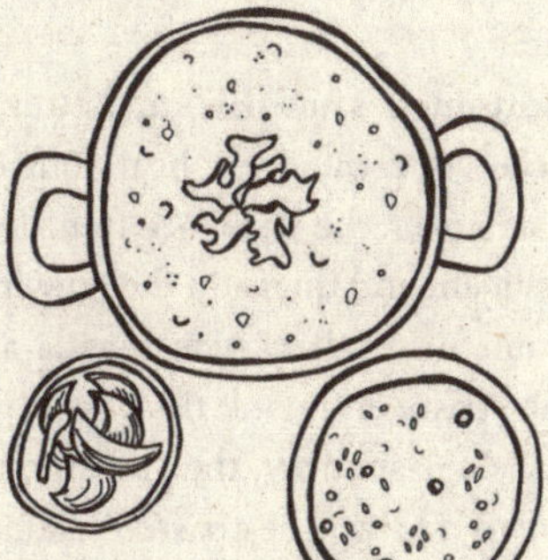

Kali Dal

1 cup black lentils (urad dal, or beluga lentils)
2 tsp tomato paste
2 tsp turmeric
3 tsp garam masala
1 cinnamon stick
3 small red chillies (chopped if fresh, or dried red chillies should be halved)
4 cloves of garlic, smashed and minced
½ a red onion, chopped very small
1-inch fresh ginger, grated or minced
1 can coconut milk
15 coriander leaves to garnish (optional)
To taste: salt, black pepper, water

Method

1. Soak the lentils overnight in cold water – the water should cover them completely. Most of it will soak into them.
2. Add the lentils to a pot of water and bring to a hard boil. Season with salt and a teaspoon each of turmeric and garam masala. The water will go frothy as it boils, the spices breaking out into bright splotches of colour. Lower the heat and allow it to simmer for about forty minutes. Try not to touch it or fuss with it during this time.
3. When the lentils are soft but still hold their shape, turn off the heat and drain.
4. In a heavy-bottomed saucepan or, better, a Dutch oven or any pot that can go in the oven, heat your oil. Just a generous enough glug to cover the base – soften the onions in this till they are translucent and then add the ginger, garlic and chillies. Fry till fragrant. Add salt, garam masala and turmeric. Then add the tomato paste and cook till it goes dark in the pan.
5. You should have a paste now; the cinnamon stick and anything else you want to add can be toasted in this. I sometimes add cloves or whole peppercorns.

6. Add the lentils into the pot and fold together. You will need to add a cup of water or stock to loosen the mixture which can then go into the oven (at 180°C) for three to four hours. This is a forgiving recipe but also one that is very easy to mould to your tastes. If you prefer a thicker dal, cook for longer. If you want it on the soupier end, add more water.
7. I like to leave the dal in the oven for as long as I dare and then adjust on the stovetop. I add a can of coconut milk twenty minutes before serving to make it thick and creamy. Many recipes add heavy cream and butter which is delicious but difficult to justify (even for me) on a weeknight. I find using stock, instead of water and coconut milk, enriches the flavours enough to get a similar unctuousness.
8. Eat with rice or naan or just by itself. Thinly sliced chillies or fried onions or coriander make a great garnish.

High on Chai and Samosa

Sadaf Hussain

One of the Hindu scriptures, the Upanishads, declares: '*Anna ka saar hi brahma hai*' ('The essence of food is the truth'), giving a great deal of importance to food. The sacred book goes on to remark that the enjoyer of food has no qualities, suggesting that God inhabits food.

In Islam, the Quranic verse 'Eat and drink but not to excess' (7.31) summarizes Muslim precepts around how much one should consume. Eating just enough ensures that a person lives a healthy and balanced life and is not lazy or lethargic which will take them away from their daily routine of work. Ammi often reminds me that our Prophet disapproved of eating food when it is too hot. He never used to blow on his food or drink, and discouraged eating food while lying down. I think he disapproved of blowing on food because the breath carries germs and impurities into the dish or beverage. Muslim families enjoy their meals perhaps like no one else. This idea can be further stretched to encompass television chef Julia Child's popular quote, 'People who love to eat are always the best people.'

Hindustani cookery is not just about indigenous dishes but also incorporates other cultures, accepting world cuisine and making this its own. We have our versions of pasta and pizza, Chinese and other East Asian food, Middle Eastern and Mughal cooking, and many more. Think of India as a vast food court where you can have a wealth of different kinds of food: vegetarian or non-vegetarian, spicy or sweet, soups or solids. You name it, and you can find it here.

Many dynasties, traders and travellers contributed to making Hindustani cuisine what it is today. Much of North Indian cookery was quickly influenced by the Muslims and their eating habits, trends and techniques. In her 2007 book *Eating India: Exploring a Nation's Cuisine*, Chitrita Banerji noted that it was the arrival of Muslims which radically reshaped cooking and eating in India. The Mughals, no doubt, brought a certain finesse and flair to the already-existing Hindustani food, alongside the creation of new and traditional dishes in the royal kitchens.

One dish that arrived long before the Mughals and became mixed up in the DNA of most Indians is the samosa. The origins of the samosa have been debated: did it come from Central Asia or North Africa, or were its origins in Egypt and Libya, travelling to our part of the world in the thirteenth century? The snack was given a makeover when the Portuguese came to India in 1498 and subsequently introduced the potato to a receptive subcontinent. The chef in me always feels that popular dishes and ingredients must travel the world to make food lovers their *mureed*.

In school, we had a samosa seller. For the rest of the day he was a street-side vendor, but during the lunch break he used to sell his gigantic samosas (as big as my hand when I was sixteen) to us kids. He'd come inside the school premises to set up his small wooden box, painted blue and with a metal mesh in front. Atop was a piece of glass covering half of the box, the perfect way to keep the samosas safe inside but also to give us a peek. The vapours on the glass used to confirm how fresh and hot this triangular deep-fried snack was, and which, back in those days, cost us only three rupees. The delectableness could have been measured by the number of students standing in line to lay their hands on a samosa. My friend and I used to take turns to buy the snack, but we'd often fight over who would get the top potato-loaded part and who the crispy bottom section. It occurs to me now that we could have easily divided the samosa horizontally in two halves, but whoever said kids could apply rational logic? The two of us would run yards chasing each other for the better part of our break.

In Jharkhand, the northeast Indian state I grew up in, we called the samosa 'singhara', also a common name in Bihar, Bengal and Odisha. A shop near our house used to make the best tiny singhara paired with chutney, alu ki sabzi, or both – which is how it is usually consumed in that part of India. The stall was set a little way off the main street, covered by a makeshift roof of bamboo and steel asbestos sheets. The floor was also rough, with a kitchen in one corner, a money counter at the other end, and enough space in between to allow at least twenty-five people to sit and enjoy the piping hot samosa with chutney or potato, along with equally hot kadak masala chai.

The combination of chai and samosa cuts across generations and geographies. The person who first wrapped a samosa in newspaper and poured chai into a kulhad must have been a genius, as these combinations can be found in almost every corner of India.

Bollywood movies taught me that when the boy visits his prospective wife, he gets chai, samosas and other snacks, along with romantic laddu sweetmeats. They say a lot can happen over coffee, but in the case of Indian matchmaking, a great deal transpires over hot samosas with chai. There was also a popular Bollywood song attributed to two of the biggest Hindi movie stars of the 1990s, Akshay Kumar and Juhi Chawla, '*Jab tak rahega samose mein alu, tera rahunga o meri Shalu*'. This song, which literally translates as 'As long as there's potato in the samosa, I'll be yours, O my Shalu,' tells us how inseparable the potato and the samosa are.

When I was a child and we used to visit my ancestral house in Sasaram, my go-to place was a small street-side restaurant selling meat samosas. I'd step up to get into the area with a neem tree in the middle, where there were a few posters of Mecca–Medina on one side, and 'Allah Muhammad' written in Arabic on another wall. A poky area, six to eight feet above the ground, was set up as the kitchen. There a woman and her young son served the hottest and crispiest samosas with green chutney onto steel plates lined with old Urdu newspapers to help soak up the extra oil. The lady would roll a thin sheet of samosa patti, stuff it with minced meat, and fry each parcel on a medium flame. This was popularly known as warqi samosa.

My maternal grandmother's recipe of this samosa is a little different and more labour-intensive than the regular samosa (please see the recipe at the end of this chapter). When she was young, the warqi samosa was her favourite. But this was an occasional snack only supposed to be cooked for sharing during Ramadan, or on other festive occasions like weddings. Nani, my maternal grandmother, recalls making hundreds of this special samosa, which were sent to my father's house as a gift before he married into the house. She chuckles and adds that Dadi, my paternal grandmother, felt stressed to see all these samosas, not knowing what to do with them, or how to find enough people to eat so many of the crisp delicacies.

This same samosa is still a popular evening snack in many parts of India, and has been part of the iftar repast during Ramadan ever since my childhood. However, the meat samosa has changed its avatar completely to become a fusion of cultures. The original recipe, which had meat and dried fruit in it, has been transformed into what are now the more familiar stuffings of spicy mashed potatoes, vegetables and paneer. The samosa is extremely customizable and in various subcontinental regions has different combinations of spices, which include coriander, pepper, caraway seeds, ginger and more besides.

I won't do justice to this topic if I just talk about the samosa and neglect chai, that other simple and very popular Indian delicacy.

Stand anywhere in India and the smell of the deep-fried triangles and bubbling chai will beckon you to street-side shops. Rest assured that almost every shop will give you value for your buck!

Chai is so intrinsically and unapologetically Indian that it wouldn't be an exaggeration to say Indians have more chai and less blood flowing through their veins. Every day, my parents have to gulp down a cup of hot masala chai after their morning prayers. In my family, everyone loves their chai differently. Some like it strong, others prefer it with ginger and black pepper, while I am partial to adding a few fennel seeds to my tea.

In the interests of complete honesty, though, I must confess that I am not an innate tea lover. Until the age of twenty-one, I was a fan neither of tea nor coffee. It was when I moved from Ranchi to Delhi in 2011 that I started bending my inclination towards the strongly intense and aromatic flavours of coffee, taken straight and black. Not until around 2014 did I start exploring the flavours of Indian and non-Indian tea leaves, along with the many preparations that we have for this beverage in my country and the wider world.

I blame my aunt for my non-exploration of the real flavours of tea till then, as well as for keeping me away from the local milk-and-masala variety. She tells me that as a kid I used to suck my thumb a lot. Now, I admit this was a bad habit and could have made my teeth crooked, but who dips a person's finger into boiling tea? That is what my aunt did to me, and it made me dislike the drink for the longest time. But don't get me wrong, she is my favourite aunt.

Then came June 2014, and I found myself in Bhopal for a short work trip. If you know anything about this city, you'll know that life here passes very slowly. Almost everyone has tea in their hand and paan in their mouths, and that's not even to mention their astonishing cooking and hospitality.

It was Sunday afternoon and I had absolutely nothing to do, so I ventured out to explore the city. I was expecting a good coffee shop, so I asked a few people to help me out. One of them told me, '*Arre kya coffee pijiyega? Aage chowk pe ek chai wala hai; uski chai pi ke to dekhe, janab; tabiyat khush ho jayegi.*' Loosely: 'Oh, why do you want to drink coffee? There is a tea seller near the next circle; try his tea, sir, he is popular and the best in this area.' I was convinced by the way words fell out of this man's mouth from between his red lips, courtesy of the paan he was chewing. I started walking to the tea shop, while thinking with each step of what else I should explore, eat or do in this city.

I stopped by the tea shop and fell in love with the rustic beauty of the place. It was just a small wooden cart with a brown gas stove in one corner. Five glass jars containing different kinds of sweet and savoury biscuits were lined up in front of the stove. Next to that was a red mat, which was the designated spot for customers to pick up their tea glasses. If they wanted to use a takeaway earthen pot, the kulhad, they had to pay three rupees extra – not a bad deal since the tea itself only cost seven rupees. I had always heard from tea lovers that chai tastes amazing when sipped from a kulhad, and who am I to question the connoisseurs? I picked up my hot cup of tea, stood next to the cart, and took pictures from every possible angle. My photography attracted many uninvited eyes towards me. Some thought I was crazy. Others were concerned, including the shop owner, who said, '*Beta chai to thandi ho jayegi* ('Son, your tea will get cold').' He was right, but I wanted to take some nice shots and document my first experience of what was going to become one of my favourite hot drinks.

I gulped down my tea (now indeed somewhat cold) and resumed my city explorations. Along the way, I took more pictures, stopped random guys to give me directions to places, and grabbed endless plates of the local delicacies poha and jalebi. Finally, I found another, very different tea place inside a popular shopping mall. I parked myself next to the counter so that I could see how the different kinds of tea were brewed and what teas people were ordering.

I called the waiter and asked what tea I should have, telling him I was open to experimentation. He advised me to try masala chai, their best-selling brew. As I was in no mood for something which I had already sampled, he further advised me to try the Darjeeling Moonshine Tea or camomile tea. Both were alien to me so I ordered both. Time was on my side. Moonshine turned out to be a black tea which was toned down with a peach extract, so essentially I had a nice cup of slightly bitter and simultaneously sweet tea. Meanwhile, camomile tea, which I now always keep in my kitchen, doesn't really have any tea flavour. However, it is very healthy and good for the senses, and of course great to drink before you hit the sack.

My nani tells me that when she was growing up in the 1940s, tea was not the most popular beverage in India. There used to be a door-to-door sales campaign for this caffeinated beverage. The salesman would come to your door, give you a few free sample sachets, and teach you how to brew the leaves in the right manner. Tea drinking was advertised as something elite, healthy and chic. But even the most passing acquaintance with Indian masala chai should know there is nothing elite about it. This nice brew is now in every nook and cranny of Muslim South Asia. Little did my nani's generation know that this hot drink would take over the entire north of the country and make people literally addicted!

Indeed, the north is high (pun intended) on tea, and they drink the beverage at least four times a day. No matter what time my parents wake up, they always start their day with a piping hot cup of tea. This is followed by breakfast, with tea again. Another cup is taken after lunch, and again as part of evening snacks. At times, moreover, to be good hosts, they drink one more cup at night with their guests if they feel like it. This last cup is a flexible option. The benefits tea brings include giving an extra kick that is helpful in the morning. In the evening when you are getting sleepy, it can lift your mood and make you feel happy before bed.

Residents of Shahjahanabad (Old Delhi) would not ask you to have tea; they'd bring tea to serve you without the exchange of any words. Their version is popularly known as dudh patti (the literal translation of this is 'milk and leaves'). Boiled and bubbling milk is poured on top of strong tea, in a concoction that is similar to coffee, cappuccino style. Bhopal serves you 'golden chai' which is only milk tea, whereas Bihar, Jharkhand and Kolkata are renowned for their kulhad/kuptee chai.

You need to boil the dried leaves to release the aroma and flavours. I was in Darjeeling in 2019 and remember visiting the tea plantations where I asked the farmers and cultivators many questions about how they pluck, dry and roast the leaves. Two of them informed me that the leaves have to be dried very thoroughly. In the olden days, they used to achieve this by sun-drying but now there are machines in the big tea estates to do the same job.

Instead of just selling chai, Indian entrepreneurs started keeping other things in their shops. This led to biscuits and other fried snacks being served with tea, as they can be stored for a reasonable duration and are easy to grab. It turned out that the perfect accompaniment for tea was the samosa.

These two dishes might have come from foreign lands, but we married them together in the subcontinent and made people happy in the most inexpensive manner.

Not just a common street food, they also make for very popular greeting dishes that are served across India in people's houses. These were also the goodies served (with broccoli instead of potatoes) to Donald Trump by Indian Prime Minister Narendra Modi on the then-US President's trip to India in February 2020.

Recently, I was watching an Indian movie in which, when the boy and his family go to meet the girl's side of the family, they are welcomed with these two refreshments. The potential mother-in-law keeps saying, 'Our daughter can make the best samosa and chai in town.' This made me turn to my parents and enquire whether they had experienced something similar in their own rishta gatherings. The answer came in the affirmative. But, they told me, along with potato samosas they had also enjoyed minced meat samosas, washed down with hot cups of ginger tea.

Warqi Samosa

My dadi and nani both followed the same recipe which I now share with you. I am adapting this recipe to suit modern measurements and kitchen equipment.

For the dough

225g all-purpose flour
20g + 80g ghee, at room temperature
¾ cup ice-cold water
½ tsp salt, or according to taste

For the stuffing

250g minced meat (chicken/beef/mutton)
1½ tbsp ginger–garlic paste
4 green chillies, chopped
½ tbsp coriander seeds, crushed
1 tsp red chilli powder
1 tbsp coarse ground black pepper
Salt to taste
1 tbsp cumin powder
½ cup fresh coriander, chopped
100g red onion chopped
Oil for deep frying

Method

1. In a bowl, mix the all-purpose flour with 20g ghee. Rub this together between your fingers to get a breadcrumb texture.

2. Little by little, pour the room-temperature water into the breadcrumbs, and knead into a soft dough. Let it rest for 30 minutes.
3. Roll the dough out and brush 20g of melted ghee onto it. Then fold the flattened dough in half and let it cool for 15–20 minutes. Repeat this process for a total of 4 times and at the end let it rest for 15 minutes.
4. In the meantime, make your minced meat (keema) stuffing by heating 2–3 tbsp of oil in a deep pan and tossing in the minced meat.
5. Add the ginger–garlic paste, green chillies, coriander seeds, red chilli powder, salt, cumin powder and crushed black pepper. Mix well and cook for 10–15 minutes.
6. Scatter fresh coriander leaves over it.
7. Add onion and mix for a further 5 minutes. Put this mixture aside and let it cool.
8. Take the dough and roll a rectangular sheet (use a sharp knife to give a perfect shape). Add the stuffing and fold into a triangular shape.
9. Repeat this process till your meat stuffing and dough are finished.
10. Cover these samosas with wet cloths and let them sit for another 5–10 minutes.
11. Deep fry in hot oil on a medium flame till the skin turns a golden brown.

My nani tells me these samosas should ideally be eaten hot with coriander chutney. Today's generation also pair them up with tomato ketchup, but this doesn't create the same magical flavour.

part two

Stories

Aftertaste

Tarana Husain Khan

Death comes with an aftertaste of taar roti.

The town crier, perched on a creaky rickshaw, had coughed and announced the demise on a whistling microphone. The news echoed through the surrounding gullies, bringing Sayedani a pang of sudden desire for the iconic Rampur-style meat curry that was served at funerals. Insensitive as it might be, this craving no longer disturbed her.

'Shh, let me listen,' she said to the children in her early morning class, who were rocking back and forth with the rhythmic chanting of Quranic verses. She couldn't quite get the name as the announcer moved away, but the dead person was from her mohalla. Soon there would be the rich, smoky aroma of taar curry and freshly baked khameeri roti. The invariable red plastic chairs, used for weddings and funerals, would seat male mourners on both sides of the gully leading to the dead person's residence, and sighing groups of burqa-clad women would tumble into the house of mourning. Maybe they would call her. On that thought, she dismissed her class.

Once *he* had brought it for her. The round steel box with its tight lid had failed to hold back the taar, the glistening vermillion red of the ghee-laden curry. In those days the curry actually shimmered like taar – strands of golden wires. She had licked her fingers holding the box, smiling. It was still quite warm and they had sat down on the mat, dipping the soft and yeasty roti into the curry, their nails turning yellow with the turmeric, feeding each other. This was their secret place on the rooftop, their world in its becoming. Later, Ammi would notice her nails and the smell of curried masalas clinging to her daughter even after several washes and gargles. Sayedani would make up a story. For now, this was life.

'They'll make a much better taar roti at our wedding feast,' he had whispered, filling her mouth with the choicest of meat pieces – succulent and lean.

She had blushed with fiery love as he wiped an imaginary dribble of curry from the side of her lip and paused to run his thumb along her lower lip.

'Sayedani-bi, open up!'

'Wait, I am coming.'

She covered her head with her crushed grey shawl as she hobbled across the courtyard. It could only be Husna at this early hour when the lazy winter sun was busy shooing away the mist, and her visit could mean only one thing.

Husna's beaming face peeped in as Sayedani unlocked the rough wooden-plank door. 'Salaam, Sayedani. Hurry up, we have to go!' she said urgently.

'Come in.' Sayedani held the door open.

Sayedani recited the Quranic verse for the bereaved – 'To God we belong, and to God we shall return' – as she turned away, only half-listening to the other woman's recital of the elaborate relationships and connections of the dead woman. It was winter, after all, and older people tended to die with greater frequency. The houses in the old town had vast courtyards and verandas, and it was impossible to insulate the elderly from icy draughts.

Husna took off her burqa and made herself comfortable on the lone wooden charpoy on the veranda. It creaked as she pulled the paan box with its betel-leaf condiments towards herself.

'It's the first female death this year. Old women seem to be hanging on despite the cold,' she laughed.

Husna was such a paan-guzzler that Sayedani dreaded her visits, often concealing a few precious leaves wrapped in moist cloth in her inner cupboard. Her paan box was nearly empty of the usual condiments. The last pinch of her favourite black tobacco, her only addiction, would be gobbled up soon. She wished she had already eaten her first paan of the day.

'Arre, I was fast asleep when Laddan knocked on my door with the news. I didn't even wash my face, just put on my burqa and ran to the haveli. Luckily, I was the first one to reach the house and Mushir sahib said, "Get Sayedani-bi immediately."' The burial is after Friday prayers,' Husna crowed, scraping the last of the katha and lime paste from the compartments and smearing it on the betel leaf. The dregs of tobacco were finally dusted onto the paan and consigned to a fleshy cheek.

Sayedani could feel the tense headache from her tobacco-deprived brain tug at her temples. They wouldn't serve any paan till after the burial.

The water was too cold for a bath and warming it over the heater would take time, so Sayedani washed her face, hands and feet. She would have to bathe afterwards, anyway. Her ice-white suit and shawl were ready for such occasions. Clothes were never a problem. She had scores of white suits and white muslin scarves given to her as charity at festivals, bismillahs and birth ceremonies, or as a reward when one of her students finished the Quran. They were always white – pure. She was assigned the role of purity.

Husna had meanwhile prepared some tea on the heater plate in the kitchen and warmed a stale roti and some leftover potato qatli. She laid it all out on the charpoy. Sayedani refused the qatli–roti. Husna folded the thinly sliced, cumin-flecked potatoes in bits of crumbly roti and ate them in between loud slurps of tea, talking incessantly about her numerous domestic problems. The tea was barely sweet, Sayedani noted. She needed to buy sugar.

'May she reside in heaven. She was a pious lady but ailing for a long time. Arre Bibi, Mushir sahib himself had to wash her and help her with the bedpan. *Tauba, tauba*! That daughter-in-law of hers is such a hussy.'

Sayedani sipped the tea slowly. It must be a relief to die. She felt less guilty as her thoughts turned once again to taar roti. Surely they would serve that rather than pulao. Not that she minded pulao, but taar roti had a deep, sensuous appeal.

'Bibi, eat something. Lunch won't be till late,' Husna burped, handing her half a roti. Sayedani declined and Husna packed the remaining qatli in the roti and tucked it in with the last sip of tea.

'Husna, clean your mouth. It doesn't look good, going to a house of mourning with red lips,' Sayedani reprimanded her.

Husna gave another guttural burp and started to clear up. She thrust her fingers into the cups and, taking the plates in her other hand, piled them on the floor of the kitchen washing area, black with moss and years of greasy curries forming sticky layers. Squatting down on the brick border of the sloping washing area, she turned on the tap and started rinsing her mouth, spitting out the red betel-coloured water into the gaping black hole of the drain.

Sayedani frowned. She would have to scour the washing area later. Husna was always so crude and unkempt. It violated Sayedani's sensibilities to have anything to do with her, but she was in need of Husna's brute strength.

Finally, they were out on the street. Sayedani, petite and bent, trailed behind Husna. The massive awkwardness of Husna's form was encased in a faded black burqa, muddy and fraying at the hem. Her dark face with tobacco-blackened teeth and red glass nose pin was veiled, the headscarf tied tightly under her voluminous chin. Sayedani herself hadn't covered her face for years now, though she still wore the burqa gown and covered her head with a scarf. What was there to see, anyway? A deeply wrinkled, tiny face, edged with stark white hair, the broad forehead and fair colouring supposedly an indicator of her noble lineage. She was a Sayedani, a descendant of the Prophet Muhammad, as was her mother, the appellation and its mantle passed down till everyone forgot her name. Sometimes she would mutter her name to herself. She had started talking to herself, addressing herself by the name given to her by her proud parents – Jameela, the pretty one.

As always, the phantom outlines of ancient kothi mansions invaded her consciousness while they traversed the gully. She had seen these huge mansions being partitioned off between brothers and cousins, the vertical build-up as sons got married, the balconies jutting out to claim the narrow sky above the gully, the lurid greens and pinks, and tiled frontal elevations proclaiming prosperity from Gulf jobs. The gully was now edged with small shops selling sundry items, which replaced the grand gates with a jostling line of signboards – 'Amanat Bhai Halwai, Khan General Store' – up to the Madarsa Kohna. There, the shops inched further into the gully, displaying garlands of paan masala pouches and plastic stands bearing garish chip packets. She always corrected her students – 'kohna' meaning old and not 'kona' as in corner. This was the oldest madrasa of Rampur, expanding inside and upward with contributions from the faithful. It even had air conditioners now, her students told her, prompting the pious to reach the madrasa well before prayer times so as to occupy places closest to the AC. Sayedani had never been inside Madarsa Kohna. Only men prayed there.

There was a woman sitting on the madrasa steps, completely covered in her burqa, her palm outstretched, the fingers curled. Sayedani froze. She could so easily have been the anonymous beggar woman. It had all been her own fault, but fate had been kind and she had survived. Sayedani slipped a coin into the cold palm. This was definitely an old woman, the grey-blue veins sticking out as she clutched the coin and touched her burqa-covered forehead in a salaam. Husna sniffed with the arrogant disapproval of the young. She herself had even worked at a construction site to feed her children. Fate had been kind to her too.

'Careful!' Husna put out a protective arm as a rickshaw trolley crossed in front of them bearing four large narrow-mouthed cooking pots and a portable clay tandoor tied to the planks. The tandoor indicated that they would serve taar curry with tandoor roti. There had been only one death in the area.

'Come, come, we're nearly there.'

It was *his* house. Once, just once, she had stood before it, a bundle hidden inside her burqa, the veil hiding her tears. She felt a deep tenderness for her younger self. No one knew her now. Mushir must be his son.

The Begum had come to know about them. Such affairs rarely remain secret where houses stand rubbing shoulders, like the pious at namaz, often with a common wall bearing a tiny door. It was easy to navigate the entire mohalla through these interconnected doorways of relationships and rumours. The Begum had called Jameela's mother for a Quran recital. Hope, youthful hope had sung in the girl's heart then, but Ammi had returned home silent and shaking from a fever.

He came, finally, after several missives through the little boy whose mother worked at his house. The prayer meeting had been arranged to convey to Ammi that he had been betrothed to the Begum's niece since birth. Jameela had sat still, listening, hardly reacting when he thrust a small bundle of money into her fist, jumped the low wall, and walked away till he was a retreating blotch over the roofs. They had spent the money.

A handsome middle-aged woman, marked with grief, received them in the inner section.

'As-salaam, Sayedani-bi. Ammi is in the room.'

Sayedani touched her forehead. She barely spoke now; Husna did all the talking.

They had left the dead woman as she had fallen on the bed, one leg half dangling, the other still on the bed, as if the act of dying had rendered her untouchable. Husna gave an angry snort and set about straightening her, smoothing the grey wisps of hair around the yellow-tinged, puffy face. Meanwhile the daughter-in-law (presumably) sobbed and narrated to the seated ladies how her beloved Amma had fallen back as she was helping her sit up.

'Ah, only yesterday she asked me to make meat curry. She loved the taar roti-style curry I make and I reminded her, "Amma, the doctor has said you can't have meat . . ."'

Suddenly two young girls started weeping uncontrollably and the women got busy consoling them. The daughter-in-law looked at them with annoyance, shoved a lady aside, and enveloped one of the girls in her embrace.

'Ya Allah, give us all patience.' She looked heavenward and started crying with loud gasps.

'Sameera, sit down, sit down. Someone get water!' Everyone now crowded around the daughter-in-law.

'Ya Allah, forgive me if I erred in looking after my Amma!'

'No, no, you looked after her lovingly for so many years . . .'

'She wet herself and this woman didn't even clean her,' Husna whispered, settling the petticoat to cover the legs. Sayedani became aware of the pungent urine smell.

She must have been a lovely woman when he wed her, although her light complexion was now mottled with grey spots and a bilious pallor; the nose stood among the ruins, regal still with its empty piercing. Sayedani looked around the room invaded by the red plastic chairs and the grieving–consoling women. It was a small room, possibly the tiniest in the large house, windowless with an old air-conditioning unit stuck on one wall, probably from the son in Dubai. The single bed on which she lay was an old *masehri*, one of a pair that she must have occupied with him; a family photograph of happy times and prayer beads on a table next to it. The women, who had stopped crying now, started whispering prayers and gossip, seemingly oblivious to the smell of sickness, medicines and stale faeces. They would speak of it all later.

Husna was by her side suddenly, nudging her, handing her a bowl of freshly ground herbal paste. She had bought the perfumed herbs as usual from an advance payment. Sayedani realized that she had been standing near the bed, staring down at the body for some time. She took the bowl, picked up the surprisingly delicate hand with long, tapering fingers, overgrown, dirty nails and the indentations of recently prised-off rings. Husna snorted again and looked pointedly at Sayedani – must be the good-for-nothing daughter-in-law.

Sayedani smeared the dark green sweet-smelling paste on the palms while Husna applied some to the feet to mask the smell of decaying flesh. Husna also tied the bloated feet together with a piece of cloth – the legs of overweight women tended to stiffen and splay out soon after death. Sayedani closed the slightly parted lips and tied a swatch of cloth around her face with a knot under the jaw. Who wanted to see a gaping, dead mouth? They followed their carefully orchestrated motions. Thankfully, someone had bothered to close the eyes. She didn't want to look into them.

He must have loved her for all those years together, bearing and bringing up two sons. A man with two sons is blessed and secure. They were waiting for the younger son on his way from Dubai. Social dynamics dictated that at least one of the sons had to work abroad while the other stayed back to look after the ageing parents.

More women were trooping in, clicking tongues and paying their condolences to the daughter-in-law who had launched forth, teary-eyed, into the story of the last meal of the deceased. In this version, she had lovingly prepared the taar curry for her Amma. Her audience approved of sating the taste buds of the dying person. What did doctors know anyway?

Sayedani covered the body with a crumpled shawl, hiding the wet petticoat. The dead woman had been reduced to wearing petticoats instead of shalwars to ease the use of a bedpan. Sayedani retreated to the veranda outside. Her stomach had been rumbling loud enough for everyone to hear.

He was dead too. The same announcement in the gully some years ago, the uneven brick-lined path lending a mournful quiver to the voice of the announcer as the rickshaw bumped along. It had only brought back memories of that terrible day, all those years ago, of Ammi's shocked face and stinging slaps – one, two, three, four. The young Jameela had shielded her face and howled. Ammi, fearful of the neighbours, had pulled her into their room, closed the door and beaten her with the stick she used to threaten the children with, calling her names the girl couldn't make sense of. She was forbidden to go out: not that she had had many occasions to do so. Till the day she died, five years later, Ammi never spoke to her again, turning away her face at Sayedani's attempts to breach the silence with pleadings, anger and finally one-sided conversations. Her daughter deliberately started missing the mandatory five-times namaz, hoping Ammi would reprimand her or wake her for the morning prayers. But Ammi had given up on her and on life.

Now Sayedani and Husna were making preparations for the bath in the tiny orchard next to the courtyard; custom stipulated that the bathwater must flow into the soil.

'Jameela, I have planted a mango tree for you,' he had said to her once. It had been drizzling for days, the perfect time to lay down roots. Yes, there was a mango tree, not very old – *their* tree. At present people were erecting a little tented area under that same tree and setting up a planked wooden bathing bed. The silver-painted pall in the shape of a bed with poles for the pallbearers, hired from the Madarsa Kohna, stood next to it.

'Nine metres cotton latha cloth, two large clay pots, loban resin, camphor, warm water, beri leaves . . . and, yes, needle and thread,' Husna was instructing a busy-looking relative who had suddenly emerged to take charge.

Finally, they settled down on a bench at one side of the orchard, away from the distinguished ladies, and began cutting and sewing the shroud. Sayedani had made her peace with becoming practically invisible. She could have been one of the Sayedanis reciting the Quran in a low musical murmur, keeping count of the volumes read and unread. It had been her fault, of course. The news of her love affair and her abortive attempt to enter this house to throw herself at the Begum's mercy had spread across their small mohalla through the ever-listening, connecting doors. Children had started dropping out of her mother's Quran classes. The few who remained were too poor to go elsewhere.

'Hmm, one to tie around the waist, one under the arms, one around the head, one to cover and, lastly, one for bathing,' Husna recited, cutting and counting, the black cloth-sheathed talisman bobbing at her throat.

Sayedani was by now hungry to the point of dizziness.

'You should have eaten something,' Husna clicked her tongue. 'Here, have this.' She unknotted her scarf edge and took out a tiny tobacco-laced paan. 'Tuck it into your cheek and no one will know.'

It would make her even dizzier, but Sayedani took it. The tobacco pulsed her body back to life.

Grey smoke rose beyond the courtyard wall with the smell of frying onions. The neighbours or relatives must have begun cooking the food for the mourners.

'Taar roti,' Sayedani murmured, and Husna hid her smile in her black shawl.

'When I was young, they used to serve the taar curry in clay bowls soaked overnight. The curry was thin enough to drink and glistened like gold,' said Sayedani, a little heady as her brain started to relax. They used to eat seated on the floor mats, the food served on low stools, and the clay bowls were replaced with fresh ones as soon as the curry became tepid. Now they had tables and chairs, but they still served palm-sized pieces of piping hot rotis, tearing them off from the large tandoori roti. You had only to open your palm and the alert serving person would thrust a warm fragment at you for the next few bites. Of course, for a funeral they would just keep the rotis in a pile next to the curry bowls and there would be no sweet dish. But Sayedani didn't care much for the sweet rice which was the usual menu at celebrations, not that she went to many celebrations these days.

They had overdone the onions. Sayedani sniffed at the faint acrid smell. The taste of the curry would be spoilt now and the colour would become too dark. Such careless khansamas! If only they had added a little bit of salt to the frying onions and paid attention, they would have turned out perfectly golden.

'Our Rampuri taar roti is such that chicken qorma would pale before it. And the way it is served . . . I went to a Meerut wedding and, Bibi, we had to stand and eat like animals,' Husna grumbled. 'And no one to give hot roti. We had to serve ourselves from big bowls. Huh, I came back hungry.' She sat on her haunches to light the camphor.

Nowadays, the taar curry was too thick and florid. The cooks even put in coconut and melon seed powders so that they didn't have to work hard at the final sautéeing, so crucial to make the ghee separate from the masala. It was more like qorma with all the aromatic spices, but it was still delicious. The fingers dipping in plastic bowls came out turmeric-dyed, and the meat pieces were soft and small enough to envelop in a bite-sized roti piece. Sayedani's molars were all gone and she could barely eat a few meat pieces, preferring to soften the roti in the curry and chew on it slowly.

Husna took off her threadbare sweater, her short kurta sleeves digging into her forearms. They laid the body out on the bathing bed. Husna scissored the clothes, slid them off from under the body, and Sayedani covered the nakedness with a sheet. Her ears were getting warm from the tobacco and her hands were tremulous; she hoped she would be able to complete her part. Husna would take on most of the work, knowing her state. The daughter-in-law and some middle-aged women stood around. To bathe the dead was a pious act, not that they even touched the body.

They divided the dead woman into their usual zones – Husna taking the turgid, swollen legs and the intimate area. The stomach had bloated up considerably by now. Husna looked at Sayedani and grimaced. The woman had probably not passed a stool and Husna would have to work to expel some, otherwise the stomach would be an unsightly protuberance on the open pall.

They turned the body to one side and Sayedani gasped. The back was covered with deep-red bedsores.

'Hai Bibi, I can see the bone!' Husna whispered, looking at the deep wound in the lower back.

Sayedani felt a rush of nausea as the tobacco congealed itself in an aching mass right below her ribs. 'Don't do anything, just wash her,' she whispered.

Husna asked one of the ladies to pour water, tenderly bathing the wounds. She took a piece of cloth and used it as a sponge to wash the intimate area. Sayedani put cotton wads in the ears and the nose, washed the hair, sparse and grey, uttering prayers loudly for the benefit of onlookers. She poured water over the distended stomach, the drooping breasts, and the arms, gently soothing the soft skin with a light touch, her hands working under the sheet. The body should observe purdah.

The first body she had bathed was her mother's, directed by her Aunt Zainab. Zainab had married a Pathan outside the community and was reduced to bathing the dead after her husband died. She had taught Jameela – at that time she still had her name – the trade, taking the young pupil with her for burials. Her few students couldn't support her. Then Husna had joined them. Aunt Zainab had tried to get Jameela married but, as the Begum had remarked to Ammi, Pathans could not marry a Sayed girl for fear that a harsh word to her might inadvertently cause disrespect to the Prophet's line. Her lineage was so exalted that she was unmarriageable to all except another Sayed, but the few Sayed families had shunned her after the scandal.

Her little group of students colonized her days with their chatter, their quarrels and her pretend anger. They were mostly girls, helping her around the house after the lessons, fetching her provisions from the mohalla shops. Sometimes they paid modest fees or brought food, though she never asked them to. If it wasn't for the funeral dressings, she would go begging on the streets. At least she had a roof over her head to hide her disgrace, bestowed by the Nawab after the merger of Rampur State into the Indian Union in 1949. They used to live in the fort area before that, where her father taught the Quran to the princes. So when the fort and buildings were handed over to the government and palaces were transformed into schools and the library, they were given a small house in mohalla Madarsa Kohna.

Sayedani and Husna finally wrapped up the body, rolling and lifting, helped by the onlookers. One piece around the waist, one under the armpits, a large scarf around the face covering the arms. Husna quickly spread a large winding sheet on the pall bed and the women helped to lift the body onto the bed. They wrapped her in a white cocoon, leaving her face open for the final viewing by the loved ones. Maybe her spirit had met his by now. They would bury her next to him in the mohalla graveyard; her sons would stand inside the grave and gently lay her to rest. The women were saying that he had purchased their conjoined burial plots. Sayedani would be buried in the same graveyard by default.

Bone-weary and freezing wet, Sayedani sat in the dull sun trying to warm herself; the water had seeped to her core despite several layers of clothing. Husna brought her a cup of overly sweet tea and they sat watching relatives pay their last respects and the final hoisting of the pall onto sturdy male shoulders as the women stood and chanted the kalima prayer. Tobacco and tea had congealed into a raw wound in her stomach. She curled protectively around it. Maybe she should drink the nauseating pink syrup the doctor had given her once. The acid was gnawing her stomach, reaching her ice-cold bones.

There was a palpable change in the atmosphere as the men returned from the burial. They didn't have to walk far, for the graveyard was at the centre of the mohalla. The cooking pots filled with curry were brought into the courtyard, and the women got back to the business of living, laying out food. The aroma of taar curry and baking rotis enveloped them. Holy texts and prayer beads were put away, the chatter became louder, and life pulled everyone back into its fold. Death receded. People always felt satisfied and at peace after the death of an old person.

Suddenly, he stood before her, his face bearing a gentle sorrow. It couldn't be him. His son Mushir touched his brow in salaam, thanked her for her services to his mother, and handed her a wad of notes.

'We are blessed that you were here to prepare Ammi on her last journey.'

'She was dear to me; almost a relative. I cannot take this.' Sayedani handed back the money, ignoring Husna's shocked face. Mushir thanked her more profusely and asked her to stay back for lunch. She shook her head, got up and put on her burqa, buttoning it slowly down to the hem.

'Bibi, what are you doing? They're serving lunch now – taar roti!' Husna hissed in her ear.

White melamine bowls brimming with red curry were being placed on the makeshift wood tables from the tent house. Women were sitting down to the late lunch with appropriately morose expressions. It would be their turn after the genteel ladies.

'And there will be a prayer meeting after lunch. They'll distribute some sweets then.'

Sayedani shook her head again, and started moving towards the entrance.

Husna clicked her tongue, quickly putting on her burqa. She couldn't leave Sayedani to walk back on her own. Maybe she would send her son with a small tiffin-carrier – that is, if they asked. She told the busy relative that Sayedani wasn't feeling well.

Sayedani felt guilty for Husna's sake as they retraced their steps back to her house. But there would be more funerals. The cold was bound to become severe and it would snow up in the nearby hills. Husna didn't say a word. She must be wondering about this sudden 'relationship'. She didn't know of the old scandal, thanks to a collective amnesia brought on by the long years of Sayedani's sequestered piety.

Sayedani took off her soaked socks and lay down in her quilt, trembling. The pain was coming in spasms and she gulped down the thick syrup, too exhausted to change or bathe. The parameters of *paak* and *na-paak*, the pure and the soiled, drilled into her by Ammi, had long disappeared. She had stopped wearing paak clothes, performing ablutions and putting her forehead to the ground five times a day to appease an indifferent God. Allah had exhausted all chances to redeem Himself.

The distance between life and death was blurred now – it was just another state she would slip into. Maybe the children would find her one morning when she didn't open the door to them. Sadiq, the naughty one, would jump into the courtyard.

The clanging of the door knocker woke her from a sleep induced by relief from the pain. Was it morning already? Husna was standing at the doorway, grinning gleefully.

'Taar roti! Allah give long life to Mushir sahib. He sent this for you, and one for me. Eat – you haven't had anything since morning. He also gave me a thousand rupees!' Husna handed her a warm black polythene bag and left.

The bag and the plastic box inside were slick with spilled gravy. They no longer used pure ghee now, substituting it with a mixture of vegetable oils. Sayedani opened the lid and inhaled the aromatic curry. The layer of grease was deep, and the masalas lay viscous on the meat pieces.

'Jameela, do you remember how Abba used to drink the curry and his moustaches would turn yellow?' Sayedani said to herself. She smiled and sat down on the little stool by the heater, warming the rotis on the skillet, dipping bits into the darker-than-usual curry. She fished out a piece of meat with the roti and put it in her mouth. 'Arre, who uses coconut? It's just made the curry sweet! All we used was fried onions and the basic masalas. Hmm . . . these deceitful cooks didn't even bother to peel the garlic! They just want a thick curry.'

She chewed slowly. The taar curry was a silken warmth curling through her.

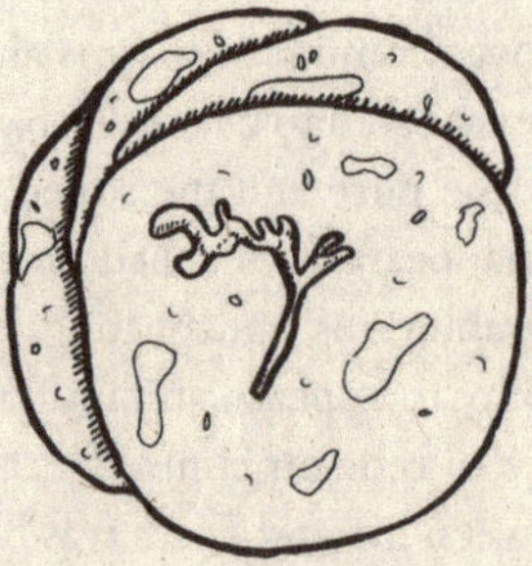

Rampuri Taar Curry

1 kg mutton or beef
500g ghee (butter if you can't get that) or ½ litre refined oil
2 large onions, finely diced
3–4 tbsp onion paste (made from the diced onions)
3 tbsp ginger–garlic paste
1 cup of dahi (curd), or yoghurt if curd is not available
10 green cardamoms
6 cloves
6–7 bay leaves
2 tsp red chilli powder (or as per taste)
2 tsp turmeric powder
3 tsp coriander powder
2 tsp green cardamom powder
1 tsp garam masala powder
1 tsp aromatic masala powder*
2 tbsp coconut powder (optional)
2 tbsp melon seed powder (optional)
½ cup milk
3 drops kewra water (optional)
salt to taste

* For aromatic masala powder, dry grind 5g each of nutmeg, star anise, cinnamon and mace.

Method

1. Heat the oil in a large saucepan or a round-bottomed cooking pot (degchi). Fry the diced onions till golden. Strain and take out the onions, putting them onto a large plate. When they are cool, dry grind them and set aside.
2. Into the heated ghee, add the whole cardamoms, cloves and bay leaves.
3. Almost immediately add the meat, onion paste, ginger–garlic paste, yoghurt and drops of kewra water (if using). Stir to mix everything, and let it cook over a medium flame for 5 minutes.
4. In a bowl mix turmeric powder, red chilli powder, coriander powder, salt and coconut powder (optional). Put this blend into the cooking pot and stir to mix the ingredients. Bring to a boil on a high flame and let it cook for 10 minutes, stirring regularly.
5. Reduce to medium flame and add 2–3 cups of water (depending on the meat). Cover and let it cook till the meat becomes tender. It will take about half an hour. You can use a pressure cooker but the taste is always better with slow-cooked meat.
6. Check the meat. If it's tender, add the melon seed powder and the milk. Keep stirring.
7. When the liquid has nearly evaporated, add the dry-ground fried onion paste. Sauté on a medium flame, adding a splash of water to prevent the curry from burning.
8. When the oil separates from the masala, add boiled water according to the desired consistency of the gravy and bring to the boil. Add the aromatic spice powder, garam masala powder and green cardamom power. Switch off the flame.
9. Taar curry tastes best with tandoor roti.

With warm thanks to Munna Bhai Khansama and Chef Suroor for their input.

A Brief History of the Carrot

Rosie Dastgir

The summer that Linda left him, Raman was bereft. After the initial shock of her flight and the gloomy absence of her in the house came the unhappy realization that the freight of domestic responsibility was now squarely on his shoulders. It wasn't so much the vacuuming that bothered him, not even the laundry, once the feat of separation of whites and coloureds had been mastered. The anguish lay in the cooking. For though Raman was many things – he taught physics at the sixth-form college down the road, and was at home with string theory and black holes and the shrinking and expanding universe – he was not a practised cook.

It wasn't as if Linda's cooking was any great shakes either, firmly rooted in the 1970s of her childhood, though he did consider making her English casserole. The ingredients were obvious. Meat and onions, definitely, tomato purée and other things, probably, though the question of exactly how to make it eluded him. The Prestige pressure cooker stood redundant on an upper shelf. She'd left it behind, a burned ember tattooed on its bottom, the indelible memory of her beef stew. No use whatsoever now without the little weight that calibrated the pressure, the tips of the handles melted like molten lava that made it impossible to marry them in alignment. There was talk of her returning to collect more things – though Raman doubted it, even as he kept the embers of that rumour glowing for their son Sami's sake because the neighbours kept asking. Whenever the boy went next door to play with Chloe, her mum always mentioned Linda, not that they'd ever been friends. Once she'd invited Sami to stay for tea, but he'd said no thanks and dashed home.

Raman was amazed. 'You didn't want to stay for the fish fingers and chips?'

Sami shook his head. 'I don't like her asking me things,' he said.

'What things?'

'About Mum,' he shrugged, splaying out his exercise books on the kitchen table so Raman could help with his homework. At least he was qualified for that.

Home was gloomy after school without Linda, the carpeted rooms muted and numb. Both of them felt her absence. Most acutely in the hours around teatime when Raman rattled around the kitchen, opening and closing cupboards in a bid to discover what the hell to cook. Left to his own devices he would instinctively have eaten meals shaped around his own carnivorous proclivities – lamb or beef curries or kebabs – though with Sami to take care of since Linda's departure, this would not wash. The boy was no fan of meat and tended to shy away from food that did not fall within a strict spectrum of white to beige to orange. Pasta was his go-to choice though Raman resisted the hegemony of this dullest of foodstuffs, baulking at the rubbery blandness of spaghetti, the slithery cables that proved so hard to wrangle when eating.

When all else failed, the humble egg came to the rescue and bailed him out. Ovoid perfection, its concentration of nutrients, and versatility made the rustling up of a nutritious plate of scrambled egg a doddle. It was the only thing that Sami would reliably eat, and so it seemed easiest to stick with this for infinity.

But infinity means forever, and the idea of it bothered him. Forever scrambled egg on toast. Forever without Linda. Forever in this house and doing the same old job. Though to be fair

Raman enjoyed the teaching and now he was the head of the physics department, which brought a modest increase in salary along with the uptick in admin. Still, lecturers could be a strange and bitter bunch. He'd had a few run-ins with them in the past, although the head herself was a cultured and gracious woman who lived alone with her dachshund in a college house on the campus. She was older and treated him with solicitude, and once they'd discussed how he squared his understanding of Islam with the complexities of the universe. The only English person who had ever done that, and he held her in quiet esteem.

If only he'd enjoyed such rapport with his wife, who taught drama at a community college south of the river. There'd been little common ground with Linda after the first flush of love and desire had ebbed. He could see that now with the benefit of hindsight, even if the rift was partly his responsibility. He should have been less eager to fit in, less intent on striving to be English. Shucking his identity, he'd done himself no favours, allowing Linda to insist on having her way. He thought of her cooking. Partly, that was his fault. Partly, she lacked flair.

When he'd first arrived in England, it was hard to lay your hands on the spices and ingredients you needed. You had to forage around in the Bangladeshi off-licences on the other side of Queen's Park to find mustard seeds and proper chilli powder, turmeric and garam masala, and sometimes he still ventured over there in pursuit of jars of hot lime pickle or a big sack of rice. He bought the spices too, so much cheaper than the supermarket, and though Linda never protested, he sometimes caught her sighing in exasperation at the tiny powdered spillages of vivid yellow and red that leaked onto the shelves. As a precaution, she isolated them at the back of the cupboard, away from her tubs of mixed herbs and the dusty shards of bay she dropped into her casseroles. The Schwartz bottle of curry powder was an outlier she'd used once or twice, sprinkled into her mince dish with – horror of horrors – the addition of sultanas.

Was he being unfair about his wife's palate? An image of Linda from before curled into his mind. Hadn't she actually loved a proper Indian meal? They used to go to the Taj Palace where she stuck doggedly to the same dishes: the scarlet tandoori chicken, the puffy naan and the vegetable curry – plus a pint of lager or two. Sometimes at the end of term they went with a gaggle of lecturers who'd order a stack of poppadoms to be devoured with gusto like crisps. He'd never tasted the blistered little synthetic discs before he came to England, and secretly found them wanting. On rare occasions he had lunch there alone, boldly choosing the brain masala, which Linda could not abide, or the special goat foot stew which was cooked for hours and known for its rich distillation of nutrients, not to mention the silken flavour.

Raman had missed the signs of Linda's affair. The crumpled Silk Cut packets in the pocket of her shearling coat when he went hunting for the car key, even though she'd given up smoking years ago. The black patent heels she stored in the footwell of the hatchback she drove to work every night. The times when she came home much later than normal, the blonde bob of her hair wreathed with smoke and something cloyingly sweet.

He didn't lecture her. The trysts with Malcolm, the sport psychologist who lived in a pretty market town up the A1, required the car, and he didn't protest when she finally moved out. He had no need of it. His place of work was a short stroll down the road, and Sami walked to school with Chloe, or Chloe's mum Iris gave them a lift if it was raining.

That autumn, it barely stopped. The lifts to school were a boon, and he was grateful. She was a decent soul, Iris, though buttressed behind a carapace of English reserve that made him slow to realize that she harboured emotions.

'About the garden,' she said to him one afternoon, her voice strained with broaching the topic over the fence.

'Oh yes. What is it?' He was innocently pegging out a row of black socks and some unintentionally pink school shirts on the washing line. She was gathering in her own – a display of tea towels printed with souvenir maps that fluttered gently on her rotary dryer – when she'd taken the opportunity to mention it. They'd barely exchanged more than pleasantries until now. Never a cross word though, and Chloe thought the world of Sami, she'd once said.

It was the change in use from flower border to vegetable patch at the bottom of their garden that rankled. She'd always had such a nice view from the back bedroom, and the change in outlook was a real pity. Was he planning on keeping it that way?

'I mean, with only the two of you,' she ventured. 'All those vegetables.'

He'd dug up the flower border when Linda left, turned over the rich clay soil with the garden fork one grey bank holiday when nobody was around to challenge him. Gone were the dahlias, the wallflowers, the pink carnations, the butterfly bush where Linda used to lie in summer on the tartan rug. In went the alu and the saag and the fragile tomato seedlings he'd found on a little stand beside wizened plug plants outside the hardware shop.

He huffed inside with the laundry basket. How could she be so unreasonable? All summer long, he'd tended and weeded, inspected the burgeoning leaves and plucked off invasive pests, spray-gunned caterpillars with soapy liquid and chased off cats caught pawing the soil. He'd watered the vegetable patch daily with run-off from the water butt by the garage and the cloudy dregs from Sami's paddling pool, and by the end of the hot spell there was a bumper crop of tomatoes. The surfeit had been dispatched in paper bags to his bemused neighbours, and the rest he'd eaten himself. Doused in salt and pepper and liberated from the watery embrace of lettuce, they made a far superior kind of salad, dressed with lemon juice and a few pungent slivers of onion.

The vegetable patch had saved him. And no matter how much Iris missed her view, there were things in the earth that he refused to disturb.

It was the exotic black carrots that were his secret pride and joy. The dark and mysterious purple tubers swelling out of sight beneath the earth that promised to be ready by winter. An aunt in Pakistan had sent him the seeds. Remembering his fondness for the magenta carrot juice, she'd slid them into the flimsy pages of a scholarly pamphlet she'd published and sent to him in the hope of reaching a wider audience. Her *Brief History of the Carrot* described how the vegetable had been harvested in the Indian subcontinent by Muslims for a thousand years before the West had stolen it – as they did with every discovery and invention – and made it their own. The idea of the carrot being colonized and changing colour gave Raman considerable pause.

The English have their kitchen gardens full of vegetables, the aunt wrote in her letter. *But these are far more delicious than their native varieties.*

The aunt was erudite and spot on. The anaemic orange kind did not even come close: with that fruity foretaste, devoid of crunch. He recalled how drearily moist it turned when grated in the coleslaw they served in the college canteen. The diced variety was no better, mingled with sweetcorn and lopped green beans in the frozen mixed bags, which Linda served alongside lamb chops and mashed potato. For years he'd eaten those dinners. Gnawed the fibres of meat from the little chop bones, chased the peas that rolled away from the curved embrace of his fork. Yet he'd never been fully converted – and now those days were past.

Over the next few weeks, Chloe came to play far more often, because of the noise and mess the two of them made, her mum said.

'Chloe thinks you don't mind,' Sami said to Raman, which was probably true. Iris was a known germophobe and fanatical tidier, judging by the frequency with which she swept the front drive and took out the hoover, spring-cleaning the family caravan both before and after their annual holidays in the breezy Hunstanton dunes. That year, however, they'd not gone. Which was odd, Raman noted, given how hot the summer had been.

When Bob told him ruefully over the front wall about Iris's little operation and how he was having to do everything these days, Raman wanted to ask more but something made him hold back.

October came. The black carrots were ready, the damp soil yielding them easily when Raman tugged at the ferny tops that sprang in rows across the sunny patch he'd sown that summer. He spread out the crop on the patio, marvelling at their earthy fatness, the purple skins ridged and speckled with soil. A far cry from their wan orange cousins, and he went in search of Iris to show her.

He found her outside in the front drive with a sponge and a bowl of sudsy water, on the verge of cleaning out the caravan for an impromptu trip over half-term.

'If the weather's not too changeable,' she added.

'I hope you're on the mend,' Raman said.

'I am, thanks.' She focused on the vegetables. 'You've been busy. Not beetroot, is it?'

'No, it's a type of carrot from Pakistan,' he said.

The revelation floored her. 'Whatever will you do with them?'

'Good question. I've been considering it.'

'How do they taste?'

He hesitated. 'Juicy, crisp,' he said, 'with a kick of spice.'

'You'd never guess it, would you?'

'You wouldn't,' he agreed.

Her response gladdened him. For that was the secret power of the black carrot, its dark allure boding sweetness, though yielding piquancy instead.

'It's also very good for you, the pigment,' he enthused. 'Healthy as well as delicious.'

She was sceptical. 'So what's it meant to do for you, the purple?'

The specifics stumped him. The aunt's recipe for black carrot kanji emphasized flavour rather than its healthful qualities, though she'd alluded to this in the pamphlet.

'Longevity,' he said after a moment. 'Supposed to be good for that, I gather.'

Chloe's mum was back in hospital again, Sami said, and most days after school the girl came over to play and stayed for tea. Branching out from the nightly scrambled egg, Raman began making curried omelettes instead, puckered golden discs speckled with tawny dots of curry powder that proved an instant hit. Sami and Chloe ate them sandwiched between two slices of white bread sitting on the settee in front of the telly. Is this what they used to call a TV dinner, they wondered, and Raman said he thought it probably was. The stranglehold of fish fingers and forever scrambled egg was apparently broken.

'That wouldn't be something I'd ever cook,' Iris said to Raman over the front wall. 'Only ever since I came out of hospital, Chloe's been asking me.'

'They're easy,' Raman said. 'All you do is sprinkle a bit of curry powder into the egg, and that's it.'

'I'll give it a try, though to be honest I'm not sure if Bob will go for it. He's not terribly fond of hot food.'

'Linda's the same,' Raman admitted, 'and Sami.'

'Is he?'

'Like mother like son.'

She held his gaze for a moment. 'Does he miss his mum?' she asked.

'We're managing,' Raman said, and looked away.

'I did wonder,' she said, 'if you were.'

The aunt's recipe for the carrot kanji was succinct and easy to follow. He washed the black carrots in a bowl of water as instructed, not bothering with the gloves she recommended to protect against the purple juice that stained his fingers. Peeling and slicing them thinly, he marvelled at how each disc revealed a starburst of deep colour like the iris of an eye, and slid the little heap into an empty glass pickle jar. Filling it to the brim with water, he watched it turn scarlet as he stirred and tipped in a generous teaspoon of salt and brown mustard seeds, adding a pinch of cumin and chilli rescued from isolation at the back of the cupboard. The aunt recommended leaving it to ferment in the sunshine for a few days to develop its particular flavour, but that was trickier than she imagined. A greenhouse was ideal, not that he had one, or the airing cupboard, perhaps, but that of course lacked daylight. In the end, he plumped for the upstairs landing window by Sami's bedroom, which gave onto the west-facing flat roof and caught the sun in the afternoons. Over the next few days, he paid visits up to the landing and gave the jar a brisk stir, impatient for it to be ready.

The taste will be slightly pungent, the recipe declared, *and the rich crimson colour will resemble wine*.

Did it? Raman held the jar up to the window to audit the results and glanced into the neighbouring garden to see that Iris was looking straight at him. He shot her a quick smile and raised the kanji so she could get a better view, though she pretended not to see.

Downstairs in the kitchen, he decanted the strained liquid into a slender pitcher and was about to test it when there was a tap at the back door. The tall figure was familiar, her muddle of dark curly hair through the beaded glass, though she'd never been over till now.

'Is everything all right, Iris?' he asked.

She lingered, insisting she wasn't stopping. 'I'm sorry, I didn't mean to be nosy just now.'

'Not at all,' he said. 'I'm glad you dropped by. Won't you try some?'

'Is it homemade wine?'

'No, no,' he smiled. 'It's black carrot kanji, a sort of fermented drink.'

'I did wonder what you'd do with them, Raman,' she said. 'Oh – and I looked it up online, what you said about them helping you live longer.'

A flicker of doubt. Had he gone too far? 'My aunt is convinced of it, and she's an expert.'

She looked at him. 'Apparently it's the anthocyanins. That colour.'

He poured out two glasses that glowed in the afternoon light. Room temperature, as the aunt's recipe specified. The taste of it was sour and pungent and strangely restorative, though not exactly as he remembered. Was some vital ingredient missing? Perhaps. Possibly. Some element that needed adding, or something he'd left out.

It struck him that Linda's departure was a gift, an opportunity to reclaim what was lost.

Iris took a sip. 'Ooh,' she said. 'Quite nice.'

The English *quite* that was always so hard to gauge.

'Do you like it?'

'I do,' she said. 'I think you've converted me.'

Black Carrot Kanji

½ kg, or roughly 5 or 6 black carrots (or orange if you can't get the black ones)
2.5 tbsp black salt (or to taste)
3 tbsp red mustard or rai
1.5 tsp red chilli powder (optional)
1 tbsp roasted ground cumin
2 litres or 8 cups of water

Method

1. Wash the black carrots and drain the water.
2. Wear gloves and peel the skin off the carrots, before slicing them.
3. In a large container add water and coarsely ground rai or red mustard.
4. Add the sliced black carrot discs and watch the water change colour.
5. Add black salt, cumin and red chilli powder. Stir with a ladle and cover with a lid.
6. Let the drink sit for a couple of days in the sun or a warm area in your house to ferment and develop its flavour. Stir it at least once a day.
7. When the taste has developed it will become a little pungent and the colour will become like wine. You can sieve the drink through a colander and discard the carrots after another two days. Transfer the drink into a glass jar with a lid and store at room temperature.

The Hairy Curry

Asiya Zahoor

Gulla was looking for a knife. He found one mounted on a metal strip on the wall. Holding its wooden handle in his palm, he turned the blade towards him, trying to assess its sharpness. It was blunt. Dissatisfied, he rubbed the cutting edge of the knife on the rough end of the cement basin to sharpen it. He was partly excited, partly apprehensive, for he had never cooked or eaten anything even close to this dish before.

Now that the knife was sharp enough, with its tip he made an incision in the grass rope that was tied around the bunch of lotus stems. The bunch fell apart, and the stems dropped into the basin. Gingerly, he picked them up one by one and examined them.

Each stem in the bunch was a hollow tube, about the length of his forearm, and with many holes in it. There were ten to fifteen stems in all. To Gulla, they looked like the stack of timber he would collect for his mother's hearth on which she baked thick cornflour bread. A month back, he had seen bunches of lotus stems at the vegetable vendor's shop in the bazaar and had asked Farooq about them.

Farooq was another boy from Gulla's village who had come to Srinagar to work as domestic help and now laboured in the same mohalla as Gulla. The two boys had got to know each other during their daily visits to buy provisions from the bazaar. Over the months their acquaintance had turned into a friendship. They confided in each other how much they missed their village and how similar their condition in the city was. Their Bibijis, both boys confided, treated them with similar cruelty. All Bibijis in the world are the same and the world is full of Bibijis, they agreed.

Pointing to a bunch of lotus stems at the vegetable vendor's, Gulla had asked Farooq if it was white timber for burning on the hearth.

Farooq had a hearty laugh before answering, 'Gulla, my brother, you are so naive! This isn't timber but a bunch of vegetables to be eaten as a delicacy.'

After all, Farooq had been working as a domestic help in Srinagar for more than two years, while Gulla had only been there six months. The vegetable, Farooq noted, was an expensive one and people from villages like theirs had neither the taste nor the money for it. Farooq also told Gulla that cleaning and chopping the lotus stems was a hard task. 'The stem has dirt in it because it is porous from within and it grows in muddy waters. It sucks up the mud through its pores.'

He added that the family he worked for had gone on an excursion to the Dal Lake one time and took him along to watch their kids. During that visit Farooq had seen lotus flowers with soft pink petals floating on the emerald waters of the lake. It was hard to imagine there could be so much mud underneath the lotus, seeping into its roots and stems.

Now, holding the knife at an angle, Gulla peeled a very thin layer off the lotus stems, then cleaned the stems thoroughly under tap water. Next he chopped them one by one into small chunks that looked like white circles with holes in them. He held each circle under the tap so that the gushing waters would clean the dirt from the pores. The cold tap water almost froze Gulla's fingers, but it was fun too. After rinsing the chunks of lotus stems he looked through the holes to check if any dirt was left. He counted the holes: there tended to be ten holes round the edge and one in the centre. He put the chunks in a deep perforated steel colander. Piled up, the lotus sections gleamed like a mound of snow.

While the chunks were draining in the colander, Gulla placed a narrow-mouthed copper degchi with a thick concave bottom on the stove. He set about boiling one and a half litres of water. Then he gathered together three pieces of black cardamom, seven of green cardamom and four sticks of cinnamon, and looked for the stone mortar and pestle to pound the spices. Bibiji had cautioned Gulla that if the spices weren't crushed sufficiently, the aromatic flavour would not be released into the curry. The pestle and mortar had been lying in a corner of the shelf for over a month and had accumulated dust. While mopping and swabbing down the shelves and floor, Gulla would leave the bigger pieces of kitchenware without dusting them. Today Gulla's hands were numb from washing lotus stems under cold water, so washing these items and lifting the heavy mortar would be a pain. Instead he picked up a handful of spices in the hem of his pheran and wrapped the spices in a fold. He held the folded cloth in his teeth and took bites till the spices were crushed into minute bits.

Then Gulla opened the fold of the pheran and shook the spices into the palm of his hand. He left his tightened fist under the tap on full. He let water pass over his fist so that it reached the spices and gave them a bath. Next, quickly opening his palm over the degchi, he tipped the spices into the boiling water. Before adding the lotus-stem chunks he held his hands over the warmth for some time. Fingers no longer numb, he added a piece of ginger and four cloves of garlic to the mixture.

Gulla then picked up another degchi, put it on the stove and poured homemade yoghurt from an earthen pot into it. In the village his mother and other women often cooked in earthen pots. 'It gives the food a fresh earthiness, adding a unique flavour,' his mother used to say. Gulla used a long-handled wooden muddler with a circular base to whisk the yoghurt. He added a tablespoon of salt to the yoghurt to prevent it from sticking to the degchi while over the flame. The muddler had wide gaps in its base and with some strenuous churning a frothy thick paste was made from the yoghurt.

The yoghurt had to be stirred continuously or the heat would produce lumps in it. Gulla kept stirring the paste with a long wooden spatula, and when his right arm started to hurt he shifted the spatula to the left hand and stirred till that one started hurting too. At intervals he scraped the thickening yoghurt from the sides of the degchi.

Bibiji came to the kitchen every now and then to check on the degchis, feeling deeply unsure that Gulla, a village boy, could manage to cook a delicacy like lotus-stem curry. But standing there for the whole process would have been tiring, and that too on Saturday afternoon when she needed to go and see her mother for an hour or so. To compensate for her absence she repeated the directions to Gulla every time she entered the kitchen. 'Ho Gulla! Ho Gulla! Keep stirring the yoghurt or there will be lumps in the curry.' She grimaced in anger.

Gulla looked slack, but his big eyes were alert. Scratching the palms of his hands, he examined his fingernails to avoid awkwardness. After a long pause he nodded his head in agreement.

Gulla was a short, brown, skeleton-like boy, his thin hair parted in the middle and oiled to the extent that even a single extra drop would have dripped down his temples. He must have been about fifteen or sixteen years of age. His stomach was a little bloated, his hands roughened from going constantly between the degchi's warmth and the cold tap. It was easy to discern that he had hardly seen any of the comforts of childhood. His small frame looked all the more minuscule when set against Bibiji's huge body, her tummy sticking out as far as her breasts. Every time Bibiji shouted, her words got inflated and seemed to push away everything around her, including Gulla.

It had been more than six months since the boy had left his hometown of Charar-e-Sharief, a village more than twenty miles away from Srinagar. He had failed the matriculation exam, after which his parents had reluctantly agreed to send him as a domestic to Kashmir's capital city in the hope that Sahibji, Bibiji's husband, would get him a government job if he put in a few years at their residence. Sahibji was an officer in the Civil Secretariat and had hinted that he could put in a word for Gulla and get him the position of gatekeeper or peon in a government office. With such a bright future ahead for their son, Gulla's parents didn't bargain and settled for a very low salary.

The boy's hands were aching again by the time the yoghurt was reduced to half its volume, and he decided it needed no further condensing. Now was the time to mix the two degchis. Gulla checked to see if the pieces of lotus stems were tender. They were soft and yet retained some crunchiness, so he emptied the pot containing the condensed yoghurt into the pot that held the boiled lotus stems and spices.

The tempering was to be done with ghee instead of oil. Into a pan Gulla put four tablespoons of the clarified butter and let this melt over a low heat. With the flame still on low, he sprinkled whole cumin seeds into the hot ghee.

Tak, tak, tak. The sound of high heels. Bibiji entered the kitchen again. The smell of naphthalene mixed with the scent from Bibiji's olive-green pashmina invaded the kitchen, but could not overcome the aroma of cumin seeds slowly roasting in ghee.

Bibiji brought down one of the many small boxes from the spice shelf. She knew exactly which one she wanted, although from where Gulla stood the boxes all looked the same. She opened the lid of the degchi and performed the last ritual of putting a magical dash of powdered mint into the curry. Bibiji returned the lid and made a gesture ordering Gulla to stay where he was. As she moved her hands, her gold bangles dazzled and her long earrings brushed her shoulders. Gulla knew that Bibiji was going to her mother's house and wouldn't be back for two or three hours. He stood near the stove, partly to follow Bibiji's orders and partly to warm himself up.

As soon as Bibiji left, Ammaji made her entry. Ammaji, Bibiji's mother-in-law, was a lady in her mid-seventies who was tall but frail. Age had not taken away the quickness of her mind but her knees ached even while climbing the two steps to the choki.

The huge wooden choki was the dining area where everyone would sit and eat. It was raised a step or two up from the floor and was separated from the cooking and washing area by a wooden scaffold about a foot high. The scaffold had chinar and tulips beautifully engraved into it. During lunch and dinnertime everyone sat around the dastarkhwan to eat on the choki. Apart from those meals, another daily ritual that took place on the choki was Ammaji's namaz. She would unroll her velvet prayer rug on the choki, and near the window facing west offered her prayers five times a day. Some distant relative had brought the rug back from the Hajj in Mecca. The colour of the rug that had faded in one place as a result of friction against her forehead showed it had been in use for a long time.

Ammaji watched Gulla doing the chores. She liked to watch him cook, and gave him an occasional tip from her culinary genius honed over decades. Gulla was untrained and uncouth but he was quick to learn. After the namaz Ammaji kept chanting over the fluorescent prayer beads rolling in her wrinkled hands. Beads that shone like a line of glow worms every time there was a power cut. She would also start to gossip about her daughter-in-law, keeping the beads rolling in her hand. Gulla shared Ammaji's hatred for Bibiji, but restrained himself. If Bibiji got the tiniest whiff of his feelings, his prospects of the promised government job would be ruined. But even a monologue was quite cathartic for Ammaji. She would give vent to all her bitterness while Gulla would act as a silent listener.

Sometimes Gulla identified with her. He had told Farooq once that Ammaji was different from Bibiji, to which Farooq dissented, saying, 'It is just a matter of situation rather than character.' Gulla didn't understand what Farooq meant, but he had his reasons for feeling qualified affection towards Ammaji. One of the reasons was that she sometimes called him by his original name, Noor-ud-Din.

Gulla's mother had once informed him, while applying oil to his hair, that she had named him Noor-ud-Din after a fourteenth-century patron saint of Kashmir, Sheikh Noor-ud-Din Noorani, whose shrine in Charar-e-Sharief was about a mile from their home. The saint, she would tell him, was a complete ascetic, so much so that he only ate the leafy vegetables that had fallen off on their own, and never allowed so much as a blade of grass to be cut for his consumption. Gulla's mother told him how she had paid several visits to the shrine of Sheikh Noor-ud-Din to make a wish for a boy when she was pregnant with him. She had given birth to three girls already and was desperate for a son. It was only with the blessings from the holy shrine that a male child was born to her. She decided to name the child after the saint as a mark of gratitude.

Whenever Gulla's mother had any trouble in life, she would invoke the name of Sheikh Noor-ud-Din. She would pick up a coin and tie it in a knot at the end of her dupatta, and when the wish was fulfilled, she would give the coin as alms to the shrine. Noor-ud-Din was a blessed name, she would say, and he was lucky to share it. It meant something close to 'divine light'.

But Gulla . . . What kind of name was Gulla, after all? What did it mean? Perhaps it meant nothing – that's why all the servants were called by this name. It was strange that in spite of having been to college for a year or two, Bibiji could not spell out his name, of all the names in the world, Gulla would think.

His train of thought was interrupted by the clattering sound of the lid being pushed against the rim of the degchi by the pressure of vapours and bubbles coming from the curry. He rushed to open the lid, which was unbearably hot. Insulating his hand with the loose sleeve of his tweed pheran, he took the lid off. The aroma wafting from the curry filled Gulla's lungs.

Lotus-stem chunks moved up with the bubbles, then drowned themselves in a whirlpool of thick yoghurt gravy. The tempering of ghee had settled like a film of gold over the pearly white curry. Bibiji had said, 'When the curry and ghee separate from each other and form different layers, that's when you should assume the curry is ready.'

Gulla couldn't believe he had been instrumental in creating such gastronomic sublimity. He was no epicure at all and still thought the best meal he had had in months was the dry bread and pickle his mother had bundled up for him when he left home six months earlier. But this fragrance emanating from the degchi was something out of the ordinary. With the big spoon he fished out a piece of lotus stem coated with some yoghurt curry into a small tin bowl. In a sweeping movement he thrust the bowl aside as he heard someone humming a Bollywood song.

It was Bibiji's daughter Zeenat, who had come back from a vacation in Delhi after two months. Holding a mirror in one hand and a comb in another she strolled to the window. Unlike the girls in Gulla's village, she never tied her hair. Farooq and other servants in the mohalla would say she looked like one of those girls on TV but Gulla didn't quite like her. He had managed to put aside some money while she was away, saving about ten rupees a day by not buying her share of bread. With the absent-mindedness of the rich, Sahibji hadn't noticed this unnecessary expense. Zeenat stood near the window while two boys from the neighbourhood ogled at her. She shut the window in their faces and went back to her room.

Gulla picked up the bowl again. With his thumb and index finger he cautiously lifted the piece of lotus stem and put it in his mouth. The velvety white curry was first to touch his palate. The softness and the tangy taste were a delight. Each of the spices had given their essence fully to the curry. Its starchy texture, carrying the spices that complemented each other, was delectable. The lotus stems were cooked properly, yet retained a certain crunchiness.

Gulla thought of Farooq. He wanted to tell him how flavoursome the curry was, but how to express something the equivalent of which one has never experienced? I will say, he thought, 'The rivers of paradise would taste like this, overflowing eternally.'

Gulla was chewing on the lotus stem when suddenly his palate resisted. He felt something hairy sticking to the roof of his mouth. He took the chewed piece from his mouth and threw it into the dustbin. Then, washing his hands, he seized another piece from the degchi. This time he chewed much faster without caring about the taste. Again, something hairy stuck to his mouth.

What could this be? Oh, it might be Zeenat's hair. Who on earth ran around the house with a comb and mirror in hand leaving her hair loose all the time like a witch? 'If any of my sisters or a woman from the village wandered around like this, her legs would be broken. May the grave swallow the girl! May lightning fall upon her!' He muttered as many curses as he knew.

Gulla was totally distraught. His heart sank at the idea of the family assembling at the dastarkhwan for dinner only to find there were hairs in the curry. His limbs began to hurt. He lay down. He buried his hands under his face to warm them up. His knees pressed up against his belly. He lay coiled like a foetus hiding in the womb. He couldn't sleep because of anxiety.

He remembered his first dinner in the family the day he had arrived from his village. It was also the day he was stripped of his name, on the pretext that remembering the names of servants coming and leaving the household was a tough task. Thus, Gulla was to be called by the name of a servant who had worked there before him. That evening Bibiji had served Gulla a plate of rice and some greens, with a piece of chicken wing on top. She had suggested that Gulla could eat on a wooden slab placed near the basin and not with the family on the dastarkhwan. Ammaji had given Bibiji an angry look. A heated argument soon erupted. While Ammaji blamed Bibiji's callousness for scaring away the help, Bibiji argued that as a result of Ammaji's being soft and indulgent with the servants they had become spoilt.

Ammaji had tightened the fist of her right hand and began beating it against her chest.

'Do you not remember how the Apostle of God treated his servant Bilal, a slave? Didn't he get him to climb over the holy Kaaba to recite the azan? We shall all return to the same soil and there will be no differentiation in the colour of our shrouds.'

Sahibji seemed agitated at the mention of the shroud, and Ammaji got the hint that she had gone overboard with her reproaches. She quickly changed her stance.

'Though the Apostle of God warns us Muslims against segregation on the basis of race and class, we are social beings after all and it's not easy to transgress social norms. May Allah forgive us all.'

There was a reverent silence for a minute and the next moment Gulla found himself eating on the wooden slab near the basin. Ammaji would not have bothered whether Gulla ate on the dastarkhwan or hanging upside down from the wall had she not wanted to incriminate her daughter-in-law. This incident had given her some success in pursuing that goal.

Bibiji on the other hand had harboured the hurt of that insult within her, and she would often take it out on Gulla.

'Ho Gulla, ho Gulla, lay out the dastarkhwan. We are late for dinner,' she shouted now.

Gulla quickly picked up the dastarkhwan from a shelf and spread it in the middle of the choki. He then placed plates, glasses and the degchi containing the lotus-stem curry and another containing rice around the dastarkhwan. At home Gulla's mother used one of her old cotton dupattas as a dastarkhwan, but here it was a true dastarkhwan. It was a thick, long cloth, mustard yellow in colour, with red and green flowers painted all over. It was divided into four equal square parts, the divisions marked by Persian couplets venerating Islamic hospitality written in beautiful calligraphy.

One by one the members of the family ascended onto the choki and sat around the dastarkhwan. Bibiji gave a serving of rice to Sahibji and then to Ammaji, Zeenat, herself, and eventually Gulla. Gulla took his plate to the slab near the basin. He scooped up a couple of morsels of rice before his hand in the plate stopped dead. He kept thinking what he would tell his parents if he was sent back. Everyone started eating. With each morsel taken by Sahibji, Gulla's heart began to pound faster against his ribs.

He closed his eyes and remembered the saint Noor-ud-Din, his namesake. 'My dear pir, if everything goes well with the dinner tonight I will come with an offering to your shrine.' He recalled snaffling the bread money while Zeenat had been away, and promised himself he would give all that change as an offering at the shrine.

Gulla was bewildered at the sudden break in his thought process when Bibiji asked him to carry the dirty plates to the sink. Sahibji was appreciating the exquisite taste of the meal. This was a real, traditional lotus-stem curry. Nadroo yakhni was the Kashmiri name for the dish, he told Zeenat. Everyone looked satiated and joyful. Bibiji took pride in her cooking, while Ammaji seemed a little irked.

Gulla couldn't believe everyone had finished dinner and no one had found a single hair in the food. He drew a long breath and thanked the saint for being his saviour.

That night, even the harshness of cold weather and the roughness of the mattress didn't bother him. What did bother him slightly was the thought of giving up his money. He wondered if rupees accumulated by stealing would be good enough to be given as alms. He would ask Farooq in the morning, he thought.

In the early hours Gulla went to buy milk and bread from the bazaar. As usual, he met Farooq and narrated to him the miracle that had happened by the blessings of the saint the previous evening.

Upon hearing the entire story Farooq burst into fits of laughter. 'You are such a duffer, Gulla. Lotus stems do have a hair-like thing going on, and these city people love them for that. When you eat the curry many times, you too will develop a taste for it.'

Gulla was astonished. 'But where does the hair in the vegetable come from?' he asked.

Farooq explained. Legend had it that a saint–poet of Kashmir was once spinning fine wool on her charkha when her yarn got tangled up. Afraid that her in-laws would find out, she threw the entangled yarn into the waters of the lake and prayed that it should turn into something delightful to the taste buds as well as to sight. As a result of her prayer, out of the knotted yarn grew lotus flowers with edible stems. The residue of the yarn remains, however, and gives the dish its slightly hairy texture.

'Do you believe this?' Gulla asked Farooq.

'No,' Farooq replied, and both laughed in unison. They decided against giving the money in alms now that there was never a hair in the curry in the first place and no intervention had been necessary from the saint. The two boys went back to their respective houses.

Ammaji unfolded her velvet prayer rug up on the choki. Down by the basin Gulla washed the dirty dishes from the previous night's dinner.

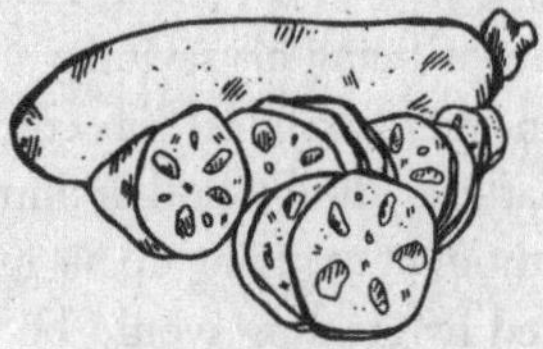

Yakhni or Yoghurt Curry

Kashmiris mostly enjoy non-vegetarian food and eat a lot of lamb. There are, however, usually two versions of each delicacy: a vegetarian version and a non-vegetarian one. The yakhni made in the story, for instance, can be vegetarian as well as non-vegetarian, while the actual curry remains the same. In Kashmiri cooking, the heat is derived mostly from red chillies and other spices, most often used whole. Yakhni is the mildest since it has no chillies at all, so people from outside Kashmir tend to appreciate this dish.

2 kg natural yoghurt
1 kg lamb (for a vegetarian version, use generous quantities of bottle gourd or lotus stem)

6–7 whole green cardamoms
3 whole black cardamoms
1-inch piece of ginger
3–4 garlic cloves (whole)
5 tsps ghee to fry
1 tsp cumin seeds
2 tsp powdered mint
6 cups water
Salt to taste

Method

1. First of all, put a thick-bottomed deep and wide pan on the stove and fill it with about 6 cups of water. Add all the whole spices, garlic, ginger and salt to the pan. Make sure the water covers the meat, and bring to boil.
2. Then cover and simmer till the meat is tender – this takes about 1½ hours. You can always strain off some of the water, retaining the whole spices, if after the allotted time there is still a lot of liquid.
3. While the meat is cooking, pour the yoghurt into another thick-bottomed pan and give it a good whisk. Put this pan on a medium flame and stir without stopping. Keep stirring till all the yoghurt begins to condense. You may then turn the heat down and only stir every now and then.
4. Cook the yoghurt down till most of the water evaporates and you're left with a thick, very pale yoghurt mix.
5. Take a pan and add about 5 tablespoons of ghee and heat it over a low flame. Add cumin seeds and roast them slightly.
6. At this stage you need to decant the roasted cumin and ghee into the main yoghurt pan and give the mixture a thorough stir. Bring everything to the boil, cover, and simmer for another half an hour or so till the meat is all creamy and yoghurty.
7. At the end, sprinkle some dried ground mint all over the dish before you serve it with rice.

8. For a vegetarian option all you need to do is to replace lamb with bottle gourd (peeled, then cut into large pieces) or lotus stem. The procedure remains the same, with the only difference being that the vegetables need less time to become tender and soft.

The Origin of Sweetness

Uzma Aslam Khan

After her father jumped from the twelfth-floor balcony of their apartment, Zulekha began to travel. At first her movements were limited to Karachi, though further north of the city than she had ever been before. She disembarked to a distinct scent, which she followed to a glass platter covered with a glass top. Beneath it lay a square of barfi. It was fairly good, but not good enough to make her stay.

Whenever she returned, her father was lying face down in the grass.

He had run a popular mithai shop in Karachi. Every day, after school, Zulekha had helped him to cut sweets into diamond shapes, decorating each one with filigree foil, arranging these in tin boxes on a shelf strewn with fresh rose petals. While her father's talent was keeping the shop crowded – he greeted every customer by name, always with generous samples, making children and adults alike feel exclusive – Zulekha's greatest contribution was her taste buds, particularly when it came to barfi. Barfi Buds, her father had called them. Before she reached the age of ten, Zulekha had learned about those microscopic hairs on her tongue, *mye-kro-vill-eye*, that sent messages to her brain about whether something was sour, bitter, salty or delicious, and whether it would sell. She was never wrong. When he introduced coconut barfi, she took one small bite and, smiling, packed a box for school the next day. By the end of the week, it was among the most beloved sweets in the shop, second only to khoya barfi (her father's favourite) and almond barfi (hers). Egg barfi, on the other hand, she quietly dismissed after one reluctant sniff, and he had thrown away the entire batch.

Her travels began to take her further. Everywhere she went, she would be offered food or drink, and when she returned, she would be starving. Her father would still be lying face down in the grass. Her mother would be screaming. The sun would be directly above them.

She began to remember things he had taught her. For instance, odour could only be detected by a human nose when airborne. How, then, had she smelled barfi under a glass lid in north Karachi, those first few times? There were no answers, and when it began to seem that her questions belonged elsewhere, she traversed time.

She arrived in a village run by Tatars, several hundred years in the past. They were attempting to make an essential ingredient of what would one day (unknown to them) become barfi: condensed milk. There were several lactating cows nearby, lowing, as friends and relatives greeted each other with laughter and the familiar Assalam-o-alaykum. A few folks were going off somewhere – to a wedding, she decided – and wanted to carry the milk, while keeping it fresh. But they were adding water to milk, instead of removing it. They also did not seem to know about sugar helping to preserve milk. When she tried to tell them, a woman hugged her and offered a sour yoghurt with something red floating inside – her least preferred vegetable, beetroot!

So she returned hungry, her father was lying face down in the grass, her mother was angry. If Zulekha could turn back the clock not by hundreds of years, but by a single hour – or a single *half* hour – she could run to the man in a black woollen Jinnah cap and white pajama who was taking off his slippers and stepping onto the balcony at 12:38 p.m., as though to offer the midday Zuhr prayer. She could hold time. She could hold him.

Time would not allow itself to be held. But the next landing it gifted her was deliciously soft – so soft it made her sigh. She was seated beside a miniaturist whose attention was turned away from her, towards a book that he was illustrating. When she lifted the book's leather cover – very slightly, so as not to upset him – she saw that it was the *Baburnama*. Letting the cover drift back down, she stared at the beautiful page. He was painting an almond harvest. His brushwork was as delicate as her taste buds, with both of them sharing a need for lavishness – he with watercolours and gold leaf, she with milk and silver leaf. As her face fell close to the page, instead of the man in a white pajama kneeling at the centre of the work, it was Zulekha herself, holding open a sack into which a man in a red tunic was pouring fistfuls of almonds – unshelled, the way her father had always bought them. She had helped him blanch the nuts, soaking them in water then flaking off each hull, her fingers peeling as the peeled almonds grew smooth. He had fed her the seven smoothest nuts, to keep her memory sharp. Then they combined the almonds into barfi dough. As the mixture cooked on a low flame, the kitchen held the scent of heaven. Her memory was sharp enough to remember, as she knelt in the centre of the painting. Around her, merchants from distant lands began to arrive, to fill their camels' saddlebags with the crop. Her sack was almost full – the miniaturist had one more almond to affix with a corner of gold leaf and glue. Then she again took her seat beside him. Placing his paintbrush flat on a stone tablet, the artist finally noticed her. 'Are you thirsty?' he asked. She was. He poured a red liquid from a silver jug into two cups and held one out to her. The taste was intensely bitter. He was smiling; the drink was pleasurable to him. He said that one day she would recall this opportunity to reside solely in the realm of sensation. One day, she would be offered the cup again. As she left him, she wondered if she would again refuse it.

Her mouth was dry as her father lay face down in the grass and Zulekha's uncles and aunts whispered in her mother's ear under the blaring sun. They were saying that what her father had done was forbidden. A life could not be taken into one's own hands. It belonged to God. It was the law. There were policemen outside the apartment complex who would harass the family if not paid. Where would the money come from? Including to look after Zulekha? Moreover, where would he be buried? Which imam would pray for him? They used terrible words. Sin. Crime. Burden. These words left her mother, who clutched Zulekha tightly, with a metallic taste at the back of her throat.

Wherever Zulekha travelled, she would either encounter the ingredients for her father's beloved barfi, or an attempt at making them. So she was unsurprised when her nose led her to the queen of all spices: cardamom. She was not, however, expecting to carry large bundles of the spice all the way to Egypt, let alone to a funeral. After the bundles were taken from her, she was brought to a tent of purification, where several men began washing a man's body with a liquid infused with her gift. There was something so peaceful and precise about their movements that she began to grow sleepy. However, when a man in a red robe made a quick cut to the body's side, she woke up. He removed the internal organs, then rinsed them in the juice of cardamom. The only organ not removed was the heart – on her instructions. She was present so they would know the heart as the centre of thought and feeling. If there was an afterlife, about which even she, as their elder, was uncertain, the dead man was going to need his heart. The brain he would not need. There was no intelligence there. They could take it away through his nose with a long hook. When they were done, they covered all the mined organs with salt. Then they stuffed the man with the remaining salt and buried him. For forty days, she prayed for his heart. On the forty-first day, his body was exhumed and washed. The dried organs were returned to his body. His skin was rubbed with oils infused with cardamom and rose. Though her nose carried the perfume, the flavour on her tongue was of salt. She had touched the body before it was oiled, and licked her fingers.

Despite what she ate or drank, it only tasted sour, bitter or salty, as her father lay face down in the grass, and a man that everyone blamed for his death stood over him. He was an old family friend who had pressured her father into becoming a business partner. Zulekha remembered that before any of this happened – before her father had stepped onto the balcony, as if to pray, before she began to travel, before she inhabited a woman's body instead of a child's – her mother told her that this man had run away with a lot of money. She told her that her father feared the shop would have to close, but did not want Zulekha to know. He wanted her to always love his sweets. Now this former family friend was here, claiming *he* was owed money, accompanied by two policemen, claiming *her father* had sinned – and her mother was screaming in a brassy voice at Zulekha for never staying close enough. More people arrived. They did not notice Zulekha run her fingers through the red streaks in the hair of the man in the grass, as she tried to turn over his face.

'I will restore your taste,' he was telling her, taking her hand. He was a child. She, the adult. They knew each other already. They were in Lahore, a city she did not know, and he pointed out places that mattered to him. Near the district courts, Government College, and Data Darbar, was his school. The walk from the school to his house inside Bhatti Gate was four miles, and he loved it because the narrow lanes of Bhatti Gate had the best sweet shop. It was towards this that he now led her. They passed a mosque with steps leading to the main praying area. The second floor was where boys, including her father, learned the Quran. Further up, a muezzin called the faithful to prayer, but loudspeakers had not yet arrived, so his call was gentle. Outside the mosque was an enormous banyan tree, with fruit bats roosting in its branches, and a fakir resting beneath them. The fakir had no tongue. No one had told Zulekha this, but she knew it, as she turned to face him. His tonsils, roof of the mouth, and the airshaft leading to his nose all allowed him to recognize and relish flavour, though anything even mildly sour or bitter caused him pain. The fakir gestured to her father, indicating that he should head to the tap to do his ablutions for prayer. But he himself kept sitting under the tree. 'I will bring you some halwa,' said her father, and the fakir laughed.

At the entrance of the mosque, Zulekha noticed a big wall clock. Beneath it, on a copper plaque, was engraved a verse:

Ghafil tujhe gharyal ye deta hai manadi
Gardun ne ghari umr ki ik aur ghata di

The moment that has passed by reminds you
Of your life being reduced by the moment that has passed by

'Hurry up!' said her father, pulling Zulekha away from the clock. As she left the fakir under the banyan tree she saw a fruit bat fanning a baby with its wings. When she closed her eyes, Zulekha was dipping her long nose into fruits and flowers and drinking nectar.

They arrived at the shop. She had expected to find mithai, and there was no shortage of this. When her father stuffed his hands in the pockets of his school pants and grinned, saying, 'One day, I want my own shop, in Karachi not Lahore, just like this, but better,' she was also not surprised. Together, they sampled it all – from rice pudding to carrot halwa to barfi made with gram flour and coconut. With each bite, Zulekha could understand how he had learned to taste, and how she had learned from him. When he inhaled, and powerful images began to appear in his brain, they also appeared in hers. At times, she was walking by the sea. Other times, her fingers brushed the velvet of a cat's paw. There was a smell that reminded her of the first time she cut her knee, and another, of the last time she heard thunder. Zulekha was not new to the pool of emotion that aromas could arouse. What surprised her, though, was that none of this had brought her father here.

The real reason he wanted a sweet shop was because it would draw people towards him, the way it now drew people towards the shop owner. The man was at the back, in the kitchen, calling out to everyone who came inside. It was a hot day, so he brought out a large silver jug of lassi with a generous dollop of clotted cream on top. He greeted everyone by name, including Zulekha and her father, as he offered them a cup, ducking back into the kitchen for fresh samples of his sweets. 'Only for you,' he said, and though he said it to everyone, they all believed him. The lassi Zulekha drank was the perfect blend of spice and creaminess. It smelled like a frangipani flower on her favourite pillow. Smell was a private mystery. Taste was better when shared: then it became ceremonial. She understood this now, as the shop filled. Her father would come to love her Barfi Buds for keeping his own mithai shop crowded.

She looked up from his body lying face down in the grass. A rabbit was chewing a carrot. Its mouth held several thousand more taste buds than Zulekha's mouth. When her mother clasped her a little less tightly, Zulekha crept out of the gate of the apartment complex and turned the corner, to their empty shop. It was hard to say how long ago she was last here. She could hear flies, and the smell that hit her was both pungent and stale. In the kitchen at the back of the shop, where her father had made the sweets, was a large clock with an engraved plaque beneath it. She recognized the verse. *The moment that has passed by reminds you of your life being reduced* . . . Beside the clock was a mirror that he had placed for her height. Now she was tall and wide-bosomed and when she ducked, she could not recognize her own face.

Those were strange lines around her mouth, inside of which many *mye-kro-vill-eye* once resided, the ones meant to rejuvenate after every two weeks. She stuck out her tongue. She pulled it back into her mouth. She stuck it out again. Her mouth drooped. Her jaw had set like a trap, into which a terrible hardness had lodged. She stuck that tongue out again and this time she was standing before her favourite photograph of her parents. They were sitting on the steps leading up to the apartment elevator. Her father was wearing a grey shirt: a bush shirt, he called it, which was funny because he was the last person to venture into a bush. Her mother was looking beautiful in a kameez with large yellow flowers. What Zulekha wanted was for her mother to always look like that. She wanted herself to always look like that too. Instead, she feared that they were both beginning to carry something heavier than a permanent head cold, with that metallic taste colonizing the back of their throats. It hadn't fully happened, yet; Zulekha, at least, was at a decision point. She wanted to keep the love, to affix it with gold leaf and glue till it stuck in the deepest crevasses of her memory – and her mother's. She wanted a ceremony.

To begin, she cleaned the kitchen. Dessert could not be crafted in an environment that was soiled, so she took her time. Next, she soaked some almonds, then put ghee and condensed milk in a large pot on a very low fire. Slowly, she added milk powder. The condensed milk was sweetened; no extra sugar was needed. She wished the Tatar woman had believed her. She had been Zulekha's first host outside Karachi, back when Zulekha travelled, and had been kind even when feeding her sour yoghurt and beetroot. Zulekha's movements were relaxed and she fell into a natural rhythm, almost a dance, as she stirred continuously in the kitchen. Other places she had been to swirled before her, in details previously overlooked. For instance, she had not only been fed peculiar yoghurt. The Tatar woman had also offered soft, warm buns filled with tiny black seeds that caught between Zulekha's teeth and filled her ears with a sound that made chewing delightful. Wanting to recreate that crunch, Zulekha looked in the pantry for seeds. She could not find the same ones, but there were sesame seeds, so she sprinkled these into the mixture and kept stirring. The milk had to thicken without sticking to the pan. But too much stirring and the milk would become lumpy. The beauty of barfi was its texture – firm yet soft, slightly grainy, like crystallized honey, and smooth. If overcooked then it became toffee, which Zulekha did not like. If undercooked, it would be dry, and the ghee would separate. Ghee should never linger on the tongue. Barfi had to feel light in the mouth, even if it wasn't.

The colour was also key. It had to be a very particular tone of gold. Who had told her this? As she watched the mixture in the pan coalesce to the right consistency, the miniaturist returned to her. He was illuminating the same page. Smiling, he said, 'You took the cup.' With his free hand, he touched her lips, softly. Curious, she put her face close to his. She had always known how to taste with her tongue, but her lips? They could taste too! They could taste his touch! Then she leaned over the page. Why had she hurried off earlier, unable to receive all this beauty before? Above the figure filling his sack with almonds blazed a sun of so many delicately painted concentric rings that Zulekha's vision began to blur. It was easier to look to the side, at the sun's margins, where mythical birds in gold leaf were taking flight. The largest was the simurgh, the messenger between earth and sky, her ephemeral tail feathers wrapping around the sun. Nearby was the divine tree, which carried the seeds of every plant, each one yielding a cure for every ailment, including grief. But at a price, for when grief became a trusted companion, leaving it behind was a risk. Most people returned to it. The tree was where the simurgh came to roost after every revolution of the sun. Now, as the next revolution was closing, the simurgh asked what Zulekha wanted – to leave, or to return? Could Zulekha not see that the time was no longer 12:38 p.m., and the sun had shifted in the sky? Did she not know that the midday prayer had come and gone for today? When Zulekha gazed again at the simurgh, the overwhelming impression was of a single unifying colour: the gold of four o'clock sun. When she looked back down at the pan in the kitchen, the colour was there.

She added a quarter teaspoon of cardamom powder, stirred the mixture one last time, and placed it on a greased plate to set. While she waited, she inhaled. It had been a long, long time since the kitchen held this fragrance, yet something was missing. She peeled the soaked almonds, chopped them, sprinkled them on top. She breathed again, now with her tonsils, the roof of her mouth, the airshaft leading to her nose. It was what the fakir had taught her, from under the banyan tree with the fruit bats, outside the mosque. But the smell now infusing the kitchen would not have met the standards of the finicky fakir. Had she learned nothing? The shop's front, where the rose petals had turned putrid around the display boxes, was spoiling all she had accomplished back here in the kitchen. Even worse were the mouldering sweets in the glass case at the entrance to the shop, where the flies were thickest. The shop's front would have to be mopped and scrubbed. It could be done in the time needed for the barfi to set.

As she worked, Zulekha fell once again into a natural rhythm. There were so many places she had seen, so many wonderful people and creatures she had met. Even more amazing was all that she would still do. She wanted her mother to share the amazement. Before Zulekha could set off again, she needed to leave behind a delicious bite for her mother, one with the right texture, sound, colour, and smell, not only as she had been taught by her father, but also the Tatar woman, miniaturist, and fakir. Her mother would take this one bite and know her daughter had grown. She would take this one bite and her life would be elastic again. She would take this one bite and know sweetness again.

When the shop's floor was sparkling, Zulekha went to a nearby stall to buy fresh roses. On her way, she could not rid herself of the thought that by throwing away the last items made by her father's hands, she had mined his organs. But those embalmers in Egypt, they had known about touch. They had known not only how to preserve a body, but how to keep it elastic. When they massaged fragrant oils into the skin of the departed, they performed rituals of love and farewell that were not endings, but beginnings. And so, returning to the shop, she scattered red petals not only on the shelves, but all across the floor. She rubbed the juice of the petals into her hands and brushed her hands over the walls, and all along the empty glass case.

In the kitchen, the barfi had set beautifully into a block. She broke off one corner and rolled it around her tongue, breathing the way she knew how, tasting also with her lips. She decorated the block with silver leaf, then carefully cut out a circle. She placed the circle on a glass platter and covered it with a glass top.

She left her offering on top of the glass case at the entrance to the shop, scattering petals all around the platter. Though she had removed everything old in the shop, her mother would know: she had left the heart.

After Zulekha closed the door to the shop, she passed the apartment complex, but did not look at the grass, the policemen, or the many people there. She looked up at the sky, and the time was right.

Zulekha's Barfi

¼ cup ghee
½–¾ cup sweetened condensed milk
2 cups (full cream) milk powder (more or less; you can use coconut milk powder if you want coconut barfi)
¼ tsp cardamom powder
100g (more or less, according to taste) almonds, soaked, peeled and chopped (or slivered)
100g sesame or poppy seeds (again you can use more or less, according to taste)
Small handful culinary-grade rose petals

Method

1. Put the ghee and condensed milk into a large frying pan and heat on a very low flame.
2. Slowly add the milk powder, stirring continuously.
3. Keep stirring on a very low flame till the milk thickens, making sure it doesn't turn lumpy.

4. Stir in the cardamom powder and seeds. (The seeds can alternatively be added at the end instead.)
5. The mixture should start to become a smooth, fudge-like barfi dough that separates from the pan, usually after 10–15 minutes. Do not overcook the dough or it will become sticky and chewy like toffee. The colour should be a soft golden hue, like four o'clock sun.
6. Remove the dough from the stove and place it on a greased plate or baking sheet to set.
7. Top with the chopped almonds (and/or seeds, if not added earlier).
8. Leave to set for at least 2 hours.
9. Once the barfi has set into a block, cut out pieces according to your desired shape. Arrange the shapes on a platter and scatter rose petals on and around them.

The Night of Forgiveness

Farah Yameen

The summer I turned ten, Bunnu Phua started hearing voices. At first, they were only the howls of the hot loo wind, filtering through the vetiver curtains, dancing with the motes of dust in the burnished slivers of sunlight. Later, they were indistinct exchanges in the backyard, punctuated by the dull thuds of the wood-apple tree's heavy fruit and the rustling leaves of the stunted guava. Occasionally, the voices were of the squirrels picking apart the fraying nylon rope holding up the swing on the mulberry tree, strung up who knows how many years ago. Later still, they came from the mesh cabinet where my mother kept the day's food, its doors opening and closing to the sound of footsteps moving in various degrees of haste.

As summer eased into sticky mugginess, the loo stopped howling, the wood-apple stopped fruiting, the squirrels conquered the swing, and the food, now unsafe in the cabinet, was moved to the refrigerator. The sprawling old bungalow, Aqil Kothi, lost a few more bricks; its whitewash, now faded to a mottled blue, peeled a little more off the thick walls. Unused swaths of the house stood gaping and empty in anticipation of a human presence. Its indistinct murmurs took form and became words, entreaties and demands from Phua's grandmother, known to all of us as Dadda.

It was Dadda who had given Phua the name Bunnu. Phua had a proper first and last name, like I did at school. But at home

I was Guddi and she was Bunnu, to everyone except me. She was my father's sister, so I was taught to call her 'Phua'. Like Phua's name, most things in Aqil Kothi were as Dadda had left them when she died ten years ago. The house was swept and mopped by nine every morning, because Dadda had so ordained. Three summers had passed since the henna tree she had planted had its last flush of leaves, yet Phua watered it every morning. The swallows' nests lodged between the wooden beams of our ceilings were never cleared out, because Dadda had deemed it a sin to evict an animal from its home. This kindness, however, did not extend to the mongooses that infested the courtyards and gardens of the house. The cats were never touched because, Dadda said, one could not be certain if they were an animal or a djinn in animal guise, and one must never offend a djinn.

Although there were two grinding stones in the old kitchen, we still used the one that Dadda preferred. Saturday lunch was always khichri, its gloopy, monochromatic yellowness offset by the assorted colours of the accompanying potato mash, tomato chutney, crisp fried onions and preserved lemons. Sundays were dedicated to pilau, speckled bright orange, and qorma.

This was, I think, on account of Phua. Her mother, my paternal grandmother, rarely spoke of her mother-in-law. Ammi, my mother, had known Dadda only in the last year of her life. So, when Dadda spoke again, so many years after dying, it was unsurprising that it was Phua she chose to talk to. And five days before Shab-e-Barat, the night of forgiveness, when souls are free to walk the earth, Phua declared to the household that she intended to cook for her grandmother.

By this time, Dadda and she had been speaking for several months. Summer was now a memory of mangoes and sherbet. My father had returned to Saudi Arabia after his yearly visit home. A thick fog and blanket-induced lethargy had settled into our mornings. Shab-e-Barat would be a long December night spent praying for the departed, shivering beside our room heaters. The only thing to look forward to was the halwa, especially if Phua made it. She would put an extra layer of silver leaf over it just for me.

There were two kitchens in the house. Ammi's kitchen was inside the house, set up once wood-fire cooking had been abandoned for the convenience of gas stoves. She had spent every day of her eleven-year marriage in this kitchen, trying to be worthy of her parents' honour, her husband's affection and her mother-in-law's approval. Once every month, a scarlet cylinder of gas would be rolled into the kitchen, its metal contours clanging against the red oxide floors.

The old kitchen jutted out from the original anatomy of the house, its walls ancient and soot-black from decades of warming fires. The stoves here were used only for festivals, at which time gigantic pots and woks would simmer over the wood fire for hours. A strong smell of mould from decades of discarded cookware hung thick in the air. Every female servant of the household had lived in this large room. Now it housed only Ajmeri and those who came to visit her. Ajmeri had been born in this kitchen into the service of the household, just like her mother before her. When her children had left to find jobs, she had stayed: who would look after her Bunnu otherwise?

It was to this room that Bunnu Phua retreated. Framed through the last of the five arches of the kitchen's facade, I could see her squatting down each morning, shifting old newspapers over glowing coals and fanning the fire until the papers caught light. Sometimes she'd stop mid-motion, as if to speak to someone.

Ammi, in whose family the dead always held their peace, hesitantly suggested a doctor. My grandmother was nonplussed.

'Bunnu *is* a doctor.'

'I mean a doctor of the mind.'

My grandmother smiled at Ammi's simplicity. My mother, with her university degree, had learned that the world existed in binaries of sanity and madness, and was caught between her faith, which believed in both sorcery and creatures that morphed into cats, and modern rationality, to which these were but collective hallucinations.

'My daughter is not mad.'

'No! But a doctor –'

'After your father-in-law passed, Dadda turned all her attention to herself,' my grandmother reminded Ammi. 'The leg piece in the kebab, the marrow in the curry, the warmest rotis fresh off the griddle: all these were now first served to her. There is no virtue in eating last, or dining on cold leftovers, when there are no men to offer the best portions to. She ate with abandon. Bunnu inherited her fondness for food, and perhaps this delayed self-indulgence too.'

'You think these voices are self-indulgence?'

'I don't know what they are. I don't know if it is her Dadda or another entity speaking to her. But she is not mad, that much I know.'

It would be indecorous and unbecoming for Ammi to argue more. Had it been her own mother, she might have continued.

Nonetheless, my grandmother's prayers grew longer each day. Besides the mandatory five sets of namaz, she started including voluntary ones too. After the namaz at dawn, she'd read the Surah Djinn from her Quran three times, until dawn's reddish glow suffused the navy-blue sky. She'd then tiptoe to Phua's room, whistle-pucker her lips and blow over her daughter's face. Those before her had used this chapter of the Quran effectively against djinns masquerading as ghosts. My grandmother was determined to expunge these beings from her daughter's life.

Late in the night, she'd wake again, the sound of the dripping tap in the bathroom of the courtyard her only companion. Beginning at three at night, she would rock back and forth, kneeling on her prayer mat, her lips moving incessantly, the sound of her tongue wet against her palate, as she recited her prayers from memory. Despite the prayers, and the alms distributed with uncharacteristic generosity, the family could not be dispelled of these voices. Phua was still in the old kitchen five days before Shab-e-Barat.

On the first day after my grandmother announced this failure, Phua made kebabs. She squatted on the floor, the arched knife clamped between her toes as she cut the meat into long ribbons, discarding the tough tissue. These offcuts I picked up and threw out, delighting over the squabbling of the crows as they fought for each piece. In my family, kebabs were a treat for special occasions. Ammi usually took the trouble only for important guests, like my father, or the ones who came calling on Eid every year. Now Dadda would be visiting after ten years.

'Don't they have kebabs in heaven?'

'There are no fires in heaven. How can there possibly be kebabs?'

This was a compelling argument. Quelled, I squatted down beside Phua to massage the yoghurt and garam masala into the meat. I stole a piece of meat to chew on and continued to watch Phua. She held out her palm with a dot of masala for me to taste for its seasoning. I swelled with pride and importance.

The person most inconvenienced by this turn of events was Ajmeri, whose role in our family alternated between abject servitude and inveterate bullying. The old kitchen was her room, and this unprovoked invasion of her space had set her on edge. She began by coaxing Phua out of the kitchen.

'Bunnu, my Bunnu, why are you blackening your hands in the coal? Look at your hair. No woman of the family has ever lit the fire on her own. What would Dadda say? Go rest, love. Tell me what you want, I'll make it.'

Phua only shook her head and said, 'No. I'll manage. I don't need rest. Could you clear out the old mesh cupboard?'

'What do you need that for?'

'I'll put Dadda's dinner there,' she said, skewering a perfect spiral of meat and laying it across the stove. The fat dripped onto the coal and sizzled.

Deflated but unbeaten, Ajmeri moved her petition to my mother's court.

Ammi had been relieved at first when Phua relinquished her stethoscope to stay at home. Never are we more aware of our inadequacies than when surrounded by those living fragments of our imagined lives.

My mother was one of those people you don't read about. She was pretty and virtuous in the eyes of the mothers of eligible sons, whose opinions on these subjects mattered. She had been raised at a time when higher education for women was viewed with much the same distrust as high fashion – it was expensive, immodest and dangerous. Ammi had raised no banners of revolt as Phua had. She had equipped herself all her life to be the perfect wife, mother and housekeeper, a woman of exquisite taste and refinement. She had prepared herself for contentment. She had not prepared herself to be sister-in-law to a woman who surpassed her in everything.

If Ammi had beautiful eyes and glowing skin, Phua had both, and curves bearing the promise of fertility and lustrous hair in addition. My mother paled next to her sister-in-law at family dinners, conscious of older women looking admiringly at Phua. Her pilau never had rice stuck to the bottom of the pot, as Ammi's sometimes did. In her parents' family, she was the second woman to have a master's degree. But her degree had hung in its frame in her bedroom, yellowing and unused, and Ammi shrank as Phua became a practising doctor.

Bunnu Phua was the pride and the shame of the family. She was the first woman in my father's family not merely to study but also to have a profession. I had heard often enough that my grandfather did not see any reason for her to continue beyond middle school. My grandmother did not oppose her husband. But Phua locked herself in a room and threatened to poison herself. This high drama ended, according to my father, when five of his cousins, who stayed with the family, took refuge in my grandfather's room since Phua had laid siege to theirs. Within three days, my grandfather's betel stash was reduced to four leaves and no lime. Someone had helped themselves to his secret bottle of rancid olive oil, which had been ageing for several years, as well as to his precious Ajwa dates. My grandfather gave in to his daughter's desire for an education, much to the consternation of the nephews who had been well pleased with my grandfather's room and the luxuries it afforded.

On the summer nights when Dadi recounted this story to Ammi as they lay on adjacent folding beds under the stars in the courtyard, she would bemoan her daughter's fall from grace. She had been a docile child, except for that one time when she fought my father for the leg piece. My father had a scar over his eyebrow where Phua had hit him with a ladle. I pretended to sleep. Ammi looked past her mosquito net at the stars and said nothing.

For the women who, like Phua, had emotionally blackmailed and defied their families into working, medicine was the only acceptable profession. Back in the 1960s a distant uncle of my father had married an air hostess, and he is still known as the uncle who married the air hostess.

Bunnu Phua went through the rigours of medicine at the local government medical college. There were some whispers that Grandfather had made a 'donation' to get her in. Ammi thought this idea was laughable. My grandfather had no desire to condone Phua's ill-mannered stubbornness. Those were his words. In Ammi's opinion, everyone was disappointed at the absence of divine comeuppance that was supposed to visit insolent women like Phua.

Nobody said much about the rest of Phua's short-lived career. She had been a gynaecologist. I also gathered from scattered conversations among adults that she had travelled too much for 'medical camps'. My grandfather, Ammi said, had often complained of her smell. He'd say she smelled like Manju, who cleaned their toilets. In truth, she smelled nothing like Manju. Manju smelled of exhaustion, detergent and unwashed clothes that she couldn't change out of until her only other outfit dried. Bunnu Phua smelled of shit, nausea and the amniotic fluid she had stepped into on the hospital's floor. She'd laugh when I'd squeeze my nose on those rare days that she returned home when it was still daylight.

Phua's peers got used to the blood and the fluids, discarding umbilical cords into gigantic buckets, diving their hands into shit in the midst of synchronous wails from parallel beds in dimly lit wards where the occasional dog from the street would check in. They learned the art of holding themselves straight as families crumpled when death visited the delivery beds.

'Your Phua,' Ammi recalled, 'began to avoid food on the days she delivered a baby. She walked about in a grey pallor, the circles under her eyes bruised blue. She used to have waist-length hair. She chopped it to shoulder length.'

I gasped. 'What did Grandmother say?'

'She got her married before things got out of hand.'

'And what did Phua say?'

'Phua chose her battles.'

It is a matter of pride to be mother to a virtuous daughter of no uncommon beauty. It is but a short step from there to the scandal of having an unwed daughter of marriageable age, and one with a career, no less. My grandmother, already reeling under the weight of this ignominy, saw Phua's disregard for the sanctity of her hair as the last straw. A Gulf-resident man was nominated in short order, much to the joy of Ammi, who had long harboured a secret hope that Phua would decide to move, and tend to a new home once she got married. But while Phua married the groom chosen for her without protest, she insisted on living with her own family. She visited his family in the summers when my uncle returned to his parents' home on vacation, also deigning to spend a few days at our house. Ammi, I felt, both admired and resented Phua for this defiance.

Ajmeri had minced no words in informing my grandmother that this would bring bad luck, and it seemed that her prophecy had finally come to pass. Ajmeri certainly thought so, as she declared from the new grinding stone. Phua had taken over the old one.

'I shouted myself hoarse. First this job. What need does she have of a job? I have delivered fifteen babies and *I* didn't need a job! Why, I delivered her, and she came out just fine. Then she refuses to go to her in-laws. I have seen this before. She says it is Dadda speaking to her. There *is* no Dadda, may Allah grant her heaven. *They* have come for her, just as they came for the milkman Shamim's daughter who would go to the hand pump without her dupatta on her head.'

Ajmeri broke down. Nobody knew who Shamim was or what happened to his dupatta-less daughter.

'Why is Ajmeri crying, Ammi?'

'Sometimes when there is so much love in your heart and you don't know how to show it, you cry.'

'Like how Phua loves me?'

My mother took a deep pause before saying, 'Yes, something like that.'

Love operated in strange ways in our family. My mother forced milk upon me twice a day because she loved me. Between her and my grandmother, they packed a bag full of leaky pickles, greasy snacks and a box of mangoes for my father every time he returned to Saudi. I suspect that nothing but the mangoes ever made it to the plane. Guests who were loved were always served three times their carrying capacity in dinner. Waist-ties were discreetly loosened under kurtas after these events. We ate more than our weight in love. But my mother's love for Phua was strangest of all.

Phua would return from work late at night, sometimes at eleven, sometimes three, sometimes not at all. Ammi would hear the turn of the key, the gentle opening and closing of the door to avoid waking my grandmother, the footsteps entering the room adjacent to hers, the clink of keys being hung on the hook next to the switch in Phua's room, the shutting of each of its four doors until the footsteps disappeared into the bathroom. Then the steps would re-emerge, moving into the kitchen, and a new set of sounds would replace the old: the chink of steel on steel, the opening and closing of the refrigerator, the lifting of lids. Ammi could tell that Phua had not bothered to reheat her food, but she never rose to heat it for her as she would have done for my father.

What Phua would find each night in the refrigerator was contingent upon the amount of love Ammi was feeling on that particular day. On the mornings that Phua had thrown her doctor's apron into the laundry for Ammi to wash, there would be a spoonful of the afternoon's vegetables, some rice and dal in the refrigerator, pushed behind bowls of yoghurt and wood-apple soaking for sherbet.

The first time Phua left home in trousers and a shirt instead of her usual salwar kameez, Ajmeri refused to cook and my grandmother sat all night before her uneaten plate of khichri. My mother went to bed in her salwar kameez, the outfit that she wore whether at home or at a party, night and day, come summer or winter; in cotton and silk, with three-quarter sleeves or full necks cut into the shapes of betel leaf or boats, every variation fading into a uniform banality. In the fridge, an uncovered bowl of khichri awaited Phua. Its surface cracked and turned a parched ochre. There was no mash or chutney.

One does not serve khichri without chutney and mash to someone who is loved.

The night after, my aunt returned as late as three. My mother roused herself to drop fresh dumplings in dal for dal pithi. Dal pithi was a rare event in our home. It was never served to guests. It was one of those intimate things that was elaborate and painstakingly made, but not considered glamorous enough for visitors.

One does not cook dal pithi at three in the morning for someone who isn't loved.

On the second day, I watched Phua slice through a mountain of onions. My eyes stung but I stayed put in anticipation of their browning. On the rare occasions that Phua cooked, she'd fry an additional handful for me to snack on. I had to beg them off Ajmeri in my mother's kitchen. When my eyes stopped watering, I noticed turnips.

'Why are you making turnips? Is Dadda weak?'

Phua laughed. 'They go into the shabdegh.'

I was not convinced. 'What's that?'

'*Shab.* Night. *Degh*. Vessel. It is meat and turnips, cooked overnight.'

'Does Dadda like that too?'

'She likes the sweetness of the turnips in the curry. It was the first thing she made for your great-grandfather after they were married.'

'Okay.'

I was beginning to doubt Dadda's tastes.

I ventured to the other end of the kitchen, and noticed the kebabs, arrayed inside the mesh cupboard. Phua was busy at the stove. Ammi always said one must not eat a guest's share before the guest. Ammi was full of wise words. But Ammi was inside. The temptation of what is before us usually outweighs the fear of what we cannot see. There is forgiveness later.

But my trespass was not forgiven. My mother stayed up that night, watching over me as my stomach twisted. Whenever the pain subsided for a few minutes, she'd ask, 'What did you eat, child? Did you have something outside?'

I'd look away each time and shook my head until I could hold it in no more.

'Ammi, is Dadda angry at me?'

She stroked my head. 'Why would Dadda be angry?'

'I had some raw meat from her kebabs. Just a tiny bit from one of the corners.'

Silence. I asked for Phua.

'She is not here,' came Ammi's reply, in clipped tones.

'Does she know I am sick?'

'Yes.'

I hid my face from Ammi to cry. What if Phua never forgave me? I prayed as I had been taught to pray, reciting at top speed and under my breath the verses from the Quran I had memorized, thinking, 'Let Phua forget this.' I promised eternal abstinence from kebabs in return.

After two days of suffering, I emerged from my sickbed on Shab-e-Barat, the day of Dadda's scheduled visit. I looked from the veranda to see if Phua was in the kitchen outside. There was no fire there, and nor was Ajmeri anywhere to be seen.

I found my mother in one of the unused rooms. According to family legend it was here that Phua had locked herself in, to persuade her father to allow her to study. My mother was standing, a cup of turmeric milk clasped in her hands, behind Phua, who had her face to the corner of the wall. This revolting concoction was my mother's idea of comfort food.

My aunt was looking at the wall, having a rapid conversation in low tones that I had never heard from her. It was as if another person was using her throat to speak.

My mother's lips were dry, and moving rapidly in what could only be protective prayers for herself.

I stood outside, not wanting to be seen.

'No, of course . . . Not my mother . . . My sister-in-law . . . She didn't mean it . . . Yes, there shall be punishment . . . No, no, no . . . Yes, she is standing behind me . . . I can't . . . I must . . .'

Phua then turned and started as if she hadn't just said she knew that my mother was standing behind her.

'Have some of this,' my mother said, her voice a whisper.

'You have to be punished.' Anger did not become my Phua.

My mother held her ground. She asked in the same whisper, 'Who were you talking to?'

'I could say it was Ajmeri who threw the food. But Dadda would know.'

'Was it Dadda you were speaking to?'

'Why do you send your daughter to spy on me?'

I hoped my mother was as shocked as I was at this accusation. A long silence followed. I could feel the anger radiating from my aunt even from outside the room.

My grandmother walked into the room with the glass we used only for Aab-e-Zamzam, the holy water from Mecca my father brought each summer. Her dupatta was on her head, as she wore it during her namaz. Her lips were moving in prayer over the water. She saw me crouching next to the door and shut it behind her.

It is a popular belief among the adults in my life that closed doors prevent scarred childhoods. I had heard my father throw a plate of food at the wall through closed doors. Behind closed doors, I had heard my grandmother tell Phua she wished one of them were dead so she could forget the pain of having a daughter such as her. This door was no different.

'She needs a doctor.'

'This is not a matter for doctors. Drink this, Bunnu.'

'No.'

'Drink it.'

There was a shriek, the briefest of scuffles, and then sobs. I heard Ammi's cup of turmeric milk crashing to the floor. A heavy voice inside screamed, 'I will return.'

The story of Phua's possession would go on to become family lore. Possessions make for the best stories. There are supernatural forces at play, suspense, a moral, and the forces of good that prevail over evil. Sometimes. Ajmeri told Phua's story in hushed tones and with many embellishments, interrupted by all the verses of the Quran she could remember, her dupatta always firmly on her head. All her recitations ended with my grandmother's intervention with the incantation-fortified Aab-e-Zamzam.

A few hours after the Incident of the Unused Room, as it would forever be referred to in the family, my mother walked my aunt to the old kitchen. I followed, keeping close to my mother. The fires were lit for the customary halwa. It was a bit late in the day for the halwa to be made in time to be shared with neighbours, but there is no Shab-e-Barat without halwa. My grandmother had retreated to her room. Ajmeri had left for the evening to visit family in the city. My mother and Phua stirred together, moving to the same silent music. The smell of roasted semolina from Phua's wok and caramelizing sugars and chana dal from Ammi's dispelled my sense of impending doom. In a voice barely audible above the scraping of the stirring spoons, my mother asked Phua, 'What does Dadda want to eat?'

Phua stopped. Then stirred again, scraping hard at the bottom of the wok, and stopped again. 'Kebab, shabdegh, pilau and sweetened rice.'

'We don't have enough time to marinate. Do you think Dadda would like a mince kebab? We could get together a qorma instead of shabdegh?'

I was put on guard duty lest my grandmother decide to emerge from her night-long prayers for Shab-e-Barat. I looked up at the sky, wondering if any of the free wandering souls of that night were in our courtyard at that moment, watching my mother and my aunt huddled close around the fire. I smelled the cardamom and cinnamon hitting the ghee, and the onions frying to an almond-gold crisp. The husky smell of arva rice cooking on a merry boil lingered under the stinging fieriness of chillies in oil. A bowl of saffron steeped in rosewater was just discernible under this olfactory chaos.

Ammi was whispering directions under her breath. Mince this, stir that. Phua obeyed, her eyes and hands moving quickly between the pots, testing a grain of rice between her fingers, turning the kebabs to char evenly, holding out a spot of masala on her palm for my mother to taste. The old dining cloth was spread on the other side of the kitchen where the mesh cupboards were. Dadda's enamel plate was at the head of the spread. The kebabs followed, surrounded by rings of macerated onion. The pilau and shabdegh came next, covered so they wouldn't get cold. Ammi put a muslin cloth over the pilau so the steam wouldn't dampen it to mush. The orange gold muzafar rice was served in a silver dish that was Dadda's wedding gift to Phua. Phua had promised I could have it when I got married. She had also rolled a paan, its leaf fresh and shiny in the firelight. My mother and Phua made their ablutions at the tank in the kitchen and sat down for the prayers of that night.

The whitewash of the walls in the courtyard gleamed under the full moon. The mongooses and cats of the bungalow slunk in the shadows, visiting the corners of the house we had abandoned. Were they perhaps inviting the souls of family members we had forgotten to their old rooms? I stared hard into the darkness to look for these ancestors of ours until I could keep my eyes open no more. Ammi and Phua waited, slouched over their Qurans, their lips moving silently.

My mother swears she heard the taps of Dadda's walking stick in its characteristic cadence that night. The smell of musk, her preferred perfume, had filled the kitchen.

'And the paan was gone, wasn't it, Bunnu?'

'Yes. Dadda never missed paan after her meals.'

KHICHRI

The pressure cooker is the best thing to have happened to kitchenkind. Slow cooking is beautiful but the pressure cooker saves hours of fretting, and all allegations of a compromise in taste are propaganda. In most cases. The khichri and its accompaniments (which, honestly, is why anyone eats khichri) come together in the blink of an eye with a couple of pressure cooker whistles. That said, possession of a pressure cooker isn't at all necessary for cooking this dish.

For the mashed potato and tomato chutney

4 medium potatoes
8 medium, very ripe tomatoes (go for the sour ones over sweet)
2 red onions, finely chopped
2 green chillies, finely chopped
1 cup chopped coriander
2 tbsp neutral-tasting oil
3 tbsp mustard oil
salt to taste

For the khichri

¾ cup split pigeon peas (toor dal)
⅔ cup short grain rice
2 bay leaves
4 cloves
16 black peppercorns
2 dried red chillies
9 cups water
⅔ tsp turmeric
salt to taste

For the crisped onions in ghee

¾ cup ghee
1 large onion, finely chopped

Note

You can adjust the amount of ghee and onions, but this part of the dish usually disappears fast. Any leftovers can be stored for at least a month and the onions will retain their crisp. The choice of fat is non-negotiable: do not substitute mustard for rapeseed oil (Canola) or replace ghee with olive oil.

Method

1. Wash the tomatoes, then chargrill them in a heavy-bottomed pan, a cast iron griddle or the oven with a splash of neutral oil. The tomatoes should be evenly charred on all sides and cooked to a mush. Set aside to cool.
2. Scrub the potatoes. If using a pressure cooker, add enough water to just cover the potatoes. Cook on a high heat until the first whistle. Then turn the heat to a simmer. Take the cooker off the heat after five minutes and wait for the pressure to release itself. Larger potatoes will require more simmer time. If cooking in a pot, boil until fork-tender.
3. Wash the pigeon peas and rice until the water runs clear. In a pressure cooker (or an open pan) tip in all the khichri ingredients and adjust the salt. Cook on high heat until the

first whistle. Turn down the heat to a simmer and take off after five minutes. If using a pot, cook until it reaches a risotto-like consistency, adding more water if needed.

4. When the tomatoes cool, remove their tops and the charred peel. Mash, with the seeds, until the tomatoes reach a uniform salsa-like consistency. Add half the chopped red onions, chillies and coriander. Season with salt and drizzle the mustard oil over the top.
5. Peel the potatoes. Mash them until there are no lumps, and season with salt. Add the remaining chopped onions, chillies and coriander. Drizzle with mustard oil.
6. Heat the ghee in a deep pan. Fry the chopped onions in the ghee on a medium high heat until just shy of brown. Take off the heat. The onions will keep cooking in the hot ghee and crisp up to a caramel brown.
7. Serve the khichri piping hot with the onions in ghee drizzled on top, with the mash and the chutney on the side.
8. The potato mash is ideally served at room temperature. The tomato chutney is best served cool.

What's Cooking?

Aamer Hussein with Sabeeha Ahmed Husain

'You have to try the biryani I make,' Mr Beg said as he stitched a cushion cover. 'I swear it would leave lords and princes licking their fingers, ma'am.'

Then the conversation turned to different types of biryani, and Beg probably dropped a few stitches as he prepared his imaginary feast.

Beg had arrived in London only a short while ago. He said he'd had a big furniture business in the Gulf. 'I employed several craftsmen, ma'am, and picked up all their different lingos. Then, one by one, they left for home when they'd earned enough money, some to Thailand, others to the Philippines or Indonesia. The business ground to a standstill, so I packed up and left for London.'

Lean and lanky, with grizzled hair and protruding teeth, Beg was a talkative man. His continuous chatter was, in Mrs Meer's words, enough to wash all the wax out from one's ears.

It so happened that Mrs Meer talked about Beg's culinary expertise to several of her friends and set their taste buds tingling. One offered her kitchen for a cooking session. 'Why not come to my place, which is more spacious, and bring your lovely apricot pudding?' another suggested. A young doctor friend from Bihar said he'd make a dish of haleem; his wife vetoed the idea because serving biryani and haleem at the same meal was profligate and the haleem could be enjoyed better on its own at another function.

For several days, as he completed the upholstering of the sofa, Beg made plans for the fantasy banquet he'd serve. When his stitching and stretching were complete, Mrs Meer requested him: 'How about a date for the promised biryani? Could you come along and cook it here next Sunday?'

Beg agreed with alacrity. The date was fixed, and he asked for some cash in advance to buy the ingredients.

On Saturday, Mrs Meer tried to contact Beg but received no response from his mobile. She thought he had probably gone shopping. But Sunday came with still no news from Beg. Mrs Meer grew anxious. The arrangement was for Beg to come and start preparing the feast in the morning. Had he misunderstood? Perhaps he intended to cook the rice at his home and bring it over?

The guests were expected at six. No sign of Beg with his biryani. *It's already four o'clock, too late to make it here*, Mrs Meer said to herself. *What next? I'll ring Memon Biryaniwala's restaurant and order a pot of that famous biryani of his that they've all been raving about to keep on standby.*

As the guests were turning out on that freezing evening in the hope of a steaming fragrant dish of rice and lamb, serving something lesser would be an anticlimax.

It was nearly five when Mrs Meer finally got hold of Beg. 'Ma'am, I'm in Birmingham refurbishing a huge mansion. New curtains, new cushions, new covers for a great number of armchairs and sofas – I'll be here for at least another week. Whatever made you think I'd be cooking for you today? Had we fixed a day, ma'am?'

'But Mr Beg, you took an advance for the shopping –'

'What advance, ma'am? Honest to God, I gratefully accepted what you gave me for my labour and I thought that you'd given me a bonus because you were pleased with my work. No date was fixed for the biryani, ma'am!'

The bell rang. Mrs Meer wearily put down the receiver and went to the door.

About seven years later, Mrs Meer received a call from a woman called Safia who said she was a skilled chef and could cook all the classic dishes, including biryani. A mutual acquaintance had suggested she get in touch to offer her services to Mrs Meer.

'Could you bring me a sample of your biryani to taste? What do you charge for one portion? If it's the way we like it, we'll order more.'

Safia arrived on a blustery Saturday in February. Torrents of rain had fallen in the morning; by noon the pavements were thick with snow. The phone rang and rang again. The girl seemed to have lost her way. Mrs Meer's grandson, Ali, who was visiting for the weekend and had been texting friends on his mobile, got to his feet with a groan, slipped on his shoes, threw on his overcoat and set off to look for her. He couldn't see much through the swirling sleet, but a female form emerged unexpectedly in the middle of the road in front of the building. Bundled up in a great coat, plus balaclava and boots, she was waving her arms about frantically. Ali gestured toward the entrance and she crossed over to greet him.

Small, plump and rosy-cheeked, Safia was about forty and looked like a Kashmiri. The rice she brought was fragrant, sprinkled with almonds and perhaps pistachios, and surrounded by tiny meatballs. It tasted fine, but it wasn't, in Mrs Meer's book, an authentic biryani: she'd call it a pilau. Safia was clearly a good cook, though, and versatile. Mrs Meer decided to have her over to cook a meal once or twice a week.

Mrs Meer learnt that Safia was a widow. Her husband had been shot at by some mad sniper while he was strolling on a Karachi street, and had died as he waited for the ambulance a witness from a nearby stall had summoned. Their child was now with Safia's mother, while she had come to London to work for a family. She wasn't only a good cook; she was also skilled at ironing, sewing and dressmaking. One day she looked at Beg's cushions and said: 'Ma'am, these covers are really old now. If you like I can make new ones for you.'

Within a week or two she produced the new covers. She said that she had made wedding dresses for various friends and neighbours in Karachi and, though her husband didn't approve, she'd enjoyed a small income from her work. She needed additional jobs in London as the money she made working for an expat businessman's family twice a week wasn't enough to live on in this city.

'Why don't you keep me here with you?' she'd say to Mrs Meer. 'I can take care of everything around the house. I can occasionally do other work here and there to supplement what you pay me. If you have no objection, that is.'

Mrs Meer found herself in a dilemma. *The girl's really useful to have around*, she thought. *She charges a lot, but she's most capable, and her confidence and ability are remarkable. But I'm not used nowadays to having someone hovering around me all day. Besides, I'll have to teach her how I like things done, and my days are fully occupied already.*

So, for the time being, the question of Safia coming to live with Mrs Meer was put to one side.

Mrs Meer's friend Parveen was constantly in need of help around the house. Every time she heard that Mrs Meer had acquired new domestic help, she'd say: 'Do send her along to me, dear.' And that was how Safia started going to her on Tuesday mornings. Parveen was well satisfied with her work.

At about this time, Mrs Meer took it into her head that insects were crawling beneath the carpet in her bedroom. When she mentioned it to Safia, she said right away: 'Don't you worry, ma'am, I'll call someone in to take care of that.' And picking up her mobile, she began a rapid conversation in a flurry of Punjabi.

A couple of days later, Parveen rang to say: 'The silly woman hasn't shown up and I've invited two friends to lunch. Can you give me the number of a decent takeaway nearby? I can't possibly stand and cook with my arthritic knees.'

A few days went by and then Mrs Meer heard from Safia. She apologized profusely. A business magnate was over from Mumbai: she had a full-time, 'live-in' job with him and needed to stay there for a few months.

'I'm so ashamed, I should have let you know. But if you should need me especially, ma'am, just call and I'll be there.'

Spring came and then summer, though that summer the rain hardly stopped for a day. Safia would phone now and again. Sometimes she had a job and sometimes she didn't. She had problems with her visa, but then managed to obtain a work permit. On occasions she would drop in with a delicacy Mrs Meer had ordered or she would come to do some small job around the house.

One day Mrs Meer reminded her about the need to get rid of the insects under the carpet. 'I'll get hold of the exterminators right away,' Safia said, and again there came a rapid flurry of Punjabi on her mobile.

A few weeks later, the exterminator called, ringing the doorbell loudly on a Sunday morning. Mohammad Ameen was an Afghan lad from Cricklewood, sturdy and green-eyed. Behind closed doors, he gave the carpet a thorough going-over, but as he left, he announced that he hadn't found a single insect that needed exterminating. 'But sister, your carpet's worn out. Just say the word and we'll fit a new one.'

Mrs Meer chuckled. 'So you sell carpets too?'

'Me an' my friends do a whole lot of things. But fitting a carpet for you, I'd do it all by myself. Beg sent me over as he couldn't find anyone else to kill them insects.'

Mrs Meer made up her mind to have two rooms re-carpeted. She chose a sandalwood shade which reminded her of the shimmering golden sands of Karachi's beaches.

Ameen arrived the following Thursday and worked diligently for a few hours laying the carpet in the first room. The next day, after only a short while, he stopped work, exhausted. 'Sister, it's my first day of fasting. Aren't you fasting too? I won't be able to do all the fetching and carrying by meself. If you'll allow me to, I'll ask my mate to come and help me. But it'll cost you another thirty pound.'

There didn't seem to be much of an alternative, with the work half done and her precious objects and other bric-a-brac scattered all over the place. 'Go ahead,' Mrs Meer said.

Not long after that the doorbell rang and Ali opened the door to a woman with reddish bobbed hair, dressed in clothes that looked as if they came from a Littlewood's catalogue. He felt he'd seen her before.

'You don't recognize me, sir. Safia!'

Ali thought how much she'd changed in just a few months.

She worked purposefully with Ameen, and by evening, the second carpet was down.

On Saturday evening, Ali had just showered and changed to go out. At five o'clock, a colleague at his university was reading a paper on art and exile, and several academics from South Asia and the diaspora would be there for a conference the next day. Safia was doing something for Mrs Meer in the kitchen when the doorbell rang. Ali hurried to the door to find Beg of the fantasy banquets standing there, lean and lanky, protruding teeth intact, his grizzled hair now quite white, though his moustache was still black. He held out his hand in greeting, but seemed not to recognize Ali. Had Ali changed that much in seven years, or was this Beg's pretence?

'I'm Beg, boss of the carpet company, come to collect my cheque,' he said.

Mrs Meer had already written out the cheque, so Ali gave it to Beg, who took it. Then he asked, 'Is Miss Safia still here?'

'Yes, come this way,' Ali said, showing him to the kitchen. Mrs Meer looked at Beg coldly, and he didn't show any sign of recognizing her.

Outside, the summer rain was pouring down. Ali picked up his umbrella and left the house.

'She's one tough lady, our Safia,' Mrs Meer said as Ali entered, looking up from the Pakistani news she was watching on television. 'You know she cleared up all the mess after the furniture men had gone.'

Ali had come back very wet and rather disgruntled from the conference, where much time had been spent talking about a series of photographs called 'Sunrise, Sunset,' taken by a Pakistani woman in the US and in Karachi. They were inspired by an Urdu children's poem that said that the cradle of the sun was in the east and its graveyard in the west; the juxtaposed images told a different story. Ali, who had lived all over the world since the age of eight and styled himself a rootless cosmopolitan, was disturbed by the photographer's advocacy of rootedness, but hadn't been given a chance to say so because there had been too little time for questions after the discussion.

'More killings in Karachi. Even during Ramadan.' Mrs Meer had switched the television off and was snipping the peel of an orange with a silver knife into fine juliennes.

'Grandma, did you meet the man who was running the company?'

'The one who came for the money was the old joker Beg –'

'Uhm. However did he get hold of Safia?'

'Maybe he passed on my number to Safia to make up for the let-down over the biryani. By the way, I asked her where she lived. "Kilburn," she said. "I live in Mr Beg's house now."'

'But Beg is –'

'Yes, he has a wife and three or four children. He's just back from spending time with them in Karachi.'

'So you think he's made Safia his second wife?'

'I never asked.' Mrs Meer was separating the orange she'd peeled into smooth segments.

'Do you think they have some sort of understanding?' Ali asked, then guffawed. 'Sounds like something from one of your Karachi soaps.'

'Can you imagine me asking her that sort of question? I'm not one of God's little soldiers. She didn't ask for my advice and I didn't offer it.' Mrs Meer had arranged the bright orange segments on a silver platter.

'Have some,' she said, pushing the plate towards Ali.

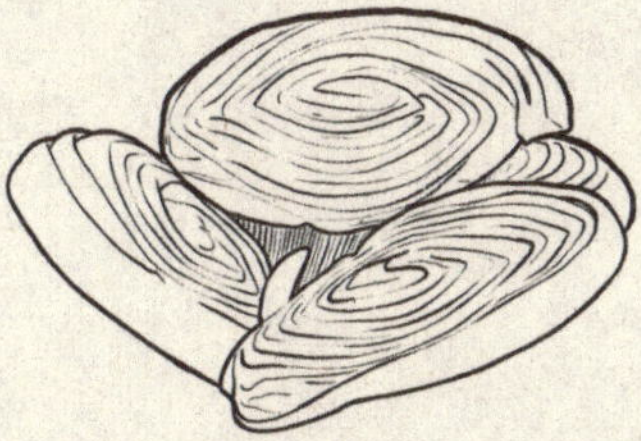

Sweet Rice (Zarda) with Orange Peel

2 cups uncooked white rice
¼ tsp orange food colouring
2 tsp grated or julienned orange zest
4–6 whole cardamoms
1 tbsp vegetable oil
1½ cups white sugar
1½ tbsp double cream
1 tbsp raisins
1 tbsp chopped walnuts
1 tbsp slivered almonds

Method

1. Cover the rice with water in a bowl and leave to soak for about an hour before draining off the water.
2. Bring a large saucepan of 5 cups of water to boil, then add the food colouring and half the cardamom pods. Stir in the

rice, reduce the heat, and cover and simmer until this is tender (about 20 minutes).

3. Fry the remaining cardamom pods in oil in another large pan over a low heat for 2 minutes. Then stir in the cooked and drained rice, along with the sugar.
4. Cover the pan and cook for 5 minutes.
5. Remove from the heat and stir in the cream, raisins, walnuts, almonds and orange zest. Serve immediately.

But There Are Angels

Farahad Zama

It was one of those lovely, warm days that sometimes grace England in autumn. The manicured garden with its close-cropped lawn and neat borders was beautiful, but Faisal still found his spirits sinking as he got out of his car at Appleby Care Home in deepest Sussex. His wife Katie must have sensed his mood because she came over to his side and took his hand in hers. He looked at her gratefully and, as always, the sight and touch of her lifted his blues.

'Thank you,' he murmured, giving her a quick peck on the cheek.

She just smiled and squeezed his hand. Together, they walked to the boot of the car and took out a picnic hamper.

The carers had brought the residents out into the garden. Faisal and Katie walked down the path towards them. A squirrel chased another across the lawn and up an oak tree, and the buzz of bees could be heard faintly as they flitted over the dahlias growing against the south-facing boundary wall. The nursing home was expensive, and a large portion of Faisal's salary went to pay for it, but seeing the residents like this, enjoying the warm sun in such harmonious surroundings, looked after by staff who actually seemed to like their jobs, made it all worthwhile. He knew that he would not be able to afford it without Katie more or less running their household from her income.

They were still holding hands and this time he squeezed hers and said, 'Thank you.'

She gave him a quizzical look.

'You make this possible,' he said.

They saw his mother and changed direction towards her. She was sitting on a painted white bench, with a cardigan around her shoulders and a blanket over her legs. Faisal hugged her, saying, 'Salaam Ammi.'

'Good afternoon, Mrs Begum. That pink cardigan looks really fetching on you,' Katie said.

'Thank you, dear.' The old lady's English was still heavily accented despite the decades she had lived in England. She turned to her son. 'Where is my bahu, my daughter-in-law?'

Faisal shot a guilty glance at Katie and said, 'She's busy with the boys, Ammi. I've got some food for you.'

'Aliya is such a good mother. Have you heard from your father?' Dementia had rolled his mother's mind back to a time when Faisal had been married for a couple of years, his sons were toddlers, and her husband was still alive. It was a time when she had probably been happiest. A time before Faisal had left south India for southern England. A time before her husband had suffered a catastrophic heart attack and died suddenly. A time before her husband's family had thrown her out and her own brothers had cheated her of her inheritance.

Faisal opened the picnic hamper. 'I've got curd rice for you, Ammi,' he said. It took him a few tries to get his fingers under the notch in the lid and open the container. The white yoghurt coating every grain of rice and the intermixed shredded coriander leaves made the interior of the lunchbox look like a lawn covered by fresh snow. One corner of the container was taken up by a rich, red mango pickle.

The fragrance of basmati rice, coriander, yoghurt and the spicy aroma of red chillies made the old lady's nose twitch. 'It reminds me . . .' she said, then fell silent, as if she had forgotten what she had remembered.

'Water,' Faisal mouthed to his wife and she handed him a bottle. The rice had absorbed the yoghurt and clotted into an almost solid mass. He poured some water into the rice and stirred it, then added some more water and stirred it again, until he was satisfied with its consistency. He took a little of the fiery, red pickle onto the spoon, then filled it with rice and raised it to his mother's mouth, feeding her as she had once fed him years and years ago, their roles reversed. He, now the adult, and she the dependant. Her eyes closed as she ate the deeply familiar, simple food of her youth.

'Ah!' she exclaimed. 'It does my palate good to eat some proper food. Pies, sandwiches and soups, bah!' Faisal smiled at her unending disdain for English food. In all the years she had lived in this country, she only prepared Indian dishes. He remembered visits to National Trust properties, in which they had opened up picnics of curries and naans on the lawns, while he had been embarrassed by the smells and had wanted nothing more than to eat salads and burgers from the café. 'Chi chi, not halal. Too expensive too. Five pounds for some lettuce leaves and a strip of pepper? You can get it for one pound in the supermarket and even cheaper if you make it yourself at home. Beta, don't be like the white people and throw your money away on frivolous things,' his mother would say. 'A rolling stone gathers no moss,' she would add, one of the few English phrases that she had learned.

Faisal always wondered what eating in a café had to do with rolling stones and moss, but he would keep silent, and grumpily eat the food his mother packed. It was only now, after his divorce and his mother's illness, that he realized how much he missed those homemade curries. Sure, he could make a few of them, but they were never as good. Many of the more complex dishes were now forgotten foods, tantalizing him by appearing at the edge of his memory, but eluding him as he tried to recapture their exact tastes and aromas. His mother had learned how to make many of those curries from her mother-in-law and had guarded those family recipes from everyone but her son's wife. When his wife divorced him, he had lost the wife of his youth, and she had taken away the children she had given him by turning them against him. But, he thought, the loss of those family dishes – the curries, the biryanis, the breads and puddings of his childhood – were as great a loss as anything else. No one else made them quite the same way they had been made in his family for generations, and now he would never taste them again as long as he lived.

'Do you remember what fun we had making this pickle last year?' Faisal's mother asked him.

'Last year?' he repeated, puzzled for a moment.

She rolled her eyes. 'You are such a scatterbrain sometimes, Faisal,' she said. 'It was just after Babul's second birthday.' Babul, his younger son, was now twenty-five. Nonetheless, Faisal remembered that far-off event quite vividly. It had been one of those days when the stars align and everything is perfect. His wife had never looked more beautiful. She had worn a parrot-green sari and, because of the work on the pickle, she had tucked the end of her sari into the waistband of her petticoat, revealing her navel, which he had always found very sexy. His sons played well together that day, with none of their usual fights. His father was still healthy, with his trademark booming laughter. His mother had clapped her hands, calling the troops. Faisal had filled a big bucket with water drawn from the well. His wife had squatted by the bucket, washing the green mangoes, scrubbing them clean and passing them to his mother. His mother had patted them dry with an old, soft sari, and chopped the tops off the mangoes before passing them to his father. His father used a sharp machete to quarter the mangoes. A serving maid scooped the pieces of the hard, acidic seed out of the mango pieces. The mangoes were then mixed with salt and spread out in the sun. Once that was done, the spices – red chillies, mustard seeds, garlic and fenugreek seeds – were similarly laid out in the sun. Faisal's mother placed a stick across the ingredients to keep the birds away. This work had taken all afternoon, and eventually the family retired into the house to cut a cake for his son's birthday.

That was just day one of the pickle-making process. Every hint of moisture had to be driven away from the ingredients, which meant several days of drying in the baking summer sun. Then the chillies and other spices were ground and mixed with the mangoes in plenty of oil for another week before they were ready. The first day the new pickle had been brought to the dining table, the aroma of the fresh pickle with its notes of chilli and mustard had made everyone salivate with anticipation. Faisal had been unable to resist dipping the little finger of his right hand into the red oil and scooping a bit of the spice into his mouth. The pickle would mellow in the coming months, but right now it was sharp and tangy.

That night, when his wife had taken the boys to bed, his mother turned to Faisal. 'Are you happy, son?'

Faisal didn't have to think about his answer. 'Yes, Ammi. I am happy.'

'Didn't I get you the most beautiful wife?'

'Yes, Ammi,' he said. 'Aliya is very beautiful.'

'Not just beautiful. She is a lovely woman inside and out. She has settled in so well with all of us. And she's given you two handsome sons.'

His mother's frail hand brought Faisal back to the present. 'Yes, Ammi,' he said. 'I remember when we made the pickle.' He raised the next spoonful of rice and pickle to her lips. As he continued feeding her, his mind wandered to the past again.

He had received a job offer from an insurance company in England. He and Aliya discussed it for days. Neither wanted to leave India and their families, but the money was too good to pass up. It would be more professionally fulfilling as well. In the end, they decided to move. He had often wondered if their decision had been selfish and the subsequent events an inevitable fallout from that original sin.

Faisal's job was interesting and his pay went up over the years. Aliya was initially lonely in their flat but as the kids grew up and started school, she too blossomed. She learned to drive and started working in a Kumon centre teaching maths and English to schoolchildren.

She became friendly with other mums in the kids' primary school, and they would all go to a nearby Starbucks where they discussed their children, their husbands, the latest diet fad, politics, fashion, parking problems and much else.

When a child was injured crossing the road near the school, the mums decided to campaign for a speed camera and for the zebra crossing to be converted to a pelican crossing controlled by lights. They wrote to the council, the mayor, the local MP and the traffic commissioner of the local police force. To keep the pressure up, they organized Slow-down Mondays. Each Monday, over fifty women (and a few men, including Faisal when he could go to work late) would turn up at the pedestrian crossing near the school and between seven and nine in the morning repeatedly cross the road back and forth. This led to long tailbacks of traffic, lost tempers, honking and general chaos.

After four such Mondays, which now required police officers to keep the peace, the authorities gave in. The women were ecstatic at their success and Faisal was full of pride for his wife, taking her to a good Italian restaurant to celebrate.

The kids grew and moved from primary to secondary school. He knew that his parents had been heartbroken by their move, but they were happy for the couple's success and looked forward to their annual visits. Those years were the happiest in Faisal's life.

One night there was a phone call. The jangling ring startled Faisal out of his sleep and he was still groggy when he said, 'Hello?'

'Faisal . . .' came an almost incoherent cry from the other side. Faisal was jolted into wakefulness as he recognized his mother's voice, and he noticed Aliya stirring next to him.

'Ammi?'

'Your father,' said his mother and collapsed into tears.

'What happened to Abba?' Faisal said. 'Talk to me, Ammi.'

One of his uncles came on the phone. 'Your father has had a heart attack, Faisal,' he said. 'It's a bad one. You had better come home.'

Aliya urged Faisal to leave immediately. The boys were in the middle of the school term and it would be disruptive to take them. Faisal agreed and was on a flight that very day, paying an exorbitant amount of money for the ticket. He didn't remember much of the journey, except that he alternated between despair and hope. A bad heart attack – Faisal thought his father would die. No, he would then think, his father was a strong man, a survivor. Surely between the doctors and the man's own will, he would pull through. Buffeted by such thoughts, Faisal reached his boyhood home to find that his father had suffered a second heart attack and passed away just hours before. Faisal had even been denied a farewell.

His mother was devastated and seemed to be in shock, saying very little and only eating when forced to do so. Faisal couldn't bear to see her in widow's whites rather than the colourful saris she normally wore, and it was a torture for him to go through the rituals associated with the death of his father. He stayed for two weeks and then came back to England, with his uncles and cousins assuring him that they would look after his mother.

His father's death changed everything. The family's main source of income was a business that was a partnership owned by his father and his two brothers. The house they lived in was an ancestral property that was also jointly owned by the three brothers. Within months, Faisal's mother was shunted off from the beautifully decorated master bedroom to a small side room that had previously been used to store odds and ends. One of Faisal's cousins had a new baby and they needed the room. And as his mother was now alone, she didn't need that much space, surely? She was excluded from all family decision-making and from festive celebrations too, as it was considered inauspicious for a widow to be part of these happy occasions. Her misfortune might rub off on the others, someone muttered. She ended up doing more and more work in the kitchen. After all, she had no husband or children to look after, unlike the other women, they said, as they piled further labour on her. She used to get an allowance from her brothers as part of her inheritance from their parents' property. That stopped. What would a widow need money for and who was there to demand her rights?

Faisal came home for his father's death anniversary and was shocked to see his mother's condition. He exchanged harsh words with his uncles and aunts and fell out with his cousins. Luckily his parents had planned to visit him in the UK and had obtained passports and visas. He made a quick call to Aliya and told her that he could not leave his mother where she was, being treated as nothing more than a drudge. His wife sounded somewhat doubtful and hoped that his mother's situation would improve over time back in India. He overrode his wife's objections and, within a week, mother and son were on a plane to Heathrow.

In certain ways, having his mother helped their household. She assisted in the kitchen and did some of the laundry. Aliya and Faisal could go out in the evenings because they now had a live-in childminder. The children's knowledge of Urdu increased enormously. But in other ways, it put a strain on them all. Faisal had read somewhere that the Chinese word for tranquillity was one woman under a roof and the word for quarrel was two women under a roof, and so it proved in his own house. Little things, like spice bottles relegated to the wrong place in the cabinet, caused the women to sulk for days. Then Faisal's mother criticized the amount of processed food that the children ate, and that caused Aliya to explode. Faisal was forced to intercede and tell his mother to leave the children alone and let Aliya bring them up as she saw fit. His mother muttered something about uxorious husbands and swept into her bedroom.

An uneasy truce developed between the two ladies and life went along, everyone treating each other with kid gloves amid the occasional dust-up. The kids grew up and left home for university. Aliya now owned three Kumon centres and employed several people to manage them. There was even talk of her running for the local city council. Faisal's career was going well too. Their personal life was cooler. They rarely went out together just on their own, though Aliya went for girls' nights out with her friends and they occasionally attended dinner parties in their social circle. Their love-life had more or less stopped and when Faisal mentioned it, Aliya said, 'What do you expect? We are not in our twenties any more.'

'We're not that old,' he replied, but his wife was adamant and there was nothing Faisal could do about it. He and Aliya were still friends and had a shared history of setting up a house, planting a garden and raising children, which outweighed the absence of sex in their relationship.

But the lack of intimacy was not only a symptom of the growing distance between them; that lack was also the cause of the widening rift. And as their connection frayed, the fights between Aliya and his mother grew more frequent. Years passed with the three of them locked in an unhappy triangle. Faisal thought it was lucky that the children, at least, were away from this mess. Whenever they came to the house, they made it clear that they took their mother's side. They exchanged barely a word with Faisal and his mother.

One evening, Faisal noticed his older son snapping at his mother. 'Hamid, don't be rude,' Faisal said. 'She is your grandmother and deserves respect.'

His son rolled his eyes. 'Dad, she's asked me the same question six times in the last hour. If she can't be bothered to remember my answer, why should I care to answer her?'

'There's still no excuse to be rude to your elders,' Faisal said.

'Whatever, Dad,' his son said, leaving the room and going to his mother.

The kids finished their education and started working. They found partners and apartments and moved out permanently. One Thursday, Faisal came home from work to find Aliya dressed to go out. 'Are you going out? What's for dinner?' he asked.

'Get your own dinner,' she snarled. 'I am not your slave.'

Faisal was taken aback by her aggressive response. 'I only . . .' he began.

At that moment, his mother came into the room and said to Aliya, 'I bet you're up to no good, going out on your own at night in that attire.'

Aliya was furious. 'How dare you insinuate anything, you old bat! You come into my house . . . You've made my life miserable since the day you landed here.' She turned to her husband. 'I've had it up to here,' she said, levelling her palm to her neck. 'You keep your mother under control. Tell her to stay in her corner and not interfere in my affairs.'

Faisal was irritated by his wife's attitude and at some level agreed with his mother's curiosity about why she was going out so frequently in the evenings all dolled up. Rather than inflame matters, he stayed silent, just noting how angry his wife was at being questioned. His silence only made his wife angrier. 'I am sick of you!' she cried. 'I want a man, not a wimp who can't stand up to his own mother. I want someone who's different.'

Faisal itched to retaliate, but forced himself to remain calm. Her harsh words cut him to the quick. Had this cruelty always been in her? Had this coldness always been at the heart of their relationship? Or was it like a worm in an apple . . . clearly foreign, but introduced so subtly that there was no sign of how and when it had made its way into the core while leaving the fruit shiny on the outside? If I were different, he thought to himself in silent answer to her barbs, I would have acted a long time ago when you stopped loving me.

Aliya burst into tears and went into the master bedroom, slamming the door hard. Faisal's mother turned to him but all she could manage was, 'I . . .'

Faisal raised his hand. 'Just go to your room, Ammi. I don't want to talk now.'

A few weeks later, when he came back from the office, his mother was crying. 'She's gone!'

'What? Who's gone where?' he asked.

'Aliya. She packed a suitcase and left.'

He was baffled. Perhaps her parents were not well and she had gone to visit them. Or even a business visit, though she had never had to travel for work before this. But why hadn't she said anything to him? Faisal walked upstairs to the bedroom and opened his wife's wardrobe. He was shocked to see it empty. How could all her clothes fit into one suitcase? He went into the en-suite and noticed that her toothbrush and cosmetics were missing. But on the counter sat his wife's black bead necklace. It was the symbol of their marriage and she never left home without it. The sight of the chain glinting under the lights took over his vision until he could see nothing else. Their marriage had problems, but this was a different step altogether. He didn't know how long he stood there before sliding slowly to the floor.

Things moved fast after that. His younger son called him. Aliya had moved into a flat and would only come back if Faisal's mother left the house. Faisal suddenly understood how his wife had left with just one suitcase while emptying her considerable wardrobe. This had been planned for a while. After all, it must have taken time to organize a flat and then slowly move her things to it. 'How long have you known that your mother was going to leave?'

'Abba, that's not important.'

'It's important to me. How long?'

'Three months. Bhaiyya knew too.'

Faisal closed his eyes. Both his sons knew and had helped their mother in secret for months. The betrayal tore into his heart. 'I can't abandon your grandmother,' he said. 'She doesn't know this country. How will she live on her own?'

A petition for the dissolution of marriage landed in the post. Faisal went into a dark depression where everything seemed too much of an effort. Aliya was asking for half of all their assets and half of his salary as spousal maintenance. A good lawyer would have pointed out that she had already taken most of their savings from the joint accounts when she left. The lawyer would have said that she earned a good income herself from her Kumon centres and there was no need for alimony. He could have pointed out that the house was required for Faisal's dependent mother. Faisal was too upset to fight any of his wife's claims. He agreed to everything and ended up giving her all his investments and most of his pension to keep the house. He found it impossible to sleep and difficult to get out of bed. Everything in the house reminded him of Aliya and mocked him with her absence. His mother seemed to be getting increasingly forgetful and frail and was no help. He didn't care about his appearance and stopped shaving. He started missing days from work. When he did turn up, his colleagues complained about his appearance and his unwashed smell. After a while, his boss sent him home and told him not to bother coming back until he was clean. About the time his divorce came through, his boss finally ran out of patience and Faisal lost his job as well.

The next three years were gloomy, and Faisal didn't remember much about them. He and his mother fell into the pit together – the house went dark with the lights hardly turned on most of the time, piles of dirty laundry littering various rooms, and unopened letters stacking up. Mould blackened windowsills and walls. All the house plants died and the garden turned into a jungle.

It might have gone on forever, but one bright spring morning, Faisal felt hungry and came down into the living room to see his mother sleeping on the sofa. A beam of sunlight from the window illuminated her, dust motes dancing in the air. She looked so small and vulnerable, and it touched something in Faisal's heart. With new eyes he looked around and saw just how bad the condition of the house was. In the past that would have acted as a reminder that Aliya had left him and made him angry, but now he could examine that thought with detachment as if it was something that had happened to someone else. It had been almost three years since Aliya had left him and he suddenly felt ashamed that he had allowed his mother to live in such squalor for so long. With an unexpected burst of energy, he decided to clean the house and make some hot food for his mother.

It took almost a month to get the house ship-shape and there were many times that he almost gave up. But each time, he had only to look at his mother to know that he must continue. His industriousness and the regular meals that they were now eating gave his mother strength, and she joined him in helping around the house. He found that he had to keep repeating his instructions to her several times, and she seemed easily confused but much happier than she had been for a long time.

When he started clearing the garden, he realized how unfit he had become and decided to make his fitness the next target. He discovered there was a walking club in the local park that met every Saturday morning for a five-mile walk. The first time he went, his feet became blistered and he crashed into a deep sleep when he got back. The next day his thighs were sore. It took till Wednesday before he got over the strain of the walk. It then took four Saturdays before the hellish trudge turned into a moderately strenuous hike.

The Saturday after that, he completely forgot about his aching muscles – not because he had become fit, but because he saw a lovely woman in the crowd. She was talking to another lady and he gazed discreetly at her animated face and welcoming smile. She looked quite young. Her blonde hair had an interesting cut, being longer on one side than the other. The longer hair was braided in the way he imagined a Swiss milkmaid would have done it. Her legs were showcased in form-fitting Lincoln-green yoga pants that had panels of transparent webbing along the sides, showing tantalizing glimpses of her toned limbs. Her top was darker green and didn't hide the shape of her impressive bust. He looked away guiltily when he noticed that. It had been a long time since he had seen, really seen, a woman – any woman – and he felt it was the wrong thing to do. She had come here to exercise, not to be gawked at by an unfit middle-aged guy just climbing out of depression.

As they were ready to set off, people milled about, causing confusion. The woman cut through the mayhem with a few crisp instructions to those around her and they all started walking. By this time, Faisal had manoeuvred close to her. 'Thanks, Katie,' the organizer said. 'You are a godsend.'

'You're welcome.' Again, the big smile. Despite the early hour, she had bright red lipstick and, Faisal thought, some makeup. So her name was Katie and she was bossy. Aliya had been bossy too, and he liked that in a woman. Then he shook his head, what the hell was he thinking? A beautiful woman like her would have no interest in him. That's if she was even single in the first place.

Lost in his thoughts, he stumbled on an uneven piece of ground. 'Are you okay?' Katie asked him.

Up close, he saw that she was not as young as he had first thought, but her smile and painted lips dazzled him and he could only smile weakly at her. God, he was such a nerd. She was just being friendly and he was overthinking it and couldn't get a word out. He took a deep breath and settled himself. 'I haven't seen you before on this walk,' he said.

'This is my first time,' Katie said. 'Are you a regular?'

'Only for the last three weeks. I was quite unfit, so I decided to join this group.'

'This walk is not enough to get you fit,' she said, with a disarming candidness.

He grinned. 'I know,' he said. 'One has to start somewhere. But why are you here? You look quite fit to me.'

She looked at him with an amused look on her face. 'So you think I am fit?'

'Yes . . .' he started saying, and then realized the implication of what he had said and blushed deeply. 'Er . . . no . . .'

She raised her neatly shaped eyebrows. 'Oh, I am not good-looking, is that what you are saying? I'm hurt.'

'No, I mean yes . . . Damn it! You know that's not what I was saying.'

She laughed and patted his arm lightly. Faisal was intensely aware of the sound of her laughter and the touch of her hand. 'I just moved into this area and thought this was a good way to meet people and make friends.'

'I am glad you did,' he said. 'I am in need of some friends too.'

And so their unlikely friendship started. On paper, they should have had nothing in common. He was a deeply introspective man, living in his mind most of the time. She gained energy from being around people. But something clicked between them. He started liking being around people again, because of her. He found that despite her generous smiles, Barbie-doll looks and flirtatious behaviour, she had an intense inner life too. She had been deeply hurt by her failed marriage to a man with anger issues. Towards the end, she had been frightened of him, though he had never been physically abusive to her. 'There are different ways to be abusive,' she told him. 'And it can actually be harder to fight against someone who is controlling and chips away at your confidence than someone who smacks you around.'

He was impressed that she had found the strength to walk away from such a relationship and told her so. And their friendship grew.

She had to take the first step, but within months they went from friends to lovers. After years of living with someone who had cut him off from physical intimacy, he found it unbelievable that Katie actually looked forward to making love. He kept expecting her to withdraw sex and use it as a weapon. It took him a while to realize that Katie really did desire his body as much as he did hers, and was astonished, as well as delighted, to learn that women could be sexual creatures just as much as men.

She met his mother a few times before Katie asked him, 'Have you taken your mother to see a doctor?'

'Why? She's not ill.'

'I think she has dementia,' Katie said.

'What!' Faisal exclaimed, and then became mute as all the clues clicked into place in his brain. I've been so blind, he thought. My poor mother . . . her increasing confusion, repetitively asking the same questions, anger at any change of routine . . . Stupid, stupid, stupid me, he berated himself and tears filled his eyes. He felt Katie's warm, soft hand caressing his cheek, and he turned towards her. She looked even more beautiful than usual in the soft focus of his wet eyes. 'I love you,' he said.

'I love you too,' she replied.

'I don't know why you would,' he said. 'I am blind as a bat, unable to see what was right in front of my eyes.'

'You keep telling me I am beautiful. I thought you had good vision,' she said. They both laughed and Faisal didn't feel so bad any more.

Less than a week later, on what he always thought of as a bittersweet day, he asked Katie to marry him and also took his mother to see a doctor.

This was a second marriage for both of them; neither wanted a big shindig and they decided on a short engagement and a small wedding with just a few people in attendance. Faisal thought for a while and decided to invite his sons. His older son put the phone down as soon as he realized that it was his father speaking. Faisal thought the line had dropped, so he called back straight away. The phone rang and rang, and no one picked up. Oh, Hamid, thought Faisal sadly. When you were younger, you couldn't wait to start talking to me as soon as I walked in through the door from work.

Faisal then called Babul, his younger son. When Faisal told him that he was getting married and invited him to the registry office, Babul immediately said, 'Abba, how could you? For three years, you claimed you were too depressed to do anything.

You even left your job so you didn't have to pay any alimony to Ammi, and now, a few months later, your depression has magically disappeared and you are actually marrying some gold-digging hussy. I am disappointed, Abba, that you are such a selfish person. I understand why Ammi had to leave you.'

It was your mother who pushed me into depression by leaving me, Faisal wanted to scream at his son. Did you once come and see how your dad was doing those three years? Did you see how your grandmother survived in a broken household? And Katie is no gold-digger. If she were, she'd be a very incompetent one, since I don't have any gold to dig after your sainted mother stripped me of everything. He didn't say any of that. Instead he replied, 'I guess you won't be coming to the wedding, then?'

There was no response and Faisal slowly put the phone down, before sitting down quietly in the chair. He was glad that Katie wasn't in the house to see his rejection. He hadn't truly expected anything else, but he was still surprised by how hurt he felt. A long-forgotten line from Shakespeare came into his head: 'How sharper than a serpent's tooth it is to have a thankless child!' *King Lear*, he remembered, lamenting his ungrateful daughters. The bard certainly knew what he was talking about.

His mother was the sole person from his family who attended the wedding and she was only half there. Even still, she smiled at everyone and told Katie that she looked beautiful, blessing her with a long married life. As if the diagnosis burst a dam that ignorance had held back, his mother's condition started noticeably deteriorating soon after. Within weeks, after she had left the house twice in search of her husband, Faisal had to make the difficult decision to place her in a home.

Faisal fed his mother one final spoonful of rice and pickle. He handed the empty container back to Katie and looked around the garden. Some of the residents were now taking a walk along the path and their quiet voices sounded like the murmurs of a brook. One of the older men went past their bench and nodded at Faisal's mother. 'It's a beautiful day, isn't it, Mrs Ahmed?'

Faisal's mother smiled and nodded. 'My son and daughter-in-law,' she announced, having one of her fleeting lucid moments. Faisal and Katie exchanged greetings with the gentleman before he continued on his walk. A light breeze balanced the warm sun and Faisal felt at peace. He had been feeling horribly guilty at putting his mother in a care home. At the back of his mind, he couldn't help but harbour a niggling thought that he had done it because he didn't want to strain his marriage to Katie with his mother's presence, as he had done with Aliya. But now, for the first time, he knew that he had made the right choice for his mother and not just for himself. 'How was the pickle, Ammi?' he asked.

'Very good. It was a little different to how I make it – Aliya must have changed the recipe slightly. It's pretty close to the original though, and much better than the shop-bought stuff you used to bring before,' she replied, her mind mixing up different timelines.

Faisal and Katie exchanged a smile and gave each other a high five. A couple of weeks earlier, Faisal had realized that they were running out of the mango pickle, but before he was able to go to the Indian grocery store, he noticed that his neighbour had put a box of cooking apples on his front lawn with a sign inviting people to take for free as many as they wanted. There were even more apples littering the grass, fallen from the tree in the middle of the lawn. An idea came to Faisal.

Katie washed the apples and he chopped them into pieces with a stainless-steel cleaver. They patted the pieces dry with kitchen towels and mixed in some salt. In the absence of the hot Indian sun, they used the oven set at forty degrees – they wanted to dry the apples, not cook them. After a couple of days, they ground the various spices in batches – Faisal was relying on his memory and on Google and YouTube for the recipe – in a little Moulinex chopper, heated the oil, and mixed the spices and dried apple pieces. They worked companionably, side by side, their hips occasionally touching. A strand of Katie's golden hair fell over her eyes and she pursed her lips and blew air upwards to try and shift it. Her hands were covered in spicy oil and she certainly could not use them. Faisal reached out and moved her hair out of her eyes and tucked it behind her ear. His fingers caressed her cheek and forehead and he felt that this was one of their most intimate acts, almost on a par with making love. His heart filled with happiness – the stars had aligned again and everything was as perfect as it could be.

He couldn't stop smiling. He had been able to recreate an iconic south Indian relish with English ingredients – replacing green mangoes with cooking apples and tropical sun with an oven, even his wife, dark-haired Aliya, with the blonde Katie as his sous-chef. He was pleased with the way the pickle turned out, but to hear that his mother thought it was close to the original was something else again. Perhaps he could try and do that with some of the other dishes of his childhood too. He knew that regardless of the results, he and Katie would enjoy the process.

Sometime later, they said goodbye and headed back to their car. With her usual perceptiveness, Katie glanced sideways at him and said, 'You seem at peace, darling.'

He thought for a moment and replied, 'You know what, you are right. I am happy.' He put his hand round her waist and pulled her to him. 'You had a lot to do with it, my love. Ammi is in as good a place as she can be. I have you by my side. I feel as if everything that happened, happened for a reason to bring me to this point, so how can I be angry at Aliya and my sons for what they did?'

'There are no villains in your story, Faisal. Just people who changed.'

He looked at her, drinking in her smile and the vivid brightness of her eyes. 'There may be no villains, Katie,' he said. 'But there are angels.'

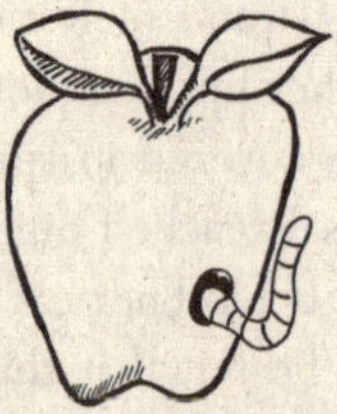

Aavakai Apple Pickle

Sharp green apples – 2 if medium-size (e.g. Granny Smith)
or 1 large (e.g. Braeburn)
2–3 tsp chilli powder, to taste
4 tsp mustard powder
2 tsp salt
1 tsp roasted fenugreek (methi) powder
1 tsp turmeric
½ cup oil
½ tsp asafoetida (hing)
Juice of a lime or lemon (optional)

Method

1. Wash and dry the green apple(s), then chop into small pieces.
2. Add salt and turmeric and mix together well.
3. Ideally, leave the mixture to marinate for an hour or so (this step can be skipped if you are pushed for time).
4. Add the mustard, chilli and fenugreek powders, along with the oil and asafoetida, and mix well.
5. This pickle will be best after at least 8 hours (the minimum resting time is 1 hour), as the flavours will properly seep into the apple pieces.
6. If the apples do not taste tart enough, add a little lime or lemon juice.
7. Serve with steaming hot rice and curd for a satisfying meal. The resulting pickle will taste good, but it won't last more than a week or so as the fruit hasn't been dried. (The traditional aavakai lasts over a year without refrigeration!)

Jackfruit with Tamarind

Mahruba T. Mowtushi and Mafruha Mohua

The tiny mosque at the edge of the backyard in our village in Jamalpur did not have loudspeakers. So the dawn azan floated in softly through open windows, almost like a whisper, calling the villagers who were still in bed to stir themselves out of deep sleep. I was wide awake as I had been waiting for the call to prayer, impatient to start the day and have it done with. I did not, however, get out of bed. I lay there listening to the rustling of mosquito nets being lifted, the shuffling of sleepy feet trying to locate sandals, of splashing water at the deep well at the back of the house and the tube well next to the kitchen, as the ritual wash before prayer was performed. And then the flutter of prayer mats being unfurled. There was a quickness to everyone's movement for there was much work to be done.

As I listened to this hushed ritual, I felt that there was something of a sehri mood to this dawn. Sehri, the meal eaten before sunrise during Ramadan to mark the onset of the day's fast, is a quiet and somewhat sombre affair, especially these days, in our flat in Dhaka.

I say quiet, but of course the sehri watchman would beat a gong and boisterously call out to rouse sleepy city-dwellers. As a young girl, I enjoyed being woken by the watchman's cry, especially because I knew that I would not be getting up for the dawn meal.

A clatter of pots and pans in the kitchen would announce that Amma was stirring dals and curries, while Abba let a pot of milk slowly simmer for the highlight of his meal, dudh-bhat, consisting of hot milk generously poured over a handful of rice and topped with puréed ripe mangoes, jackfruit or bananas.

As part of the ritual around his dudh-bhat consumption, Amma, without fail, would remind him that he had less than a minute to finish his meal. Abba, not fazed by the ticking clock that Amma kept pointing to, would take his time. Right on cue, the watchman would begin his countdown to the dawn azan that culminated with the declaration, 'Sehri time is over!' The voice of the watchman would gradually die down and the clinking from the kitchen subside, as I drifted in and out of sleep. During those dawns I had an overwhelming sense of being cocooned in comfort and safety. The last thing I'd hear would be Amma and Abba settling down for the post-sehri prayer. All was well in this corner of the world.

This particular dawn, I did not feel a sense of comfort; instead, unease hung in the air. The morning prayer was over and the house, bursting with aunts, uncles and cousins, filled with whispers, for none of them wanted to disturb the sleeping children.

All of a sudden, the main doors thunderously swung open and I heard Chotonani's familiar loud voice: 'Do you have a final estimate of the number of people coming today?' For the past few days, we had become used to her abrupt appearances, flinging doors open with the force of a nor'wester wind, and breathlessly hurling a hundred questions at no one in particular.

'Do you have an estimate of how many kilos of onions are required?'

'Is there an estimate of how much rice should be cooked?'

'What about an estimate for the overall cost?'

'During Jahangir's wedding, I made sure that we had estimates for everything!'

And on and on it went. She was not convinced when Amma pointed out, respectfully, lovingly, that there was no need to worry about estimates since the cooks had already provided a detailed list of items and quantities needed. Our youngest great-aunt continued to burst into rooms and fire her questions about estimations at us. She used the English word 'estimate', but pronounced it 'eshtimet', to signify, I suppose, the seriousness of the matter. The younger cousins started calling her 'our eshtimet nani', while the elders grew weary of her theatricality.

As the sun rose and the house filled with light everyone was up and about. Breakfast was being served. But I lay under the mosquito net and wished that the day would continue and conclude without my participation.

Soon the inner courtyard was milling with friends and neighbours who had come to help with the preparations for the day. Mounds of vegetables had to be washed and chopped, and bags full of whole spices, neatly lined up in the veranda, needed to be ground.

It was the day of my nani's chollisha, a memorial service for the departed on the fortieth day after death. We were expecting four to five hundred people to come, pray, converse and feast in memory of the woman who reigned over this household for many decades. I did not feel ready for such a final goodbye.

The sounds coming from the courtyard were numerous and varied. It felt almost festive, and I found it impossible to stay in bed. I got up but, still not wanting to be part of the commotion, opened the door that led to the eastern side of the house and sat on the cold stone steps.

This part was thickly shaded with jackfruit, mango and areca nut trees. To the right stood a cluster of lime and guava trees and to the left the flower garden which had turned into a veritable jungle ever since Parvin aunty had left after her wedding. It was overrun with tangled hibiscus and thorny rose bushes.

The areca nut trees formed a natural fencing around the house, beyond which was a field. There was a time when the field was full of trellises heavy with bitter melon, bottle gourd and snake gourd. Beyond that field was the railway line. When the blue, weather-beaten trains of the Ekata Express and Teesta

Express whooshed by, children ran onto the field, screaming and waving at the commuters who always waved back, sometimes with handkerchiefs or towels. Perhaps Nani wanted to leave the field open for the village children who were thrilled by the novelty of encountering trains from such close proximity. The earth rumbled when the trains passed by, shook the wooden panels and corrugated tin roofs, and sent a tremour right though our bellies.

As a child I spent many languorous hours in that part of our compound with my cousins and Rupban, my grandmother's help, who ushered us into the grown-up world, took us on long walks along the river banks, showed us which trees had the sweetest mangoes, and recounted the juiciest village gossip.

I remember one afternoon many years ago when Rupban plucked a few baby jackfruits, or muchi, while we gathered around her like devoted followers to listen to her explain the mysteries of babies. Unlike the spiky, thick skin of ripe jackfruit, in the muchi-state the fruit has smooth, pale green skin. She carefully washed the fruit and then, sitting down on the low stool, used a long, curved blade attached to a flat base to slice the muchi into matchsticks. Her hands moved deftly as the pieces fell neatly into the bowl placed under the curved blade.

'No, babies do not come out of their mother's belly button.'

'But Anu aunty said . . .' Binu, my cousin, interceded.

She was cut short by Rupban. 'Such silly ideas you have. I must say, you city folks are like farmed chicken: flabby and stupid.'

I looked at my scrawny arms but dared not contradict her. She mixed the sliced muchi with tamarind pulp, crushed green chillies, salt, a sprinkling of sugar and some mustard oil. It was crispy, tangy, salty and hot, but the tears that ran down our cheeks were not entirely from the heat of the chillies. We were scandalized by Rupban's revelation.

I suppose gustatory recollections are a form of autobiography, for the taste of the muchi is forever entwined in my mind with all the details of that afternoon. Of that particular expression on Rupban's face, a combination of disdain and amusement. Of Parvin aunty giving us a curious look when she saw us huddled and teary-eyed but, seeing the quantity of chillies in our little bowls, smiling, and slipping back into the house. For us, Rupban symbolized the fun and adventure of those hot summer holidays.

Like many of my fellow Bangladeshis I have a tendency to associate pungent, spicy fruit preparation with after-school snacking, that twenty to thirty minutes of freedom when we were released from school and waited for our parents to pick us up. We would rush out of the school gates and gather around the fruit vendors selling green mango bhorta, a concoction of thinly sliced mangoes mixed with chillies, mustard oil and salt, or a similar concoction of boroi or jujube bhorta. My favourite was ripe kodbel or wood-apple mixed with black salt, chilli powder and kashundi, a sauce that is a cross between a chutney and a pickle, made of green mangoes, mustard, chillies and ginger. There would also be vendors selling hog plums, sliced open like a flower, sprinkled with salt and chilli powder and mounted on a stick, like a lollipop. The ice-cream wallahs would be there as well, but I do not think they were as popular as the fruit wallahs.

I was beginning to feel hungry but didn't think there was much prospect of breakfast at such a late hour. Yet soon Paru aunty came up with a plate of many-hued Elokeshi pitha and a mug of sweet black tea. I gave her a grateful look. How quickly she was filling up the space left by Nani's departure.

What a treat to have these rice cakes, which have the most poetic of names: Elokeshi, a woman with untied, tousled hair. It brings to mind an image of a girl, standing on the banks of a river, her long thick hair tangled in the wind.

I also can't help remembering the story of Elokeshi of Tarakeswar in West Bengal. In 1873, the sixteen-year-old Elokeshi, from a genteel Brahmin family, was murdered by her husband for being seduced by an elderly mohant, the head priest. The story goes that Elokeshi went to the temple to seek pregnancy-related advice; it was here the mohant raped her. The tragic affair became the subject of numerous popular theatrical productions, Kalighat paintings and Battala woodcuts. People revelled at the salacious and violent nature of the case that blatantly castigated Elokeshi, the supposed goddess of the home, as a transgressor of respectable, wifely duties.

Although the name Elokeshi evokes a sense of wild sensuality, the pitha is rather dainty, crispy and light as air. Agrahon, the eighth month of the Bengali calendar, marks the Nabanno or autumn harvest celebration. Nabanno means 'new food' and pithas – cakes and dumplings made with newly harvested rice – are the most important part of the Nabanno festival.

Pithas are usually filled with jaggery or date molasses and grated coconut. Some are made with ripe palmyra palm, some have intricate floral designs etched on them, some are steamed, some deep-fried, some wrapped in banana leaf and roasted in open fires, others are soaked in cream or simmered in milk. The variety is stunning.

To make pithas, new rice is pound to a fine grain in the traditional wooden dheki, a contraption fast disappearing even in the most rural parts of Bangladesh where machine-operated mills have surfaced to economize on time and cost. After the rice was ground, children were allowed to play on the dheki as the women sifted the ground rice to yield a fine powder. We would emerge from the kitchen covered in a dusty layer of rice powder.

Most pithas are made from rice flour, but some, such as khaja, are made with wheat flour. For this snack, the batter consists of the flour with water and a little oil, while sometimes milk solids are added. The thick batter is formed into cylindrical shapes and deep fried in oil. The hot khajas are then dunked in sugar syrup.

There is a reference to khajas in one of the Jataka stories, where Buddha's disciple Sariputta alludes to his partiality for this sweet pitha. In the Jataka story it is called pitthakhajjaka, but in today's Bengal the name has been shortened to khaja. An exquisite variety of ceremonial and festive pithas appear in the twelfth-century Sanskrit poem *Naishadha Charita*. Later, the fifteenth-century Bengali texts, *Chaitanya Charitamrita* and *Chandimangal*, would recount one of the earliest cases of the art of pitha-making.

During the Pitha Festival, stalls appear all over Dhaka – in supermarkets, at street sides, on university campuses, selling pithas from various regions of the country. During this season, each house in the village becomes a pitha-making factory!

In Bangladesh our lives are structured by three calendars. The Gregorian calendar signifies our official time (office time, school time, election time), the Bengali calendar marks our folk rituals, and the Arabic calendar organizes our religious festivals.

Each festival is marked by distinctive foods. If pitha-making is the main ritual of the eighth month of the Bengali calendar, then halwa-making is the definitive culinary activity on the fifteenth day of Sha'ban, the eighth month of the Arabic calendar.

The night of the fifteenth of Sha'ban is known as Shab-e-Barat, the Night of Forgiveness. Devout Muslims stay up all night praying for forgiveness. But before the night of prayer begins, there is a period of feasting. My memories of Shab-e-Barat are tied to Dhaka, where the old bakeries would be busy making their special fish-shaped breads with jewelled eyes!

Carrot halwa, walnut halwa, semolina halwa, chickpea halwa and a myriad of other sweet dishes would be made with the same degree of fervour with which prayers are observed. The heady aromas of cinnamon, cardamom, cloves, ghee, saffron and burning incense hung in the air. Just before evening set in, trays filled with halwas cut into rhombus shapes would arrive from neighbours and Amma would be busy filling up trays with our own halwas, covered with delicate muslin cloths, to take to neighbours in our turn.

On Shab-e-Barat, Amma also prepared duck bhuna, a dish that is heavily spiced with a thick sauce that clings to the meat. This dish would be served with rice-flour rotis, paper thin, perfectly round and almost translucent. More than anything else, the delicate rotis symbolized for me the sacredness of the night. Luckily, the day after Shab-e-Barat is a national holiday, for who can go to work after such feasting and praying?

The last dish Nani had cooked for us was on a Shab-e-Barat. She had come to Dhaka to spend some time with us and although her health was failing, she insisted on cooking at least one dish. She prepared kaon chaler kheer, a dessert similar to rice pudding, made with foxtail millet, milk, date molasses, bay leaves and cinnamon. Often slivers of almond are sprinkled on top.

I could have sat on those cold steps, shaded by jackfruit trees, for hours, recollecting all the dishes that Nani had prepared for us over the years. Feeding her large brood of grandchildren during the holidays, when we would all be crammed into the house, fighting over the best morsels, the most comfortable bed and the softest pillows, was the joy of her life. But it was time to join the throng.

The courtyard felt like a large, open-air kitchen. There were huge bowls of chopped bottle gourds, potatoes, pumpkin, aubergine and okra. A vegetable curry was one of the dishes to be served that day.

Over a huge, makeshift stove a man was dry roasting an unimaginable quantity of mashkalai dal. It took me many years to adjust my palate to the taste of mashkalai with its distinctive earthy undertones and mucilaginous texture.

My first memory of this dal is supremely unpleasant. It all began with a death in the family. We had just returned to Bangladesh after a few years in Algeria, our palates slightly altered by Maghrebi flavours. Amma's uncle from Shyampur had passed away, and the news reached us in the evening. We travelled in haste by the night train to attend the funeral.

It was well past midnight when we arrived at Jamalpur station. I was hungry and cold, but the greyish concoction from which peeked bits and bobs of stewed garlic and chilli looked less than enticing. The moment my fingers made their first contact with the dal's cold and slippery viscosity I recoiled.

Having thus equated this dish with the sordid business of death in the family, mashkalai and I kept a safe distance from each other for many years.

In the courtyard children were laughing and shouting, examining the pots which were so large that a child could easily fit into one. They declared that such a pot would be an excellent hiding place.

A long table was placed on the veranda with platters full of betel leaf, areca nuts, slaked lime, chewing tobacco and khair, a thick, chocolate-coloured paste made from boiling heartwood chips of acacia tree with water. It has an astringent taste and is a favourite condiment for paan, though the end result is horribly stained teeth.

Everyone was free to have as many paans as they wanted. Anu aunty stationed herself next to the table and was busy chatting and handing out paans to all and sundry. She first folded the heart-shaped leaf lengthwise and then rolled it into a funnel, smeared the inside of the funnel with a little slaked lime and khair, then added sliced areca nuts and tiny pieces of moist and slightly sweet tobacco leaves. She is an expert at making betel leaf parcels.

In the far corner of the courtyard, preparations were underway for the main dish, beef pithali. A cow had been slaughtered early that morning in a field nearby. Mounds of meat were cut into large chunks.

Standing next to the head cook, who was supervising the meat preparation, was Zafar uncle, engaged in what looked like a serious conversation. Whenever cooks are brought over for large family events, be it an engagement party, a naming ceremony for newborns, or a wedding ceremony, Zafar uncle would be seen amongst them, asking innumerable questions and sometimes stirring the large cauldrons of food.

Many of the men in my immediate and extended family are keen cooks, but for Zafar uncle it was almost an obsession. His obsession started soon after his wedding, when to their disbelief everyone discovered that Zafar uncle's new bride could not stomach the smell or taste of fish. The mere sight of fish was enough to make her violently ill. Everyone was shocked, for who has heard of a Bengali who cannot tolerate fish?

Within a few days the story of the bride who did not eat fish spread through the village and throngs of people came to catch a glimpse of this strange woman. The new bride only smiled politely as others questioned her odd dietary ways. 'So you eat meat only?' 'Can you eat vegetables?' 'Do you drink tea?' 'And what about dal, does that make you ill?' 'I suppose you cannot stand dried fish either?'

Zafar uncle was not disconcerted by this discovery. First he took over the responsibility of cooking fish, but very soon his wife became a secondary presence in the kitchen. His fish curries were heavenly, though I am partial to Amma's macher jhol, especially when prepared with winter vegetables.

Amma is fussy when it comes to preparing a fish. It has to be cleaned numerous times to get rid of the sliminess. She then smears the pieces with turmeric and salt and lightly fries them – for a minute or two – in mustard oil. Amma has a fervid dislike of people who skip this process. Macher jhol should have a light, refreshing taste and so spices are added sparingly. Amma always complained of Manwara aunty's macher jhol, which contained such inordinate quantities of vegetables and an odd assortment of greens that eating it was like walking through a virgin jungle with a machete in hand!

But for my aunt food was preventive medicine. She judged her curries by the quantities of vitamins: zinc and potassium and other such healthy minerals. She spent hours consulting little booklets on medicinal plants, herbs and roots, and subjected her children to all forms of homemade concoctions.

In this healthy-living venture, my aunt's only supporter was my father, whose knowledge of and enthusiasm for such roots and herbs matched hers. At one point, my father even suggested that Amma might want to emulate her sister's cooking. In response he received from Amma one of her signature looks, a single raised eyebrow, very much like Madhubala in the classic Bollywood blockbuster *Mughal-e-Azam*. But while Madhubala's arched look signified seductiveness, Amma's raised eyebrow denoted pure fury.

When we returned from our stay in Manila, we spent two weeks at Manwara aunty's place in Narayanganj before moving into our flat in north Dhaka. By the end of the first week, I was tired of her high-vitamin curries and was thoroughly reprimanded by Amma for 'approaching the dinner table like a prisoner approaching the gallows.'

I never knew that mealtimes could herald such dread. I yearned for Amma's bottle gourd with shrimp, fried cauliflowers with panch phoron, the five-spice mix essential to Bengali cooking, potatoes with bitter gourd and murgir jhol, chicken curry with cubes of potatoes in a thin gravy. It was the ilish season but even the ilish dishes looked like vegetable allotments. We were all delighted when Parvin aunty came for a short visit and took over the kitchen. I still remember the ilish pulao she cooked for us.

Like most Bengalis, I too am a little obsessed with this fish. Although ilish can be found all year round in the Bay of Bengal, it is only when this relative of the herring leaves the sea and swims upriver to lay eggs that it becomes attractive to the Bengali palate. The longer the fish stays in the river the more it loses the saltiness and some of its oiliness. So the fisherman patiently waits for it upriver, far away from the mouth of the delta. A general excitement is felt when the first ilish arrives in the market, and ilish prices make national headlines. I could not believe the treatment that was meted out to this jewel of the river in Manwara aunty's kitchen.

For the ilish pulao, fragrant rice is mandatory. This dish is perhaps the best example of a Bengali-inspired Mughlai dish. It combines the use of yoghurt and warm spices like cinnamon, cardamom and cloves with the Bengali obsession with fish.

Parvin aunty was our in-house Mughlai chef. After her marriage she surprised everyone by enrolling in cooking classes specializing in Mughal cuisine and became an expert on biryanis, pulaos, kebabs, qormas, rezalas and various kinds of parathas.

Although these dishes are enjoyed by all, they do not reflect the soul of Bangladeshi cuisine. More often than not, rather than having a rezala we would have a bhuna, of which there are many variants. In Sylhet, this meat dish is prepared with shatkora, a citrus fruit that is used mainly for its thick but wonderfully scented rind. In Khulna, beef bhuna is made with chui jhal, the stem of the long pepper plant. Then there is the famous mezbani beef of Chittagong which, along with the usual spices, includes a paste made with poppy seeds, mustard, nuts and copious amounts of chillies. The dishes of this part of Bangladesh are known to be fiery. In Jamalpur and Mymensingh, pithali is the meat dish of choice for family feasts.

However, during Eid celebrations our village home seemed to me to resemble a Mughal court. The scent of qorma, kofta curry, pulao, vermicelli pudding and carrot payesh wafted through the courtyard. Before lunch my cousins and I, along with all the other children, would parade around in our new clothes. For a few hours the village turned into a fashion show. Each household that we passed would invite us in and offer us rice phirni and other sweet dishes in dainty, porcelain bowls.

The cooks in the courtyard were now preparing to make the pithali. One of those large pots that the children wanted to requisition for their games was filled with chunks of meat. The head cook with furrowed brow proceeded to add handfuls of turmeric, dried chillies and pastes of coriander, cumin, fennel and black pepper. The women of the village spent many hours preparing the spices because, unlike in cities, village cooks are not fond of packaged spice powders. Whole spices were freshly ground with a little water to create wet pastes.

The cook also threw in ginger–garlic paste, sliced onion, salt and oil, and proceeded to mix everything well. 'The mixing should be done with care and patience,' he explained to Zafar uncle, 'so that each piece of meat is well covered.' He then added some water and with the help of two other cooks placed the pan on one of the makeshift stoves which were lit with bundles of dried jute stalks. The burning stalks would add a wonderful smokiness to the dish.

After fifteen minutes the heat was lowered and the meat was simmered for two hours. At this point the cook added the ingredient which gives this dish its name. Finely ground rice was mixed with water to create a very light batter, or pithali as it is called. This pithali of fragrant rice not only thickens the gravy but also adds a distinctive taste to this curry. The pithali must be added slowly and as it is poured in, the curry is stirred continuously to prevent the batter from clumping. Once the pithali is thoroughly mixed, handfuls of whole green chillies are added. The meat is cooked for a further twenty minutes over a low heat.

Meanwhile, in another pan of hot oil, the cook threw in whole cumin, cinnamon and bay leaves, followed by sliced onion and garlic. Once the garlic and onion turned a deep golden colour, the tempered oil, along with the fried onion, garlic and whole spices, was poured into the meat pot.

Amid all this cooking, friends and family shared news and gossip, groups of great-aunts and aunts recounted memorable events of Nani's life, her wedding day, the day she stumbled upon her married brother-in-law with his arms around the wife of his cousin, and the day that the Pakistani army came all the way to her courtyard.

As if these stories were not commotion enough, BBC radio was blaring away in the background. Chotonana, Amma's youngest uncle, made it a point to punctuate his day with commentary on world affairs from Reuters, Voice of America and, of course, the BBC. According to Chotonani's estimation, this was a sign of his high intelligence and fine education. The volume was always turned up so that everyone could hear it and perhaps attain that elusive level of intelligence. Most of us only got bad headaches.

Yet there was one aspect of Chotonana that his wife Chotonani disliked vehemently. It was his habit of smoking the handheld hookah. It was not the smoking of hookah that she frowned upon, but that particular kind of hookah which was used by field workers and labourers. Chotonani felt that this lowered the status of our family, but after years of fruitless persuasion she came to accept this as another one of her husband's foibles.

It was not only Chotonani who disapproved of this habit. Chotonana's elder brother, Boronana as we called him, would often be heard castigating his younger brother for being stubborn and uncouth. As if to set an example, Boronana spent his afternoons smoking from an elegant brass hookah, with its long, slender tube, while reclining on an easy chair in his well-maintained garden. As Nani would often say, this was not casual smoking but a calculated performance staged to impress us all.

He would be joined by his youngest daughter, Reba aunty, who would sit next to her father, her long hair arranged just so over her shoulder, reading the latest novel by Humayun Ahmed, Bangladesh's most popular author. As much as I was impressed with Boronana's graceful performance, my secret desire was to try out Chotonana's handheld hookah, made with coconut shell. He looked far more relaxed and happier than Boronana did, puffing away at his hookah in his immaculate garden.

The sun had passed its highest point, the Zuhr prayer was over. Our backyard was full of people sitting down in rows on bamboo mats with squares of bright green banana leaves in front of them, since the chollisha meal is served on banana leaves.

The village youths volunteered to serve the food, while the elders looked on, pointing to the man in the second row who needed more dal, or the little girl in the far corner who had no meat on her banana leaf. The guests were fed in several batches.

Our feasting continued well after Asr prayers. The mashkalai dal tempered with mustard oil, chopped ginger and whole fennel, although not as good as Nani's dal – the aroma of which had something of the earth in it – was greatly appreciated. But it was the beef pithali which garnered the greatest praise.

As we all tucked into our steamy rice covered with rich, piquant pithali, I was struck by how the chollisha preparation is a poignant celebration of communal harmony. The congregation of relatives distant and near, of friends and neighbours, did not denote a farewell ceremony but rather a cementing of Nani's presence within the very foundation of the house.

That night there was a soothing calmness in the house, and even Chotonani was quietly contemplative as she chewed her paan. I sat next to her and asked, 'Nani, what is your estimation of this day?'

'A grand affair worthy of her.'

I knew then that although Nani would be much missed, I would always keep returning to this old, crumbling house and to our natal village on the banks of the Brahmaputra.

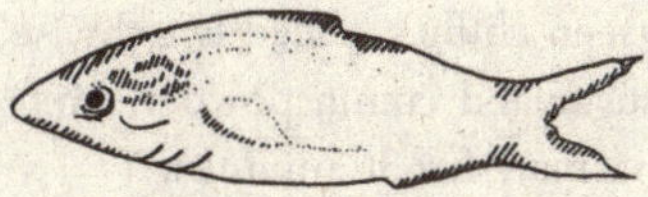

Ilish Pulao

For the ilish

6 medium pieces of ilish (or salmon if you can't get ilish, though it won't be the same)
½ cup yoghurt
½ cup crispy fried onion (baresta)
1 tsp green chilli paste
1 tsp garlic paste
1 tsp cumin powder
4–5 green chillies
salt to taste
½ tsp sugar
4 tbsp vegetable oil

For the Pulao

2 cups aromatic rice, pre-soaked
8–10 black peppercorns
4–5 cloves
4-inch piece of cinnamon
3–4 cardamoms
2 bay leaves
½ cup sliced onion
1 tsp ginger paste
1 tsp garlic paste
Salt to taste
4–5 green chillies
5 tbsp cooking oil

Method

1. In a mixing bowl add yoghurt, crush the crispy baresta into it. Add the green chillies, sliced lengthwise, along with garlic paste, salt, sugar and cumin powder. Mix well. Add the fish pieces and marinate for 30 minutes.
2. In the meantime, wash the rice and let it soak for at least 30 minutes, before straining.
3. In a saucepan, heat 4 tablespoons of oil. Remove the fish from the marinade and put the marinade mix into the hot oil. Wipe down the marinade bowl with a little water so as not waste any of the marinade mixture. Cook the mixture, on a medium heat, for a few minutes, then add the green chilli paste and continue to cook for a few more minutes, stirring continuously to prevent the mixture from burning.
4. Add the fish and reduce the flame to low. If the mixture feels too dry you can add a little bit of water. After 3 minutes, carefully turn the fish pieces over and cook them on the other side for a few more minutes. Remove from heat and keep them aside.
5. In another pan, warm 5 tablespoons of oil, and add the whole spices (cloves, peppercorn, cinnamon, cardamom and bay leaves). Add sliced onion and fry until lightly browned.

6. Add the drained, soaked rice and sauté it, stirring continuously until the rice is well roasted, about 4 minutes.
7. At this point add ginger and garlic paste and stir for another 2 minutes. Then add 4 cups of warm water. Alternatively, you can add one cup of coconut milk and 3 cups of water. Cook the rice, covered, until most of the liquid evaporates.
8. Gently place the fish pieces on top of the rice, pressing the pieces down gently, and pour the gravy over the fish. Add a few whole green chillies, cover and cook on a very low heat for 20–25 minutes.

Hungry Eyes

Sophia Khan

The Poetess and her son live on the border of the vast refugee camp that lies between Us and Them. Sometimes when the wind is right – or rather, wrong – they can smell its foetid stench. The Poetess rolls shut the windows and lights incense made in France. The boy hides beneath his bed until his airways are cleared of all but heliotrope and myrrh. The wall is high and topped with glass but the line it draws is thin. Some days there is perilously little separating Us and Them.

They got out early – early enough to have segued seamlessly into Us but, as the Poetess keeps reminding her reluctant son, they are in fact part of the great human tide, the teeming masses. It is something she will allow no one to forget. Her poetry has won prizes now. She spoke at the UN. She cannot abandon the fount from which her inspiration draws. She tosses and turns between her satin sheets, the haunted eyes of an eight-year-old orphan burning through the air conditioning. *Eyes burned dry by suffering*, she scribbles in the notebook on her nightstand, *grey eyes stark as ash*.

On Saturday, as she often does, she rouses her son early. They volunteer in the camp several days each month. *They are you and you are they*, she tells him, though he dreams now in a foreign language: neither that of their conquerors nor of their homeland. She reads him the poetry of exile – albeit in translation because she doesn't speak their native tongue well enough for verse. Like most of the elite, her education was the product of colonial leavings and she never truly mastered her own language. When she spoke it in her mountain convent, nuns rapped her knuckles and it wasn't long before her mother tongue was another tongue. The boy listens to her politely as pixellated soldiers slaughter zombies behind the blank screen of his eyes.

The Poetess and her son have a secret. They are not there just to distribute blankets, to feed the hungry, to stroke the ravaged hands of those who clawed their way to freedom, those who hadn't the contacts to secure passage out on one of the last flights. They are not there to teach her son history. They are not there to reap imagery for her poems ('Excruciatingly transcendent,' raves the *New York Times*). They are there, sifting eternally through the human refuse of imperial aspiration, in search of the boy's father. They left him, and she cannot forgive herself.

She never really loved him. The marriage was not her choice. She was young and beautiful; he, older and unrefined. She was vibrant, brilliant. He, immensely wealthy, too wealthy to decline. He mocked her literary aspirations mercilessly. She looked down on him. In their native land she was renowned as the poet of the people. He was a landowner whose whims could change ten thousand lives. Of the people, he had nothing kind to say. *They're all bastards*, he used to tell her. *There's no poetry in poverty. Your adoring acolytes are nothing more than pretty toys. They grow fat and corrupted and you say their artistry has evaporated as you discard them for the next lithe young thing you want to fuck.*

He disgusted her. He was a boor. In bed, she could not get enough. He was her connection to the people, whose voice she was although she barely spoke their tongue. Secretly, he idolized her: his young and charming wife. He called her his tiny dumpling. He did his best to understand her life. He grasped very little of what she wrote except that it was good. She imagines him crying out for her as he dies. She prays that he is alive. For years, she hunts amongst the refugees. Perhaps some part of her loves him, after all.

Mama, says her son, tugging on her scarf. He points to a man younger than his father ever was, a man with a heroic moustache and a defeated stance.

No, she whispers, shaking her head. The boy is uncharacteristically shy here amongst the refugees. He clings like a limpet and either cannot or will not speak the language in which he was raised. When other children show interest in him, he pulls away. She sends him to give an old man a packet of the sandwiches they make together on Friday nights. He looks back at her dolefully as he goes. His accusing gaze burns into her, but then so do many other pairs of eyes. She is a striking figure anywhere and she stands out particularly here, among the many shades of grey. The Poetess has adopted native dress following her flight to the foreign land. Before, her wardrobe consisted of garments with the names of Italian men sewn into the labels. Now, she wears bright, flowing scarves and armfuls of prettily tinkling bangles. She is a sight to behold on television. Though she rarely picks up her son any more, sometimes he still runs to her for comfort and his weight shatters her bracelets, leaving little nicks along his thighs.

She turns her attention to the young man with the heroic moustache who, she's been told, writes sonnets. She's curating an anthology of the dispossessed, which, along with all her other acts of nobility, will one day win her the storied Swedish Prize. By the time she's coaxed the man's battered journal away from him, her son is gone. He's not with the old man. He's not kicking around the deflated football with the other boys. He's not splashing by the pump.

The Poetess barrels through the crowd, blind with panic. She's heard terrible stories, stories of organ theft, human trafficking, rape. But they know her here. They love her. She'd thought her son would be safe at her side. The problem is, he left it. The old man, whose eye sockets proved to be empty, patted the boy's face with a disconcerting intimacy, implored him in the name of a god who surely could not exist. The boy ran. He had to get away.

But at the Border of Us and Them, he is just a boy. No one believes he is the Poetess's son. The Poetess's son never leaves her side. They all know that. *I live here*, he tells the soldiers, fluent in their tongue. So too are many refugees. He shows them his video game, the latest model. So too have many of the refugees. He names his school, the local library, his favourite bakery. The refugees once had the internet. They too could know these things. They send him to the infirmary, where a brusque nurse shaves his head though he protests he hasn't got lice. She doses him with worm medication and roughly gives him some injection he's no doubt already had. *Ungrateful wretch*, she hisses when he bites her, flinging him back out into the dust.

He finds himself in line, a battered tin plate hot in his hand. Tears stain his cheeks but he's run out of energy to cry. *Lost your parents?* asks a boy about his size who has somehow retained his head of curls. He nods. *Me too.*

They ladle mush onto his plate and he thinks of the sandwiches he and his mother made last night. Just egg, but no wonder the refugees clamour for them. He chokes down a mouthful, then another. Silent tears run down his face.

When he looks up again, the sunlight blinds him. Before him is a vision. An angel in an emerald scarf swoops down from heaven to embrace the little boy who spoke to him in line. Her bangles clink. Her joyful tears salt his plate of toppled mush. Her slim fingers are so soothing in his curls. The boy closes his eyes and breathes in her perfume. *Mother*. His back is to her and for one endless, impossible moment, he forgets the twisted corpses he saw beneath the rubble.

Then: he's wrested away, flung to the ground. He reaches out to grasp salvation and gets only a scarf.

How could you think he was me? the little bald boy howls. *How could you? How could you?* She cannot quite name the emotion in his eyes but it is notably grown-up. Later, she thinks perhaps she saw a glint of hatred.

It takes months for his hair to grow out. When it does, his cherubic curls are gone. He has a leading man's raven waves, which he demands to have cut in the barbershop into which she cannot go. He comes out redolent of Brylcreem and adulthood. He never again runs to her to be picked up.

Years pass. The Poetess wins grants, titles, prizes and honorary degrees. She appears often on television, exhorting the world to help the people for whom she speaks. She likes to tell the story of how she helped her maid get a hysterectomy after her fifth child. Charity begins at home. She does not tell them how the maid protested that bearing children was easy for her and she loved each baby more. She tells them only how she prevailed: made the illiterate woman See Sense, Hear Reason and Accept Responsibility. The applause is thunderous when she speaks. The audience shed tears. The Poetess gets a facelift and looks too young to be mother to her son.

The boy grows and grows. Fed on foreign foods, he grows to tower over his slight mother. The smell of spices nauseates him. He will not eat with his hands. All he remembers of Before is the blast.

It happened on a Wednesday, which was the best day, chicken sandwich day at the elite academy where he first began the unknowing of his native tongue. There had been unrest in their city, though he hardly knew it then. He knew only that it was February and it grew dark early, and in those precious few hours of daylight he was kept indoors. He did not know that tensions had been mounting, that his parents had already booked passage to the foreign land. He knew his grandparents had gone, half his friends had gone, there was a substitute teacher at the school. He was dimly aware that his parents argued when they believed him to be asleep, his mother begging his father to leave.

Not yet, not yet, he remembers the refrain. *Too much to do here.*

And then the house in flames. Rubble in the streets. *It was targeted. You must go.* Speeding to the airport, still in his school uniform. *Where is Papa? Where is Papa? When will Papa come?*

They never found a body. Shortly after, the silent war washed over their streets. The combatants who until then had fought Somewhere Else were suddenly ransacking the zoo. He heard they ate the elephant. On his fifth birthday he'd ridden Queenie up and down the monkey avenue. They burn and loot, blow up the backdrop of his childhood. The television shows a country wracked by war. One of *those* countries. His mother is quick to shut it off. *That is not your home*, she tells him. *Your home is here*, she taps his temple. But it isn't. His home is the land where he is growing up.

The truth is, the Poetess cannot reconcile the images that flash across the screen with her own history. True, she lived in a violent land fraught with violent happenings but the madness had always been Over There: a friend's gangster of a husband kidnapped, a former schoolmate murdered for belonging to a minority they'd barely acknowledged when they were young. They hadn't thought it could happen to them, they with their organic tomatoes and spanking new iPhones. They posted on Instagram. They'd attended Coachella. They could not be refugees of war. But they are. The camp is full of people who were once like them, children her son might have known at school. After the day she almost lost him, he becomes aware that the only thing which separates him from the ragged creatures with hungry eyes is luck. The fragility of his existence frightens him, and as he grows older, he grows better at finding reasons not to face it.

We cannot forget who we are, she tells him, realizing he never knew. He was too young for personhood when they left their native land. With a sigh, she lets him skip one weekend, then another. There is always a birthday party, a track meet, a school activity. It is why they are here, isn't it? So he can have a better life. If she insists, he still helps her with the sandwiches, but she suspects he purposely misaligns the bread. She goes alone to the camp, smiling bravely through her tears. Sometimes, news crews follow her. Orphans hug her. Widows clutch her as they weep. She keeps a delousing comb behind her bathroom mirror and, despite the warnings, sprays herself liberally with Deet. On camera, she is always perfectly composed.

When will their suffering end? she rages, one perfect tear running down her cheek. Her mascara is waterproof.

Your mother is a saint, says her son's friend admiringly, pausing the image on the screen. They can do this now: pause things on live TV. The boy makes a noncommittal sound. He knows his friends have crushes on his mother. She is so very exotic beside their own loafen progenitors. He wishes for a mother who could bake.

She's looking for my father, he says, letting spill the secret they've always kept. *She thinks maybe he's lost his memory*. As he says it, he wonders why they've been so reluctant to admit this to others. His friend, if anything, only admires the Poetess more following this revelation.

When he gets home, he asks his mother if she really believes amnesia exists other than as a plot device for bad TV. She is stung more by the cruelty of his tone than by the question. She sees the man she thought she'd left behind is here. He's taken a new form. When she goes through the family album, she sees the future for her son and hopes his hairline holds up better.

The Poetess has been going alone to the camp for years now. Her son has entered secondary school and he sees no point to sandwiches that are not for him. He's old enough to be some protection, but she's never needed that. The people worship her. She is everybody's friend. *Someone's looking for you*, the whisper goes up. She wonders who it is. Could it be her husband, returned to her from the dead? She could use his help now that their boy is hatching oh so painfully into a man. She goes to the camp daily hoping that it is.

But it is not. It is her maid from Before, the one whom she took to get a hysterectomy. A decade of war has turned her into a crone. A decade of peace and plastic surgery has kept the mistress young. They were the same age once, but now they are centuries apart.

Where are your girls? asks the Poetess, embracing her. The woman is a board between her arms.

Dead. They are all dead. Her voice is flat.

And we cannot have another.

The husband steps out of the shadows then. She had not seen him lurking in the dark. She'd met him only once and all she knew about him was that he loved his wife.

What he does next to the Poetess he does not do out of lust or passion. He does it because, in their country, it is the worst way to punish a woman, worse even than death.

She never speaks of it, not even in a poem.

The Poetess adopts a new look. She casts aside her bright cottons for fine neutrals in unbleached textiles woven by indigenous peoples in far-off lands. She lops off her hair and allows it to fade tastefully to silver. For jewellery, her rule is diamonds; under a carat and over an IF. Her work takes a turn to the experimental: words strewn over the page like confetti, making no overt effort at form or meaning. It doesn't matter. She is famous enough by then that academics imbue every syllable with significance. One Professor, a starchy sexagenarian loafen as the parents of the boy's dreams, asks her out after a reading. She accepts. *I thought amnesia was a literary construct?* she says, when her son protests.

Some might say the Professor is too old for her. Some might say he is not accomplished enough. At the end of the day, though, he is one of Us. The Poetess and her son receive passports of a pleasing hue. They leave their airy apartment for a well-appointed bungalow on the outskirts of a new town. There are no refugees there. Even the gardener was born on the soil in which he toils. When her son asks her if the distance is the reason she no longer visits the camp she sniffs. *Some people revel in depravity. They do not wish to better themselves.*

He doesn't really care.

Until: two teenage heads, curls damp and puppyish with sweat, hunch over a screen.

No, he says, *it's bad. It's wrong. It's not for me.*

But he cannot tear himself away.

She is twelve, maybe thirteen, and her eyes, they are so green. She is not wearing much – an emerald scarf – and her gaze begs him to save her. To rape her. He slams shut the screen.

The next day he comes back, the day following that. *You can have her for ten thousand*. He decides he will raise the cash to save her.

He cannot bring himself to ask the Poetess. It's his turn to be the saviour. He boils up a batch of eggs, sandwiches being the only avenue he knows of to salvation. But the refugees are resourceful now. They no longer trade in snacks. Soon, he's conveying tape-trussed packets back and forth across the border. The Poetess tails him to a part of town where the Professor has told her she mustn't go alone. She watches him exchange a stack of cash for some unmarked envelopes and decides she doesn't want to know. The blurry photo in his wallet is something she's still trying to unsee. A mother's love may not know bounds but she won't risk it by crossing borders.

Saturdays she sometimes helps him, shelling eggs over the sink. When he notices her noticing him slipping glassine envelopes beneath the bread, he snatches back her spatula and asks her why she's there. *I thought some people revel in depravity?* A year ago, she might've followed up with, *Do you?* Instead, she retreats to her writing room and tries to come up with something new.

Months pass. The boy turns down more girls than he can count. Some are pretty. Some are scarred. Some are so young they do not know to be relieved when all he does is offer sweets. The men, they laugh and laugh. He thumbs the fraying paper in his pocket and saves every cent he makes. He has the cash and then he asks, *Tell me, do you know?*

They're ebullient with understanding then. In a week he goes from a bore with a bleeding heart to a bad boy down for action. In a week he has an address. He makes his way down an unlit alleyway, a dirt ditch full of shit. He crawls over the rooftops thinking, *Right now, here now, this is it*. He's higher than he's ever been, his pockets full of sweets. With his freshly shaven upper lip he's any refugee's wet dream.

He falls down through the awnings. He falls down to the floor. As his mother used to warn him, this is not a place he knows. He's filthy as he's ever been, filthier than he was the last time the line blurred. Undeterred, he hurries on.

Stop, cries a voice he can't quite place. *Stop*, cries a man who is used to issuing orders, who has ordered him around before. He stops.

You boy, you come here, and because something impels him, he goes.

The man who's summoned him is a beggar. The man who's summoned him is much too decrepit to be anyone he knows. And yet, there's something so compelling about his gravelly baritone. The boy falls to his knees before him. He cups his bristly chin. His fingers trace the ravaged face. The effects of the gases are something everybody knows. He feels the old man's furrowed brow. He feels his pitted cheeks. He feels the empty eye sockets that are so common now. Feeling him, he runs and runs as though he could un-know.

He doesn't tell the Poetess. He keeps it to himself for a month, more. Then one day: *It's Le Creuset, that's not yours to take*. His pretty sandwiches stuffed slapdash into sacks.

Furious, he tells her what he's seen. His mother is not interested. The Poetess isn't buying it.

He takes her to the alleyway. He takes her beyond the crowds. He takes her to the huddled beggar who, for one confused, hopeful minute looks up at her blindly and asks, *My dumpling, is it you?*

For a moment she is still, paused as though by TV remote. Then her pretty nose wrinkles with disgust. *How could you?* she asks, turning to her son. *How could you! How could you imagine he is anything like Us?*

Egg, Aubergine and Tomato Curry

2–3 small aubergines
6 eggs (to be soft-boiled)
1 onion, minced
4 cloves garlic
2 tbsp olive oil
½ tbsp harissa
2 tbsp tomato paste
½–1 tsp ground cumin
8–10 medium tomatoes, diced
1 large capsicum or red pepper, diced
¼ cup chopped parsley or coriander (or both)
⅓ cup crumbled feta cheese
Salt and pepper to taste

Method

1. Cube the aubergines and soak in salt water to remove any bitterness. Dry them on a tea towel, then toss with 2 tbsp olive oil and salt and pepper to taste. Roast at 430°F/220°C until crispy and golden brown and set aside.
2. While you are waiting for the aubergine to roast, boil your eggs for 6 minutes on a rolling boil. Set aside.
3. Sauté the onion in olive oil until translucent. Add the garlic.
4. When fragrant (1–2 minutes), add the harissa, tomato paste and cumin.

5. Stir and add the tomatoes and capsicum.
6. Cook over a low heat, stirring occasionally until all the ingredients meld together (about 20 minutes). Stir in the roasted aubergine.
7. Cook for an additional 1–2 minutes.
8. Halve the soft-boiled eggs and nestle them gently in the tomato sauce and simmer briefly to warm.
9. Remove the pan from the heat.
10. Sprinkle with the chopped herbs and crumbled feta cheese. Serve with naan.

Afterword: Dessert

Siobhan Lambert-Hurley

It is September 2019, and I find myself sitting before a semicircle of immaculately groomed schoolgirls in an airy classroom in Lahore. The small private school caters to girls from poorer urban districts who have lost their parents, often in traumatic circumstances. Some of them appear shy before their visitors, a rather motley assortment of researchers from the UK and a local university. Others are outspoken and highly articulate, eager to ask questions of their foreign guests in particular: Why are you interested in us? What made you want to study Pakistan?

I tell them a now well-rehearsed story: of how, as a child growing up in a small town in western Canada in the 1980s, my class at school – not unlike theirs, sitting before me – did a unit on 'countries of the world'. We made flags and factsheets and tried on costumes, and, to foster a sense of human bond, signed up for a penfriend. What an archaic notion the latter seems now when paper letters rarely come but global communication is immediate!

Of Irish descent on my father's side, I wanted to learn about where I supposedly came from, and thus chose Ireland as my letter's preferred destination. But – I tell the girls – somehow, serendipity stepped in and my missive to a hypothetical penfriend ended up in the wrong 'I' pile. Not long later, I received a neat letter in a blue airmail envelope with curious foreign stamps – not from Ireland at all, but India. My interest in this part of the world was piqued.

Why do I recount this story within a story here as a bookend to this collection of food writing? Because of where my mind wandered as I told the anecdote: to dessert. Or, more precisely, to carrot halwa. Contained within one of those precious, early letters from India was a response to my naive nine-year-old query: 'But what do you eat?' In my penfriend's tidy hand came her mother's recipe for a strange sweetmeat. I could prepare it myself, she suggested, and then know – not just by description, but by taste, by the experience of my own tongue – what my new pen pal liked to eat.

I duly accompanied my mother to the local supermarket – a vast warehouse of a very North American kind – to assemble the ingredients:

- 1 kg sweet red carrots (though I had only ever seen the ubiquitous orange variety)
- 2 litres whole milk
- 1½ cups sugar
- cashews and raisins to taste (Californian raisins were common, but would I have known how to identify a cashew? I imagine my mother explaining that they were something like peanuts).
- ghee to fry the cashews and raisins and a spoon to garnish (Ghee? What was that?)
- green cardamom powder (Surely some kind of exotic potion.)

We certainly wouldn't have been able to source red carrots or ghee in our small west coast town at that time. And I wonder if cardamom was available either. My parents had one single friend of South Asian descent (via East Africa) – perhaps he had stepped in to bolster the ingredients?

I have only a vague memory now of preparing the strange mixture with my mother's help. We must have followed something like the following simple method:

1. Grate the carrots.
2. Boil the milk to reduce it by two-thirds.

3. Add the grated carrots and cook until soft and all the milk has evaporated.
4. Add sugar, checking for taste.
5. Fry cashews and raisins in ghee before adding to carrot mixture.
6. Add green cardamom powder.
7. Garnish with ghee (optional).

I can't remember whether I liked this hybrid halwa on first taste. The memory is too overlaid by all the times I have happily consumed gajar ka halwa since. For, ultimately, intrigued by my penfriend's regular letters over many years, I ended up studying South Asian Studies at university, undertaking a PhD in colonial Indian history that led to an academic career, and, of course, visiting the countries of the subcontinent more times than I can count.

My penfriend and I eventually met in Delhi when I went to India for the first time in 1993 – ten years after we had begun our correspondence – and, most recently, we met there again in November 2019. Over a sumptuous Punjabi meal (rounded off with gulab jamun, rather than halwa), we reminisced, talked about our families and caught up on what we were doing now. Why, she asked, was I in India this time?

Our editor, Claire Chambers, intimates in the introduction that this anthology is part of a bigger academic project – and it was this project that I was in India to launch last November. We call it by its main title, 'Forgotten Food', for short, but the subtitle is more revealing of its intended themes: 'culinary memory, local heritage and lost agricultural varieties in India'. The big questions revolve around how we might use food history and literature to invigorate local heritage agendas: to bring economic and cultural benefits to struggling communities and to foster a sense of social cohesion. What we learn from the past may even inform food production in the future.

Our broader project, as with this anthology, centres on Muslim South Asia – conceived broadly here to incorporate

Muslim communities in India, Pakistan and Bangladesh, as well as the diaspora. The main justification is the vicious assault that Muslim communities have experienced on their food cultures in contemporary India. This assault has resulted, most devastatingly, in so-called 'beef lynchings' accompanied by the closure of slaughterhouses and meat shops on which so many depend for their livelihood.

Our response is to target those intensely rich food cultures from India's cities with significant Muslim heritage for recovery, preservation and renewal. Such an approach enables culinary exchange across South Asia's deadly borders too. We pursue our aims in different ways. Oral history is used to capture culinary memories where there are no written records. Historic cookbooks and food writings are gathered from archives and families to document changing food cultures. Creative writing becomes a vehicle, as in this book, for individual expression and gustatory memory.

And, as I write, the project's first crop of a now rare heritage rice is ripening in a field outside Rampur in north India. The hope is to identify its specific characteristics – smell, taste, texture – lost to high-yield strains. Perhaps those flavours and features may be incorporated into new varieties that are, at once, still drought-resistant and rich in nutrient in future? Or, as new markets open for heirloom products, might this heritage rice offer another option for local producers?

At the heart of our project is partnership. Claire is a scholar of literature, but I am a historian. As academics, we work together with other historians, sociologists and, rather unusually for those in the arts and humanities, plant scientists. Our base is my own institution, the University of Sheffield, in the UK, but our team is international. Vital is the dialogue fostered with non-academics, including heritage practitioners, cooks, street vendors and authors. That collaborative impulse underpins *Desi Delicacies*.

And so, I can tell my penfriend, this current project takes me back to where I started: her carrot halwa for dessert. To understand a culture and its history, we must engage with the preparation, cooking and eating of food. Food is not just a necessity; it permeates our memories and enlivens our stories. It enables us to evoke another time and faraway place, even as we keep one eye on the future. Food can divide us, but also bridge the gaps. Over a meal or even one dessert, friendships are forged, and a lifetime of adventures launched.

Biographical Notes

Nadeem Aslam is the author of five novels, *Season of the Rainbirds* (1993); *Maps for Lost Lovers* (2004), which was longlisted for the Booker Prize, shortlisted for the IMPAC Prize, and awarded the Kiriyama Prize and the Encore Award; *The Wasted Vigil*, described by A. S. Byatt as 'unforgettable … tragic and beautifully written'; *The Blind Man's Garden* (2013); and *The Golden Legend* (2017). Born in Pakistan, he now lives in England and is a Fellow of the Royal Society of Literature.

Claire Chambers is Professor of Global Literature at the University of York, where she teaches literature from South Asia, the Arab world and their diasporas. She is the author of *British Muslim Fictions* (2011), *Britain Through Muslim Eyes* (2015) and *Making Sense of Contemporary British Muslim Novels* (2019). She has also published a collection of her essays entitled *Rivers of Ink* (2017). Finally, she co-edited (with Caroline Herbert) *Imagining Muslims in South Asia and the Diaspora* (2015) and (with Nafhesa Ali and Richard Phillips) *A Match Made in Heaven: British Muslim Women Write About Love and Desire* (2020). Claire is Editor-in-Chief (with Rachael Gilmour) of the *Journal of Commonwealth Literature* and is a Fellow of the Royal Society of Arts.

Rosie Dastgir is a writer and novelist, born in England to a Pakistani father and an English mother. Her novel *A Small Fortune* was published by Riverhead in the US and Quercus in the UK, and she is working on a second. Her writing has appeared in publications including the *New York Times* and *Sunday Telegraph*, and her short stories appear in various anthologies. She has written and presented a short drama and documentary for BBC Radio, and is a Teaching Fellow in Creative Writing at Queen Mary University of London. Rosie lives in Hackney with her husband and two daughters, and is a contributing writer for *Spitalfields Life*, the East London blog. The family previously lived in Brooklyn, New York.

Kaiser Haq is a Bangladeshi poet, essayist and translator, and currently Professor of English and Dean of the School of Arts and Humanities at the University of Liberal Arts Bangladesh. He has been a Commonwealth scholar, Senior Fulbright scholar, and Royal Literary Fund Fellow. His publications include *Published in the Streets of Dhaka: Collected Poems*; *Pariah and Other Poems*; the translated volumes *Selected Poems of Shamsur Rahman*, *Selected Poems of Shaheed Quaderi*, *The Wonders of Vilayet* and Tagore's *Quartet*; *The Woman Who Flew* by Nasreen Jahan; the retold folk epic, *The Triumph of the Snake Goddess*; and the edited volumes *Contemporary Indian Poetry*, *Padma Meghna Jamuna: Modern Poetry from Bangladesh* and *Collected Poems of Shahid Suhrawardy.*

Sarvat Hasin was born in London and grew up in Karachi. She studied Politics and International Relations at Royal Holloway College, London, and then took a master's in Creative Writing at the University of Oxford. Her first novel, *This Wide Night*, was published by Penguin India and longlisted for the DSC Prize for South Asian Literature. Her second book, *You Can't Go Home Again*, was published in 2018 and was featured in *Vogue India*'s and *The Hindu*'s end-of-year lists. She won the Moth Writer's Retreat Bursary in 2018. Her essays and poetry have appeared in publications such as *On Anxiety*, *The Mays Anthology*, *English PEN*, and *Harper's Bazaar*.

Sabeeha Ahmed Husain was born in 1924 in Indore, India, and passed away in 2020 in London, UK. She came to Karachi as a bride in 1948 and divided her life between working for women's welfare, studying vocal music, and bringing up a family. Her son,

Aamer Hussein, was born in Karachi in 1955 and came to study in England in 1970. He is the author of two novels (notably *Another Gulmohar Tree*) and six collections of stories (including *The Swan's Wife*), and divides his time between London, Karachi and Islamabad. 'What's Cooking?', his story for this collection, was originally written in Urdu. It was amplified and transcreated very freely by Sabeeha Ahmed Husain, to whose memory 'What's Cooking?' is dedicated.

Sadaf Hussain is the author of *Daastan-e-Dastarkhan* and works in Delhi as a consultant chef. He was also among the top contestants of *MasterChef India* in 2016. He loves storytelling and is passionate about exploring the background stories and origins of food, running a food website on the same concept, www.foodandstreets.com. He is a TEDx speaker and has food shows on YouTube. As a kid, Sadaf really wanted to be the fattest child in the world, which made him fall in love with food. He likes to come up with nostalgic stories and weave them into the dishes he creates. He travels across India and outside to find and learn new and old recipes.

Sauleha Kamal is a PhD candidate and Overseas Research Fellow at the University of York, researching post-9/11 South Asian narratives in the context of human rights and politics. She holds an MPhil (English: Criticism and Culture) from the University of Cambridge, where she was a Chevening and Cambridge Trust scholar, and a BA (Economics and Social History and English) from Barnard College, Columbia University. Her scholarly work, essays and fiction have appeared in various places including *Postcolonial Text*, *The Atlantic* and *Catapult*. She was a writer-in-residence at Yaddo in Saratoga Springs, New York in November and December 2019.

Tabish Khair is the author of a number of critically acclaimed novels, poetry collections and academic studies. Born in Ranchi and educated up to his master's in his small hometown, Gaya, India, he studied for his PhD in Copenhagen after a few years as a journalist in Delhi. He currently teaches at Aarhus University, Denmark.

His most recent book is the novel *Night of Happiness* (Picador India, 2018).

Sophia Khan was born in 1985 in Islamabad, Pakistan. She studied English at Haverford College and received an MFA in Writing from Sarah Lawrence College. Her first novel, *Dear Yasmeen*, was published by Periscope UK in 2016 and also by HarperCollins India, Diana Verlag/Random House, Germany and Eksik Parça, Turkey. It was shortlisted for the Shakti Bhatt First Book Prize and the Karachi Literature Festival Getz Pharma Fiction Prize. Her second novel, *The Flight of the Arconaut*, was published by Westland Books in early 2020. Sophia's short fiction has appeared in Oxford University Press's *In the New Century: An Anthology of Pakistani English Literature 1997–2017*, *The Aleph Review*, *Kestrel* and *Commonwealth Writers* in connection with the short story prize shortlist.

Dr **Tarana Husain Khan**'s articles on Rampur cuisine, culture and oral history have appeared in *Scroll*, the *Wire* and *DailyO*. She wrote a monthly column on Rampur cuisine, 'Food Fables', in *DailyO*. Her historical novel, *The Begum and the Dastan*, is currently in press with Tranquebar Westland. Her book *Rampuri Cuisine: Food Fables, Memories and Recipes* will be published by Penguin India in 2021. Her novels, *I'm Not a Bimbette* (2015) and a sequel *Cyberbullied* (2020), were published by Juggernaut Books. She founded the Rampur Book Club in 2016 to promote the reading of world literature in Rampur, and hosts a website on Rampur's cultural history: www.taranakhanauthor.com. Tarana is currently working on the Global Challenges Research Fund and Arts and Humanities Research Council-funded research project, 'Forgotten Food: Culinary Memory, Local Heritage and Lost Agricultural Varieties in India'.

Uzma Aslam Khan is the author of five novels translated worldwide to critical acclaim. These include *Trespassing*, recipient of a Commonwealth Prize nomination in 2003; *The Geometry of God*, a *Kirkus Reviews* Best Book of 2009; *Thinner Than Skin*, nominated for the Man Asian Literary Prize and the DSC Prize for South

Asian Literature, and winner of the French Embassy Prize for Best Fiction at the Karachi Literature Festival 2014. Khan's most recent novel, *The Miraculous True History of Nomi Ali*, twenty-six years in the making, is the first known fictional account of the Andaman Islands preceding and during the Second World War, when they were occupied by the British and then the Japanese. Hailed by Pankaj Mishra as 'a master lesson in the art of historical fiction ... brilliantly excavating a forgotten past of several societies and honouring its human complexity with a narrative of delicate precision', the novel was shortlisted for the Tata Literature Live's Best Book of the Year Award for Fiction 2019 and the Karachi Literature Festival–Getz Pharma Fiction Prize 2020. Visit her at http://uzmaaslamkhan.blogspot.com or follow @uzmaaslamkhan_writer on Instagram.

Siobhan Lambert-Hurley is a cultural historian of modern South Asia with particular interests in women, gender and Islam. She currently works as a Professor of Global History in the History Department at the University of Sheffield. Her latest publications include *A Tent of One's Own: Three Centuries of Travel Writing by Muslim Women* (co-edited with Daniel Machrowicz and Sunil Sharma; Indiana University Press, 2021), and *Elusive Lives: Gender, Autobiography and the Self in Muslim South Asia* (Stanford University Press, 2018). Her current project, out of which this anthology comes, is funded by a Global Challenges Research Fund and the Arts and Humanities Research Council partnership award for 'Forgotten Food: Culinary Memory, Local Heritage and Lost Agricultural Varieties in India' (2019–2022).

Sanam Maher is a journalist and author based in Karachi, Pakistan. For more than a decade, she has covered stories on Pakistan's art and culture, business, politics, religious minorities and women. Her work has appeared in the *New York Times*, *Al Jazeera*, *BuzzFeed*, *Caravan*, *Roads and Kingdoms*, and the *Times Literary Supplement*, among others. Her first book, *A Woman Like Her: The Short Life of Qandeel Baloch*, an investigation into the murder of Pakistan's first social media celebrity, was published in South Asia in 2018, the UK, Australia and Europe in 2019, and the US and Canada in 2020.

Sisters **Mahruba T. Mowtushi** and **Mafruha Mohua** spent their formative years in Dhaka, Algiers and Manila. Mahruba is an Assistant Professor in the Department of English and Humanities at the University of Liberal Arts Bangladesh (ULAB). Her research and writing interests cut across South Asian and African literature and cultural history. She is currently preparing a manuscript on East African and Bengali literary exchange in the twentieth century. Mafruha teaches Modernism and Postcolonial Literature in the School of English and Drama at Queen Mary University of London. Her general area of research is modernism in relation to colonialism, especially that of the British Empire. She is currently preparing a monograph on T. S. Eliot, which examines his work from the perspective of the Empire, as well as researching Bengali modernism.

Rana Safvi is a renowned writer, scholar and translator. She is the author of *Where Stones Speak: Historical Trails in Mehrauli, the First City of Delhi*; *The Forgotten Cities of Delhi*; and *Tales from the Quran and Hadith*. Her blog, www.ranasafvi.com, is a repository of her writings on Indian culture, food, heritage and age-old traditions. She lives in Delhi with her family.

Bina Shah is a Karachi-based author of five novels and two collections of short stories. Her novels include the critically acclaimed *A Season for Martyrs* (2014) and the feminist dystopian novel *Before She Sleeps* (2018). She has been a regular contributor to the *New York Times*, *Al Jazeera* and the *Huffington Post*, and is a frequent guest on the BBC. Bina is a graduate of Wellesley College and the Harvard Graduate School of Education, and is an Honorary Fellow in Writing at the University of Iowa. She is currently the president of the Alliance Française de Karachi and writes on issues of women's rights and female empowerment in Pakistan and across Muslim countries.

Farah Yameen started out as a filmmaker, discovered it was not her calling and moved to public histories and digital archiving. Her public history works deal with diverse subjects: cultural geographies and the individual, democratic movements, personal histories of journalism and, lately, food. She considers herself a dabbler. Her short story in this anthology is her latest exercise in dabbling, this time in fiction writing.

Asiya Zahoor studied at Oxford University and the University of Kashmir. She has written books and articles on the literature of exile, Kashmiri literature, Muslim identity, South Asian literature and psycholinguistics. Her film, *The Stitch*, won the Critics Award for Best Film at the Second South Asian Film Festival and has been screened at prestigious festivals internationally. Her latest collection of poems is *Serpents Under My Veil* (2019). She is a Fellow of the Ford Foundation and has recently won the Sanford Taylor Fellowship at Cornell University. She is currently working at a college in Baramulla, Kashmir.

Annie Zaidi is the author of *Bread, Cement, Cactus: A Memoir of Belonging and Dislocation*, *Prelude to a Riot, Gulab, Love Stories # 1 to 14*, *Known Turf: Bantering with Bandits and Other True Tales*, and the editor of *Unbound: 2000 Years of Indian Women's Writing*. She is the recipient of the Nine Dots Prize (2019) and The Hindu Playwright Award (2018) for her play, *Untitled 1*. Her work has appeared in various anthologies and literary journals including *Griffith Review, Aleph Review, Massachusetts Review, The Charles River Journal* and *The Missing Slate*.

Farahad Zama is the author of four novels and a collection of short stories that have been translated into twelve languages. Farahad's first novel, *The Marriage Bureau for Rich People*, was a Richard & Judy and *Daily Mail* Book of the Month, and he was shortlisted for Best New Writer of the Year at the British Book Awards, Best Published Fiction at the Muslim Writers Awards, and the Melissa Nathan Award for Comedy and Romance. Farahad works in an investment bank, lives in south London with his wife and two sons, and keeps mightily resisting getting a dog.